The Politics of Co-Opposition

The Inside Story of the
2021-24 Co-operation Agreement
Between Plaid Cymru and Welsh Labour

I pondered all these things, and how men fight and lose the battle, and the thing that they fought for comes about in spite of their defeat, and when it comes turns out not to be what they meant, and other men have to fight for what they meant under another name.

William Morris, *A Dream of John Ball*, 1888

(quoted by Ioan Bowen Rees in *The Welsh Political Tradition*, 1961)

Cover photograph: First Minister Mark Drakeford and Plaid Cymru Leader Adam Price signing the Co-operation Agreement, 1 December 2021. (© Welsh Government)

The Politics of Co-Opposition

The Inside Story of the
2021-24 Co-operation Agreement
Between Plaid Cymru and Welsh Labour

John Osmond

welsh academic press
Cardiff

Published in Wales by Welsh Academic Press, an imprint of

Ashley Drake Publishing Ltd
PO Box 733
Cardiff
CF14 7ZY

www.welsh-academic-press.wales

First Impression – 2024

ISBN
Paperback: 978-1-86057-168-8
Ebook: 978-1-86057-169-5

© Ashley Drake Publishing Ltd 2024
Text © John Osmond 2024

The right of John Osmond to be identified as the author of this work has been asserted in accordance with the Copyright Design and Patents Act of 1988.

Every effort has been made to contact copyright holders. However, the publishers will be glad to rectify in future editions any inadvertent omissions brought to their attention.

Ashley Drake Publishing Ltd hereby exclude all liability to the extent permitted by law for any errors or omissions in this book and for any loss, damage or expense (whether direct or indirect) suffered by a third party relying on any information contained in this book.

All rights reserved. No part of this publication may be reproduced, stored in a retrieval system, or transmitted, in any form or by any means without the prior permission of the publishers.

British Library Cataloguing-in-Publication Data.
A CIP catalogue for this book is available from the British Library.

Typeset by Prepress Plus, www.prepressplus.in
Cover design by Welsh Books Council, Aberystwyth, Wales

Contents

Acknowledgements vii
Preface by Professor Gerald Holtham ix
Foreword by Professor Leighton Andrews xii
Introduction xv

Part I
Plaid Cymru & Labour – Contrasting Approaches to Policy and Governance 1
1.   A Huge Step Forward   3
2.   View from the Back Row   20
3.   The Carmarthenshire Connection   39

Part II
The First 100 Days of Plaid's New Leader – A Week-by-Week Diary 2018 73
   15 October – Touching Base   76
   22 October – The Shadow Cabinet   79
   29 October – Adam Meets Theresa   83
   3 November – Economy Front and Centre   84
   12 November – Nuclear Option   88
   19 November – Party, Programme and Performance   95
   26 November – Brussels   99
   3 December – Black and Blue on the M4   109
   10 December – Carwyn   113
   17 December – Something Out of Nothing   122
   29 December – Scenario Gazing   124
   2019
   7 January – Dublin   127
   14 January – The Nation's Perfect Son   130
   21 January – The Dud Report   135
   4 February – Time is Slipping Away   140
   11 February – Plaid Cymru Newydd   142
   18 February – Nova Cambria   144
   25 February – Polling Our Way   146
   4 March – The Group Implodes   150
   11 March – Upping Our Game   153
   18 March – The Speech   159
   Blown Off Course   164

Part III
The Agreement 169
4. Negotiating the Agreement 171
5. Senedd Reform 188
6. Personalities and Politics Intervene 213
7. Nation Building 227

Afterword – The Welsh Experience of Contract Parliamentarism 247

Appendix - The Co-operation Agreement 257

Index 278

Bibliography 289

Acknowledgements

My first debt is to Adam Price for giving me the opportunity to work alongside him in the Senedd for four years, from 2018 to 2022. Without him neither the Co-operation Agreement nor this book would have happened. One way or another, as both journalist and activist, I have been closely involved in the story of Welsh devolution from the early 1970s. So, it was an enormous privilege to be able to witness at first hand the process of Welsh democracy in action when we were negotiating the Co-operation Agreement with Welsh Labour, between June and December 2021. I am grateful for the comradeship of Steffan Bryn and Siân Gwenllian MS in that endeavour, along with Adam Price himself.

I am also grateful to Gerald Holtham, Professor of Regional Economy at Cardiff Metropolitan University, and Leighton Andrews, Professor of Practice in Public Service Leadership and Innovation at Cardiff Business School, for providing the Preface and Foreword. Their perspectives are especially insightful due to both having a Labour background. Professor Holtham was Director of the Institute for Public Policy Research during the 1990s and chaired the Welsh Government's independent Commission on Funding and Finance for Wales 2008-2010, while Professor Andrews was Labour AM for the Rhondda 2003-2016 and Minister for Education and Skills and for Public Services in the Welsh Government from 2009-2016.

I should like to pay tribute to the small, but highly professional and often extraordinarily young, teams working for Plaid Cymru in the Senedd, at Westminster, and at party headquarters in Tŷ Gwynfor. Especially helpful to me during my *sojourn* in the Senedd were Sioned James, Steffan Bryn, Mabli Jones, Esyllt Meurig, Carl Harris, Emily Edwards, Gwennol Haf, Aled ap Dafydd, Nia Medi, Fflur Arwel, Ben O'Keeffe, Geraint Day, and Carmen Ria Smith, now the youngest member of the House of Lords, Baroness Smith of Llanfaes.

Drafts of the manuscript were read by Peter Finch, Ceri Black, Geraint Talfan Davies, David Williams, Eurfyl ap Gwilym, Cynog Dafis, and Rhys David. All made helpful comments and suggestions, most of which I have incorporated. As ever, however, responsibility for the contents, any errors and omissions, are entirely my own.

My final thanks are to my publisher at Welsh Academic Press, Ashley Drake, whose editorial support and political insights are a tonic in equal measure.

John Osmond
Penarth
August 2024

Preface

John Osmond's revealing account of the Co-Operation Agreement between the Welsh Labour Government and Plaid Cymru – the first example of Contract Parliamentarism in the UK – is a wide-ranging reflection on what it did and did not achieve. Written from a Plaid perspective and an insider's viewpoint, it describes how it served Plaid's longer-term objectives and, indeed, what the prospects for those objectives are. The verdict is on balance strongly positive, though flaws are acknowledged.

For those approaching the Co-operation Agreement with little prior knowledge of Welsh politics, the first part of the book usefully outlines the circumstances that led to the Agreement. In important respects, Welsh Labour and Plaid Cymru have converged in the post-devolution period. Labour buttressed itself against Plaid by taking a Welsh-patriotic stance. It did so by stressing that Welsh political culture was to the left of New Labour and the party's chosen identity reflected that position – 'Classic Labour' in Rhodri Morgan's phrase. Under Conservative governments in Westminster it made a point of asserting it stood for the Welsh interest and tended to blame difficulties on 'London'. Meanwhile, Plaid moved left in its social and economic policies as it attempted to attract support in post-industrial areas, outside its rural Welsh-speaking heartland.

However, this convergence did not remove mutual suspicion and, indeed, further intensified rivalries. The personal rapport and trust between the two leaders, Mark Drakeford and Adam Price, was, as Osmond explains, critical to the formation of the Agreement. Both were innately left-leaning Welsh speakers from Carmarthenshire with an intellectual bent.

Plaid Cymru wished to avoid the perils of being the minor partner in a coalition with Labour, which occurred between 2007-2011 and which proved electorally disadvantageous. Hence the search for Co-Opposition, to use Adam Price's apt phrase. Plaid wished to retain a distinct identity in the hope they could be the major party in a different coalition after 2021. In the event, those hopes died as

Brexit put an unbridgeable gulf between the Conservatives and Plaid. It also temporarily raised Conservative support in Wales while Covid later raised the profile and popularity of Mark Drakeford. At the 2021 election Plaid relapsed to third party in the Senedd without any prospect of power. The Co-operation Agreement became the party's only means of influencing policy, while for Labour it ensured they could pass a budget and key legislation without ad hoc horse-trading.

A singular aspect of John Osmond's account is the diary of his first 100 days as Adam Price's Special Adviser, which takes up the second part of the book. The entries detail the meetings and machinations leading to the setting of Plaid's policy proposals and the negotiations which saw some incorporated in the final Co-operation Agreement. This section, which is discreetly revealing about intra-party tensions, provides essential source material for historians and has a certain fly-on-the-wall fascination, especially for those with an interest in Welsh politics and a knowledge of the individual politicians involved.

The book's third part reviews what the Cooperation Agreement achieved in a longer perspective. It strongly reflects Osmond's confidence in the inevitable success of the programme he espouses. You could say he has a Welsh equivalent of the Whig view of history. Whatever the appearances, the real story is of slow but inevitable progress that will culminate one day in an autonomous Welsh polity and nation. Setbacks are acknowledged but do not disturb his conviction. The goal will not be achieved by a single political party but by a number working together on individual steps along the road. After all, the story goes, Wales has survived as a nation against the odds and has now acquired a government and political system for the first time since 1536, if not 1282. From a shaky start the Welsh National Assembly, now Senedd, has acquired legislative and limited fiscal powers. A legal jurisdiction must surely follow. The Cooperation Agreement, by ensuring the enlargement of the Senedd to have enough members both to constitute a government and to provide enough independent members to hold it to account, has facilitated another step along the long, bumpy but irresistible road.

The Co-operation Agreement, then, apparently gave the Welsh devolution process another stride in an onward march. However, there was a substantial catch. Plaid Cymru wanted a more democratic electoral system for the enlarged body, like the Single Transferable Vote, but Labour insisted on a closed list system as a condition for enlargement. Yet, by reducing voter choice this seems likely to reduce voter turnout in Senedd elections from already modest levels. While seen as necessary by insiders, enlargement is doubtfully popular with the public at large many of whom are resentful at the expense, coming at a time when both public services and private incomes are squeezed. Time will tell whether Plaid's concession on the electoral system will result in a check rather than a boost to devolution by increasing public disengagement from the institution.

Osmond provides a detailed account of other disputes and how, after initial resistance from Labour, the negotiations ended up with a wide-range of policies. In effect, Osmond asserts, Plaid provided Labour with a substantial part of its programme for government. Significantly, however, Labour was not prepared to entertain any substantive innovations in policy for the economy. Notably, Plaid's commitment to re-establish a Welsh Development Agency, crucial it believes for effective policy delivery, was off the table.

Osmond gives an informative, insider's perspective on the conditions that are necessary to make such cross-party deals possible. In the first place the personal chemistry between the major personalities has to work. Then the parties themselves have to align in their willingness to co-habit. The experience of the Co-operation Agreement is testimony that when these two aspects come under pressure, when the personalities and politics change, such accords can easily fall apart. Nevertheless, the Co-operation Agreement lasted for most of its intended three years. It proved an innovative and imaginative alternative to a coalition that, because of the relative strengths of the two parties following the 2021 election, was unattainable. It is an open question, however, whether it is likely to be repeated.

Nonetheless, after future Senedd elections, when parties search for mechanisms to achieve a working majority, politicians in Cardiff Bay will be able to refer to this book to see what can be learnt from Wales's first experience of Contract Parliamentarianism. In the meantime, for those wishing to know the inside story of an historic period in Welsh politics, this is a timely and thought-provoking book that seeks to persuade but also to inform.

Gerald Holtham
August 2024

Foreword

From memory, the first time I met John Osmond was around 1990 when his TV production company, *Agenda*, was filming a programme about the campaign to get funding for Gaelic Language television in Scotland into the 1990 Broadcasting Act. I was coordinating the parliamentary aspects of the campaign at the time. But I had been reading the writings of the 'old warhorse', as he calls himself in this book, for far longer: probably since around 1980 when he and others set up the radical magazine *Arcade* in the aftermath of the failed 1979 devolution referendum. Newly resident in London, I kept in touch with what was happening in Wales through publications like *Arcade* and others.

John has been a writer, think-tanker, activist and latterly a political adviser throughout the devolution journey and a journalist for decades before. He's been as much workhorse as warhorse, as his output has been prolific, and he helped to shape the Institute for Welsh Affairs into an important institution in Welsh public life. The present book continues his intellectual adventure in the unexplored regions of the devolved world, combining anthropological investigation of the dynamics of the Plaid group in the Senedd through the 'fieldwork' of six months of his personal diary, with reflections on Welsh political leadership in the fraught period after Brexit. He notes 'the often circular, mind-numbing, time-wasting character of professional politics' and the ways on which day-to-day events in the Senedd can distract from a party's overall strategy. I particularly enjoyed his analysis of the relationship of the speech-writer to their principal, as he described the process of working on speeches for Adam Price.

The book is an original examination of the Co-operation Agreement between Welsh Labour and Plaid Cymru which endured from 2021 until the middle of 2024: something which Price himself has described as 'Co-Opposition', which John adopts for his title. That tells you immediately that the perspective of the book is John's perspective, his take on the events in which he was involved. There will, doubtless, be other accounts and interpretations of that period,

Foreword

and I look forward to reading those. But this is the first attempt to address them.

John's interpretation sits very clearly in the tradition of his previous writings since the 1980s, and the general theme can perhaps be summarised in one simple passage:

> 'If Labour has become more politically Welsh, Plaid has had to face the reality that building the nation involves engaging with the greater part of the country and not just those regions where it feels most at home.'

He refers to Plaid's traditional role, as he sees it, of pushing Labour in a more radical pro-devolution direction. As I said, this is John's interpretation: it would not be mine, and others will have their own views.

That being said, the book gives a fair-minded account of the development of the Co-operation Agreement after the realities of Brexit and Covid knocked Plaid's strategy of leading a Welsh Government after the 2021 Senedd elections off-course. John identifies the significant role of Mark Drakeford and Adam Price as the leaders of the two parties, and doubts that, without them, the Agreement could have happened at all. He notes the need for the Agreement in the face of the much more aggressive and strategic 'muscular unionism' of the Conservatives at Westminster, seeking to halt devolution's 'forward march'. John ends by looking forward to possible further co-operation between Welsh Labour led by Eluned Morgan and Plaid Cymru under Rhun ap Iorweth's leadership, and wonders how devolution will develop with Labour in power in Westminster.

The book will have interest to politics scholars, as well as students of Welsh history. The kind of Co-operation Agreement that transpired after 2021 is one which has only been tried in a few other territories and never before in the UK: in academic language, it is known as 'Contract Parliamentarianism'. John reminds us that following its announcement, the Presiding Officer of the Senedd, Elin Jones MS, had to take legal advice as to whether Plaid Cymru could still be regarded as an independent political group in the Senedd, or whether they should be regarded as part of the Welsh Government. He also acknowledges that Plaid made a claim for ministerial positions.

John puts much of the development of the Agreement in historical context. He looks back to the Richard Commission, published 20 years ago in 2004, in his consideration of the size of the Senedd. In discussing one of the economic policy ambitions of the Agreement, from Plaid's position, he looks back on the abolition of the Welsh Development Agency during Rhodri Morgan's 'Bonfire of the Quangos' and rehearses his and others' criticism of that. It is not a perspective I share but it is useful to be reminded of that side of the argument in contemporary terms. Similarly, he reflects on the making of the Welsh Baccalaureate during the first Assembly and what he believes to be the resistance of civil servants. Overall, John considers the Agreement in the context of the history of Plaid-Labour co-operation in the Assembly and Senedd since 1999.

There have been all too few reflective writings on the *political practice* of devolution in Wales. John has added an important additional volume. This is part of the story of the making of Wales since 1999. It is a story we are still writing and still making.

Leighton Andrews
August 2024

Introduction

Shortly after his election as Plaid Cymru's leader in September 2018 Adam Price asked me to become his Special Adviser. I had supported his bid for the leadership and looked forward to the energy I was sure he would bring to Plaid's progress, but I was immersed in undertakings of my own and, notionally at any rate, retired. Did he really need a 72-year-old warhorse?

He convinced me he did. There was a project to hand. Given a fair wind, a shake-up of the party organisation and some strategic vision, there was an outside chance that Plaid could lead a government following the 2021 Senedd election. This was important, not just for the party, but to give Wales a new start after 20 years when for much of the time the country had been treading water. Arguably the future of Welsh democracy itself was at stake if, election after election, the result was a foregone conclusion.

As I became immersed in my new role, it was intriguing to discover exactly what it was. Special Advisers are wholly dependent on those who hire them. The concept of advice is embedded in the job description, but it is seldom asked for directly. Instead, most of the time the task is to listen, not just to the politician in question, but to those around him or her, to get a sense of the way things are going, and whether they are heading in the right direction. You are to act as a sounding board, to be empathetic, but also a critical friend. You are a go-between. You can be contacted at any time. You attend a constant round of meetings. You travel about, literally carrying bags and bundles of paper. You write endlessly – policy and position papers, memoranda, speeches, even manifestos. More often than not these are unacknowledged, ignored, discarded or amended out of recognition. Your greatest strength is invisibility; your greatest weakness visibility; your greatest opportunity access; your greatest threat irrelevance.

An ongoing challenge was to extricate myself from the day-to-day, not to say hour-to-hour immersion in the immediacy of politics, and take a longer view. Our sights were supposed to be fixed on the

2021 Senedd election but events constantly diverted our gaze. Most immediate was the fall-out from Brexit, a maelstrom and calamity that sucked the lifeblood from forward planning. Scarcely had that been settled, at least for the time being by the December 2019 'Get Brexit Done' election, when we were overtaken by the Covid-19 pandemic. This was a further calamitous event, overwhelming in its impact. The combined effect was to throw the idea of a Plaid-led minority government completely off course. Somehow, we had to find an alternative, more realisable objective. Following the year-long production of our manifesto for the May 2021 Senedd election, this became the Co-operation Agreement.

Part I
Plaid Cymru and Labour – Contrasting approaches to policy and governance

Chapter 1 provides an overview of the Agreement that Plaid negotiated with Welsh Labour in the wake of the election. There is no doubt that the breadth of its policies, and the novel political arrangements that accompanied them, came as a surprise to most observers. Few had anticipated the extent of the programme, which covered 46 commitments. They included free school meals for all primary-aged pupils, expanding free childcare to all two-year-olds, action on the second homes crisis, and reforming the Senedd. The Agreement was not a formal Coalition, but neither was it confined to providing support in matters of confidence and the budget, in return for modest concessions. Instead, it was a hybrid arrangement in which an opposition party is engaged in the implementation of policies though a delivery unit within the government.[1]

Chapter 2 explores some of the underlying differences between Labour and Plaid Cymru's approach to policy and governance. It is important to understand these, since both parties come from the same Welsh radical tradition that emphasises social justice, community and solidarity. Even on constitutional matters there is less to separate Welsh Labour and Plaid than in the past. Both now agree that sovereignty rests with the people of Wales and not the centralised British state. Welsh Labour advocates a federal solution

---

[1] The full text of the Co-operation Agreement is contained in the Appendix.

Introduction

to Britain's constitutional backwardness, while Plaid Cymru has adopted a confederal alternative, following the recommendations of its Independence Commission in 2020. Moreover, the subsequent Independent Commission on the Constitutional Future of Wales, established as part of the Co-operation Agreement, found that both federalism and independence were viable options.

Despite this, however, Plaid and Welsh Labour still have distinctive approaches to their priorities and the way they should be implemented. Much of the story of the Co-operation Agreement is how these were exposed and then blended together in a spirit of compromise. It is also a story of how this was achieved because of the leadership of two Carmarthenshire-born politicians. The Agreement was, of course, driven by events, the fall-out from Brexit followed by the impact of the Covid pandemic. Together they framed the immediate background to the 2021 Senedd election and were determining factors in its outcome. At the same time, the Co-operation Agreement would not even have been contemplated, let alone successfully negotiated, had it not been for the inclination, ideology and personalities of Adam Price and Mark Drakeford, the Plaid and Labour leaders. Their hinterland and political philosophies are explored in **Chapter 3**.

Part II
The first 100 Days of Plaid's new Leader – A Week-by-week diary

The central part of this book provides an insight into the background of the Co-operation Agreement. A contemporaneous weekly diary, it records the episodes that led Plaid Cymru to fall back on its traditional role – to pull a governing Labour party in its direction, and in the process exert a powerful influence on the future direction of Wales, short of exercising power on its own account.

The diary covers the six-month period of what Adam Price called our 'first hundred days'. As they reached their end, it looked for a dizzying moment as if Plaid was on course to achieve our objective of leading a minority government. Adam's leadership was established, and the party doing well in the opinion polls, well enough it seemed to reach our goal.

Then the diary stops. With the benefit of hindsight, I can see that subconsciously I realised that if it continued, I would be recording something completely different to the project we had started upon six months earlier. In short, the politics of Brexit were taking over. We were sucked into the fruitless vortex of a Westminster crisis about the terms on which Britain was to leave the European Union. Endlessly circular arguments revolved around how these were to be decided, whether through a further referendum or a general election, or possibly both.

During this time the character of the Conservative Party in the Senedd was changing before our eyes. In the early years of the National Assembly, that was to become the law-making Senedd, the Conservatives appeared to be adjusting to the political realities of a more self-confident Wales. Re-branded and bilingual, they wanted to make devolution a success. They were changing their approach and identity in line with a moderate Christian Democratic position within the European mainstream. So much so that in the wake of the 2007 election, Plaid Cymru briefly considered forming an alliance with them, along with the Liberal Democrats, in what became known as a Rainbow coalition. Following the 2016 election, the Conservatives actually supported Plaid's then leader Leanne Wood in a tied vote to make her First Minister.

These memories were the backdrop for the project Adam had embarked on at the beginning of his leadership in 2018, but any hope of such a prospect now disappeared. Under its new ill-tempered leadership, the Conservative group in the Senedd adopted a stridently pro-Brexit, anti-European, and ultimately anti-Welsh position. There were no circumstances in which Plaid could contemplate having anything to do with that trajectory. The hope that circumstances might contrive to propel Adam Price into the role of First Minister at the head of a minority government was collateral damage. In short, the project on which we had set out so optimistically six months before was no longer realistic. A new mission needed to be identified.

This quickly appeared in the form of developing a new political programme for Wales. In the ensuing months it became evident that if Wales was to make any significant constitutional advance it could only be achieved in a partnership between Plaid Cymru and Welsh Labour. In truth, this had always been the case, as had been shown in 2007 by the One Wales coalition between Labour and Plaid that led to the successful 2011 referendum on legislative powers. This became clear once more in the months leading to the 2021 election. Coincidentally, as this realisation dawned, I was elected Plaid Cymru's Director of Policy at the party's October 2019 conference in Swansea. More than ever before, Plaid Cymru's central purpose was to be the source of a policy programme so compelling that it would be persuasive with other progressive forces, Labour in particular.

By then Plaid had been through the elections for the European Parliament in May 2019, which were won convincingly by the newly formed Brexit Party. In short order, the Brexit process reached its denouement with Boris Johnson's 'Get Brexit Done' Westminster election in December. These events were quickly followed by the Covid pandemic. Together they created an entirely different backcloth for the 2021 Senedd election than the one that had been had envisaged when Adam Price became leader in 2018. Instead, they provided the circumstances that led to the Co-operation Agreement.

Part III
The Agreement

The third part of the book tells how Plaid Cymru negotiated these turbulent changes to find a way to achieve considerable influence in an alliance with Welsh Labour through developing radical policies for Wales and influencing their implementation, rather than directly gaining power for itself.

Chapter 4 provides an insider's account of negotiating the Agreement which was aimed at lasting three years, to December 2024. It also explains the circumstances that led to it being on the agenda. Largely due to the Covid pandemic, in which Mark Drakeford achieved an unprecedented profile and justified approval ratings, Labour equalled its previous best performance in a Senedd election, in 2003 and 2011, winning 30 of the 60 seats. These were enough to allow it to continue governing on its own. Nevertheless, Mark Drakeford sought to govern in a constructive relationship with Plaid Cymru. One reason for this was his need for a more radical and expansive policy agenda than was to be found in Welsh Labour's minimalist manifesto. However, the most telling reason was an acute sense that, due to the hostility of Boris Johnson's Westminster government, the powers of the Senedd were being systematically undermined. It was illuminating, not to say startling, when one of the Labour negotiators told his Plaid counterparts, 'They're coming for our country not our parties.'

Chapter 5 is devoted to an account of Senedd reform which was regarded by both sides as the most effective response to this pressure from Westminster. The preamble to the section in the Co-operation Agreement containing this commitment declares, 'With devolution under threat from this Conservative UK Government, we must send a clear message to Westminster that the Senedd is here to stay and decisions about Wales are made in Wales.' Fundamentally, of course, the reform agenda is about much more than standing up to Westminster centralisation. It was the Senedd's next step in creating a fully-fledged Parliament.

Chapter 6 describes how the Co-operation Agreement was brought to a premature end, in May 2024, six months before it was due to run its three-year course. As the chapter title suggests, that was due to the intervention of new personalities and political dissension. By then, for a variety of reasons, both Adam Price and Mark Drakeford, the leaders who had been responsible for devising the Agreement, had left the scene. Their replacements, Rhun ap Iorwerth and Vaughan Gething, though in public at least, supporters of the Agreement, did not have the same personal investment in its programme. The immediate reason for the Agreement coming to an end, though, was the flawed and controversial character of Vaughan Gething's campaign for Welsh Labour leadership between January and March 2024. At the core of the dissension was a £200,000 donation he received from a businessman in his constituency who had been convicted of environmental offences. It was this continuing controversy that persuaded Rhun ap Iorwerth to withdraw Plaid Cymru from the Agreement in May. Nevertheless, the chapter goes on to argue that much of the content of the Agreement had by then already been achieved. It also suggests that it may have laid the foundation for another iteration of the Agreement in the wake of the 2026 Senedd election.

Chapter 7 places the Co-operation Agreement at the centre of Plaid Cymru's mission, which is to build the nation. The historian Prys Morgan likened institutions to a 'rib cage for nationality'.[2] Certainly,

---

[2] P. Morgan, 'The Creation of the National Museum and National Library' in J. Osmond (Ed.), *Myths, Memories and Future; The National Library and National Museum in the Story of Wales* (IWA, 2007), p.21.

Introduction

this is a function of the institutions he referenced that were founded in 1907, the National Library and National Museum. He described the period between the 1880s and 1914 as the first age of devolution. With the creation of the National Assembly and its evolution into a Senedd we are living through the second age. For Plaid Cymru the significance of the Co-operation Agreement, with Senedd reform at its heart, is its continuation of a nation-building process. Plaid are determined that, in turn, this will propel Wales to the brink of devolution's third age, which will herald independence.

Ultimately, the Co-operation Agreement will be judged by how far it brings improvement to the everyday lives of the people of Wales, and especially the more disadvantaged. On that score, among a raft of policies, Plaid can point specifically to free school meals for pupils in the primary sector, the expansion of free nursery care for pre-school children, tackling homelessness, promoting a new system of fair rents, securing record funding for flood defences, and protecting payments for farmers.

The Co-operation Agreement gave Welsh Labour a programme for government that was sure to be implemented because of the enhanced majority of votes in the Senedd it also delivered. As for Plaid Cymru, it ended ten years in the wilderness of opposition and placed the party in a stronger position to achieve an even more influential role in the life of Wales in the decades that lie ahead.

Part I

Plaid Cymru and Labour

Contrasting Approaches to Policy and Governance

1
A Huge Step Forward

With the Co-operation Agreement, two parties that a matter of months earlier had been in bitter opposition came together to agree a programme for government. In the process they discovered that they had a good deal in common. Both parties were left of centre, pro-European and social democratic, and placed greater value on co-operation than competition. Even on the question of the constitutional future for Wales, where most difference could be found, both at least wanted progress, and to make an advance. Both also shared an intense antipathy to the Conservative government in London, which was pursuing the hardest of Brexits. Not only that, the Westminster government had no compunction about widening the gap between the well-off and those struggling on low incomes. Moreover, aided by Brexit, it was intent on centralising power at the expense of the devolved governments in Cardiff and Edinburgh.

The Co-operation Agreement offered an innovative mechanism for its implementation. It was not a formal coalition, with Plaid Cymru Ministers in the Welsh Government, as had happened with the One Wales agreement in 2007. Neither, however, was it limited to the 'confidence and supply' model in which, in return for limited policy concessions, an opposition party agrees to support the budget and not to oppose the government in a vote of confidence. Instead, it was a hybrid arrangement, with a shared delivery unit within the Government, populated by two designated Plaid Senedd Members as Political Leads and two Special Advisers. This was the conduit through which Plaid was to communicate and negotiate with Welsh Labour Ministers to implement the Co-operation Agreement.

Meanwhile, Plaid remained an opposition party or, as Adam Price put it, in 'Co-opposition'. The model was completely new in UK governance experience. However, it had precedents elsewhere, notably in Sweden, New Zealand, and Malaysia. In academic parlance, this kind of arrangement is known as Contract Parliamentarianism.[1]

With 30 seats in the 60-member Senedd, First Minister Mark Drakeford could have opted to continue as a minority Government, one vote short of a majority, brokering deals to get his budget through year by year.[2] Instead, he chose greater stability and a far more ambitious policy programme than the one he had announced following the May Senedd election. He described it as capturing 'how Welsh politics works – by finding common ground and sharing good ideas',[3] adding:

> 'We can achieve more for people in Wales by working together and the Co-operation Agreement is both a response to the external challenges we face and a chance to build on the opportunities in our future.'[4]

In an account of Welsh Labour's National Executive meeting that approved the Agreement, he was reported as saying that the content of the Agreement was 'entirely in keeping with Labour's principles, whatever claims might be made to suggest that they were principally Plaid policies.'[5] A Plaid Cymru special conference voted by 94% to support the Agreement, following which Adam Price declared:

> 'Almost a quarter of a century ago, people in Wales voted for self-government for Wales, with a promise of a new type of politics. They placed their trust in a new democracy with an instruction to work differently – inclusively and co-operatively. In the face of the pandemic and a hostile Conservative government in Westminster – a government determined to do everything it can to undermine our long-contested national institutions – it is in our nation's interests for the two parties to work together for Wales.'[6]

---

1 See T. Bale and T. Bergman, 'Captive No Longer, but Servants Still? Contract Parliamentarianism and the New Minority Governance in Sweden and New Zealand', *Government and Opposition* (Cambridge University Press, March 2014).
2 Labour was a vote short of a majority because David Rees, Labour MS for Aberavon, was the Deputy Presiding Officer.
3 BBC Wales, 1 December 2021.
4 *Western Mail*, 23 November 2021.
5 D. Williams, *NEC Reports*, 20 November 2021 (darrenwilliams.org.uk).
6 *Western Mail*, 27 November 2021.

A Huge Step Forward

In the two weeks following its announcement, the Plaid Cymru communications team in the Senedd logged 320 reports and commentaries on the agreement in print media outlets across the UK and judged 70% of them as positive. Quoting Adam Price, the *Western Mail's* banner front-page headline declared, 'Labour-Plaid deal "huge step forward".' Inside, its editorial commentary chided some Plaid critics who opposed their party co-operating with what they saw as a staunch unionist party:

> 'Those members of Plaid who blame their leaders for reaching a deal with Labour which contains many policies that they have been campaigning on for years need to take stock of reality. The demography of Wales is such that Plaid will not win a majority at the Senedd any time soon. That a party which came third in this year's election has such influence on the winning party's governing programme is something they should celebrate, not condemn.'[7]

Ifan Morgan Jones, then Editor of the online news service *Nation Cymru*, observed:

> '"Vote Labour, get Plaid; vote Plaid, get Labour", said one Conservative Senedd member in reaction to the confirmation that the two parties had come to a co-operation agreement. The problem with this as an attack line is that I suspect that many voters from both parties would think, "Yes, fine." It's not fair to say that Plaid Cymru and Welsh Labour are interchangeable. Even as Welsh Labour have shifted in favour of more autonomy for Wales, Plaid Cymru have shifted, too, towards full-throated support for independence. But on the main animating issue of Welsh politics today – the attempted post-Brexit roll-back of devolution by the UK Government – both sides find themselves very much on the same team.'[8]

Stephen Bush, then the *New Statesman's* Political Editor, said that in negotiating the Agreement Plaid had pushed Welsh Labour to the left. He noted, too, that many of the commitments required a good deal of policy development. Because of this he judged that it was preferable for Plaid to have Special Advisers inside the government pushing the

---

7   *Western Mail*, 23 November 2021.
8   I. M. Jones, *Nation Cymru*, 22 November 2021.

Agreement's policy commitments, rather than a full-scale coalition with Ministers sharing collective responsibility:

> 'That's probably a bigger prize than ministerial offices: a lot of the most far-reaching bits of the agreement involve a degree of consultation and policy development, whether it is in the development of a national care service, or reforms to council tax. These are policy commitments where the work of Spads will be as important, if not more so, than that of ministers.'[9]

In its assessment, the Institute of Welsh Affairs looked back at the first 20 years of devolution which, it judged, had had little practical impact on the everyday lives of most Welsh people. This was because of the Senedd's limited powers coupled with a lack of ambition and self-confidence from the Welsh Government. However, the Co-operation Agreement suggested a corner had been turned:

> 'Proposals to increase the size of the Senedd, explore introducing rent controls, reform council tax, end homelessness, introduce tourist taxes, and introduce universal free school meals are policies that, at last, speak to a self-confidence in Welsh decision-makers to change the lives of people in Wales rather than attempt to disrupt the present system as little as possible.'[10]

According to an evaluation by a contributor to the UK Constitutional Law Association's website, the Agreement's establishment of a Constitutional Commission, coupled with Senedd reform, marked 'a definitive milestone in enhancing the powers of the Senedd and furthering the coming of age of Welsh devolution.'[11] Plaid's former MP and Senedd member for Ceredigion, Cynog Dafis, described the Agreement as bringing together radical social democracy with nation-building:

---

9   S. Bush, *New Statesman*, 22 November 2021.
10 W. Henson & H. Thomson, *IWA Analysis: Our View on the Welsh Government & Plaid Cymru Co-operation Agreement*, 23 November 2021.
11 G. Evans, *Welsh Devolution and the Co-operation Agreement* (UK Constitutional Law Association blog, 30 November 2021). Gareth Evans is a Lecturer in Law at the Hillary Rodham Clinton School of Law, Swansea University.

'Speaking as one who observed Welsh Labour at close quarters in the first Assembly, I find their current reincarnation almost unrecognisable. For Plaid, all those years of earnest policy-development, of trying to reconcile vision and practicality, now promise to come to fruition. Dig beyond the headline-grabbing free school meals and tackling the holiday-home issue and you will find a range of potentially transformative nation-building measures: two publicly-owned bodies, for housing and renewable energy; our national history mandatory in the school curriculum; support for devolution of broadcasting and an intention to build a distinctive Welsh media landscape; working towards an integrated national public service; an expanded and more proportional Senedd – are just a few examples.'[12]

There was, of course, opposition to the Agreement, largely from the Conservatives. For instance, Clwyd West's Senedd Member Darren Millar said:

'It does nothing to address the crisis in our NHS; nothing to improve our ailing Welsh infrastructure; and nothing to fire up our sluggish economy. Prioritising more politicians and constitutional reform over action to secure treatment for the one in five on an NHS waiting list or improving take home pay for the low paid is appalling. Yet again, Plaid has betrayed its voters with another deal that cements a failing Labour administration into power for years to come.'[13]

Unusually, a political story from Wales drew the attention of the *Daily Telegraph*, in particular the Agreement's pledge to take 'immediate and radical action' to tackle the number of second homes in Wales. This, the *Telegraph* noted, included a cap on their number; measures to bring more homes into common ownership; a statutory licensing scheme for holiday lets; greater powers for local authorities to charge council tax premiums; and increasing taxes on second homes. The paper's leader writer concluded:

---

12   C. Dafis, 'Plaid Cymru and Labour's radical, nation-building agreement has made Wales an exciting country to be in once again', *Nation Cymru* (23 November 2021).
13   *Western Mail*, 22 November 2021.

'The agreement is essentially the enactment of a socialist/nationalist agenda for which the Welsh people did not vote. It would be hard to imagine a programme more designed to scare investment away from the Principality and damage its growth prospects.'[14]

Of course, to claim the policy programme lacked democratic legitimacy ignores the fact that Labour and Plaid combined had secured 60% of the votes and 43 of the 60 Senedd seats (more than the two-thirds required to secure Senedd reform).

Perhaps the most balanced assessment came from the Director of the Wales Governance Centre at Cardiff University, Professor Richard Wyn Jones, a seasoned commentator on Welsh political trends. He observed that although, in the run-up to the May Senedd election, Plaid Cymru and its leader Adam Price had exaggerated the party's prospects and failed to manage expectations, the Co-operation Agreement had produced far more gains than could have been imagined in the immediate wake of the poll:

'The fact of the matter is that Plaid Cymru and the people of Wales in general have seen the best and worst of Adam Price in recent months. However, due to a combination of favourable circumstances and, yes, some of Price's special talents, Wales is entering a new phase in our political history. Time will tell exactly what the new programme for government will bring and the unique arrangement put in place to oversee it. But, in reading the agreement, it is difficult to avoid the conclusion that the programme is in many ways more to the taste of the national movement than even the One Wales agreement of the period 2007 to 2011. It is also difficult not to believe that the fact that the Labour Party in the Welsh Parliament has endorsed the agreement is a sign of a significant shift in its attitude.'[15]

A party of policy

As explored in Chapter 4, at the start of the negotiations Labour sought to restrict the parameters of an Agreement to ten short headings. In part this reflected the party's weariness after 20 years

---

14   *Daily Telegraph*, 22 November 2021.
15   R. W. Jones, 'Plaid Cymru wedi'r cytundeb' [Plaid Cymru after the agreement], (*Barn*, December 2021 to January 2022, Issue 707-708).

of being in government. Over two decades it had expended a lot of energy in Whitehall battles to secure more funding and acquire more powers. It also had to contend with the instinctive conservatism of the civil service in Cathays Park. In the process, what it might actually do in terms of policy had tended to take a back seat. On the other hand, in opposition Plaid had a freer hand to be more expansive and imaginative. This was reflected in the Co-operation Agreement that emerged following six months of negotiations. Of its 46 commitments, a large proportion emanated from Plaid Cymru's May 2021 Senedd election manifesto — 28 compared with four from Labour's, with a further 14 drawn from both. Plaid's manifesto set out five headline priorities, to:

1. Extend free school meals to all primary school children and improve early years Welsh-medium childcare and education.
2. Launch a £6bn Green Economic Stimulus to create 60,000 jobs.
3. Cut the bills of average council tax payers.
4. Provide free personal care for older people at the point of need, ending the divide between health and social care.
5. Meet the climate and biodiversity emergency, in particular by establishing Ynni Cymru [Energy Wales] as an energy development company.[16]

Apart from the second commitment, all of these were secured by the Co-operation Agreement, without which either they would not be happening or aspects of them would be pursued in a diluted form, with less funding and at a slower pace. There was a shared acknowledgement that implementing the commitment on social care depended on the financial implications of decisions made in Westminster. Accordingly, the Co-operation Agreement committed to:

'Set up an expert group to support our shared ambition to create a National Care Service, free at the point of need, continuing as a public service. We will agree an implementation plan by the end of 2023. We will continue to better integrate health and care and

---

16 Plaid Cymru, *Let Us Face the Future Together:* Senedd election manifesto 2021, p.10-11.

work towards parity of recognition and reward for health and care workers.'

It was notable, however, that the second priority – a package to stimulate the economy and deliver green jobs – was not part of Labour's agenda in negotiating the Co-operation Agreement. Neither, in Plaid's view, was the essential mechanism for making this happen – the re-establishment of the Welsh Development Agency that Labour had abolished, as part of its so-called 'Bonfire of the Quangos', in 2004. Labour refused to countenance this, and was extremely wary of the spending implications of any major commitment to economic development and job creation.

Conversely, though, Labour was willing to entertain nation-building policies that did not involve major expenditure. Crucially for Plaid, these included Senedd reform and the establishment of a Constitutional Commission to make the case for greater powers for Wales. In addition, other Plaid Cymru nation-building priorities included:

- The creation of *Unnos*, a national construction company to improve the supply of social housing.
- Welsh history as a mandatory part of the curriculum.
- Creation of a National Gallery for Contemporary Art.

These initiatives would not have been on the political agenda without the Agreement. It is true that many of the commitments were made easier to negotiate by an increase in the Welsh Government's budget that became apparent some months after the election. There was an extra Treasury allocation of some £1.6bn for 2022-23, mainly due to Covid. Nonetheless, the Agreement was a vindication of the priority Plaid Cymru had given to the development of its manifesto, a priority some critical voices in the party claimed had diverted attention from building a more effective vote-winning organisation.

All political parties aspire to win votes, achieve office, and implement their policies. To a great extent these motivations are inter-related. After all, a party must secure votes to gain office, and thereby power to put their policies into effect. Nonetheless, depending on their circumstances and value systems, parties tend to prioritise, or at least give greater emphasis to, one of these motivations over the other two. Of course, it can be argued that the choices they make are more a result of the circumstances that parties find themselves in, rather than an ideological preference.[17]

Welsh Labour is essentially an office-seeking party. Indeed, since the advent of the National Assembly in 1999 it has entered into no fewer than 14 cross-party deals to secure power, ranging from full-blown coalitions (with the Liberal Democrats in 2000 and Plaid Cymru in 2007) to more limited deals, pacts and compacts.

Circumstances have made the Welsh Conservatives largely a vote-seeking party. It is true that in the period leading up to the 2007 Assembly election the party attempted to modify its approach. It became more centrist and Welsh-focused, to an extent that for a brief moment a three-way 'Rainbow' coalition between it, the Liberal Democrats and Plaid Cymru became a distinct possibility.[18] However, since that time, Conservatives in the Senedd have become less enamoured with Welsh as opposed to British identity, have moved to the right, and certainly since Brexit, have become identified with so-called 'muscular unionism'. This is shorthand for the desire of the Conservative government in London to reduce the powers and influence of the devolved governments, and even to encroach on their powers by, for example, offering funding inducements to Welsh and Scottish local authorities. The result is that the Welsh Conservatives now have very little prospect of cross-party collaboration, leaving them no alternative but to resort to increasing their vote as their overriding objective.

For Plaid Cymru, until Adam Price became leader in 2018, putting its constitutional objectives and policies ahead of gaining office had consistently been its priority. Arguably this had been the position since it was founded in 1925, and certainly since the creation of the National Assembly. There were two watershed moments, the first in 1999 within months of the first elections to the National Assembly, and the second in 2007.[19] In 1999 Plaid played a leading role in the

---

17 For a discussion of these variants see W. C. Muller and K. Strøm (Eds.), *Policy, Office, or Votes? How Political Parties in Western Europe Make Hard Decisions* (Cambridge University Press, 1999).

18 See J. Osmond, *Crossing the Rubicon – Coalition Politics Welsh Style* (IWA, 2007). In this early period, emphasising a Welsh approach was easier for the Conservatives because either they had very few Welsh MPs at Westminster or none at all.

19 Attention to these episodes has been drawn by R. W. Jones, 'Plaid Cymru wedi'r cytundeb', *op. cit.*

overthrow of Alun Michael, the Labour leader in the Assembly, despite this being to the party's electoral disadvantage. If the unpopular Michael had remained in office there was every prospect that Plaid would have garnered votes in the following election. However, Plaid's leaders judged that, given the fragility of devolution due to the slender majority in the 1997 referendum, his presence threatened the national project. Accordingly, they gave priority to that rather than the narrower electoral interests of their party.

Similarly, in 2007 when Plaid Cymru was faced with the chance of pursuing a Rainbow Alliance that would have made its leader, Ieuan Wyn Jones, First Minister, it opted instead to become the junior partner in a coalition with Labour. This was partly because this course meant greater government stability, with the Liberal Democrats being regarded as a less than reliable partner. But it was mainly because the deal with Labour guaranteed the constitutional advance of full legislative powers for the Senedd, that duly took place following the referendum in 2011.

Forming a minority government

However, in the autumn of 2018, when Adam Price became leader, a narrow window of opportunity appeared to open in which, following the upcoming election in 2021, there was a possibility that Plaid Cymru could form a minority government. The reasoning was as follows. Firstly, immediately after the 2016 election, in which Plaid emerged as the second party to Labour, the other opposition parties, including the Conservatives, joined together to vote for Plaid's leader Leanne Wood as First Minister. Her vote tied with Labour's Carwyn Jones, and in the talks that followed Plaid agreed a Compact with Labour. In return for concessions in a number of policy areas, Plaid allowed Labour to form a government.

The episode had given Plaid hope that the precedent might be followed in 2021, with the Conservatives backing a minority Plaid government in which it might expect to have some influence, rather than handing Labour a further term of office. The scenario advanced was that Plaid could be voted in as a minority government even if Labour was still the largest party in the Senedd. For this to happen Labour would have needed to lose a few seats and finish with a total in the mid to high twenties, and Plaid would have had to gain seats taking its total to the high teens. Given the state of the polls – and given also that Labour was poised to elect Mark Drakeford as their new leader, who was at that time relatively unknown and lacking the profile and presence of his two predecessors, Rhodri Morgan and Carwyn Jones – the scenario was surely within the bounds of a reasonable possibility.

When Adam Price embarked on his period of leadership in September 2018 it was envisaged by party strategists that the period to the May 2021 election would unfold in three phases:

- Phase One: the six months to the Spring conference in March 2019 during which changes would be made to put the party on a more robust campaign footing.
- Phase Two: 18 months from Spring 2019 to end of 2020, when Adam Price would undertake a country-wide campaign, visiting every constituency.
- Phase Three: the May 2021 election campaign itself which would start in January 2021.

That was the plan. The 2021 election was envisaged as being presidential in style, with Adam Price's qualities of experience, presence and projection being pitched against those of Mark Drakeford who, by comparison, was regarded as somewhat retiring and certainly less charismatic.

The plan appeared to be working for the first six months. Indeed, opinion polling suggested that it was eminently achievable. In early March 2019 an ICM poll for BBC Wales put Labour on 34%, Plaid 27%, Conservatives 23%, Liberal Democrats 7%, and UKIP 5%. This would have given Labour 25 seats, Plaid 19, Conservatives 14, and the Liberal Democrats and UKIP one each.

Very soon, however, the strategy began to falter, unravel, and then be completely overwhelmed by the force of events. The first was Brexit and its associated melodramas at Westminster. The European Parliament election in May 2019 completely diverted attention. In its wake came the Brecon and Radnor by-election in August, in which Plaid stood down in favour of the Liberal Democrats as part of a 'Unite to Remain Alliance' forged with them and the Greens across Britain. Plaid engaged in intense negotiations on this deal at Westminster. It was also part of large-scale demonstrations and marches in Cardiff and London in an effort to build momentum for a second referendum on European Union (EU) membership. This effort drove through the

Autumn until it crashed on the rocks of Boris Johnson's snap general election in December, dominated by his campaign to 'Get Brexit Done'.

Then, within a matter of weeks from February 2020, the world was subsumed by the Covid pandemic. Over the course of the subsequent 18 months that led to the 2021 Senedd election, Covid fundamentally changed people's lives and perceptions. In virtually every respect the Senedd election came to be fought in the shadow of the pandemic.

For many people across Wales – undoubtedly the majority – the Covid emergency brought Welsh institutions, the Senedd and the Welsh Government together with its First Minister, sharply into focus for the first time. For instance, until the pandemic hit, most people in Wales thought that decisions about the health service were the responsibility of the government in London. Most had low awareness and little knowledge of the Welsh Government and the significant powers it exercises, particularly over health and education.

Above all, the pandemic made many aware for the first time of the role and personality of the First Minister. From being scarcely visible, and a rather academic and hesitant figure at that, Covid shot Mark Drakeford into the forefront of public attention. He appeared daily in televised press conferences instructing the nation as to what they could and could not do in their personal lives – whether they should stay at home, when they could go out to exercise, who they could see and in what numbers, including their extended family, where they should shop, whether they could go to pubs, whether and where they could travel.

Polling confirmed that people found the First Minister's cautious, considered, and step-by-step approach reassuring and admirable, certainly when contrasted with Boris Johnson's reckless, chaotic boosterism. The slogan on Drakeford's media podium was *Diogelu Cymru/Keep Wales Safe*, which became the branding for the Welsh Government's distinctive response. What had been seen by many in the political world as Drakeford's weaknesses now became his strengths. Even his television delivery, characterised by a somewhat ponderous tone and odd pauses but no verbal hesitations or audible 'ums', was interesting and worked to his advantage.

The key dynamics that influenced the May 2021 election outcome were revealed in extensive polling undertaken by the

Wales Governance Centre at Cardiff University. Mark Drakeford's presence and performance during the pandemic utterly transformed his image. By the time of the Senedd election he was a significant electoral asset. When asked why people had supported Labour, the following answers came to the fore, represented by a word cloud:

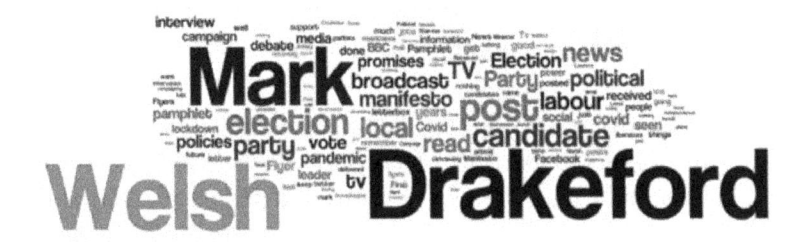

Figure 1: 'Word cloud' summarising the electorate's attitude to Welsh Labour in the 2021 Senedd election

There was a further development, also associated with the pandemic, that fatally undermined Plaid Cymru's aspiration to lead a minority government. In January 2021 the Conservative leader Paul Davies was forced to resign after it was discovered he had been drinking alcohol with others in the Senedd just before Christmas, in possible breach of Covid rules. Davies was consensual, centrist, and pro-European. It was possible to conceive that he might support a minority Plaid Cymru government. On the other hand, his successor Andrew R.T. Davies was much further to the right. He was abrasive, more aligned with Westminster priorities, and had campaigned against Britain's membership of the European Union. He quickly made it clear there were no circumstances in which he would vote for Adam Price to become First Minister.

For all these reasons, as Plaid Cymru approached the May 21 Senedd elections it reverted to being a party of policy. This was reflected, first in the detailed attention Plaid gave to the preparation of its Manifesto; and then in its internal assessment of how it should deal with Labour in any negotiations about a governing relationship once the election was over. There was a calculated anticipation in naming the Plaid Manifesto *Let Us Face the Future Together*, a riff on the title of Labour's famous 1945 Manifesto *Let us Face the Future*.

Labour and Plaid approaches to collaboration

In the months before the May election there was a widespread view across the parties, and in the press and media, that the outcome would result in collaboration between Labour and Plaid, even if not an outright coalition. There was little expectation that Labour would perform significantly better than in 2016. Indeed, it was expected that the Conservatives would perform well and repeat their successes of the 2019 general election in Labour's north-east Wales 'red wall' seats.

Certainly, this was Labour's view, and experience had taught them they should prepare to reach out to Plaid. In the previous election they had won 29 seats, two short of a majority, and that had proved difficult to manage. As Jane Hutt put it in 2007, when she was Labour's Business Manager and Chief Whip:

> 'Surviving as a minority government in the period up to 2007 with 29 seats was extremely difficult. We did manage to get most of our programme through but it proved very difficult with the budget. After May 2007, to think we could manage with 26 seats without a stability pact or a coalition was naïve. We would have been constantly firefighting to a point where we would have been unable to deliver our mandate.'[20]

In the run-up to the May 2021 election Mark Drakeford was quite open about such a prospect recurring. For instance, he told the *Financial Times* that he would welcome a deal with Plaid. He pointed out that the 2007 One Wales coalition between Labour and Plaid had worked well, 'The key thing is whether there is a policy platform on which we can agree,' he said.[21] A few weeks earlier he had set out his position in more detail:

---

20 J. Osmond, *Crossing the Rubicon – Coalition Politics Welsh Style* (IWA, August 2007), p.50. Jane Hutt was interviewed on 18 July 2007. Labour had won 30 seats in 2003 but in 2005 that fell to 29. This was due to the resignation from Labour of Peter Law, AM for Blaenau Gwent, in protest at Labour using an all-woman shortlist to choose a Westminster Parliamentary candidate in his constituency.

21 A. Bounds, 'Wales finds greater belief in self-government amid pandemic response' (*Financial Times*, 5 April 2021).

'The history of devolution tells you that no party has ever secured a majority in our electoral system. I have worked in governments with members of Plaid Cymru, the Liberal Democrats, and people of no political party at all. What has always mattered to me is the policy programme. If we need to work with other parties, I'm not interested in political fixes. I'm not interested in approaching it on a who gets what kind of basis. The reason we've had successful governments with other parties is that we've started with hammering out a common policy platform that different parties can sign up to. I spent the summer of the year 2000 going every Saturday down to the Bay to meet a man called Michael Hinds who was the senior adviser in the Liberal Democrat party. The two of us worked our way through policy positions that in the Autumn we were able to present to the First Minister and Mike German, Leader of the Liberal Democrats, as not a done deal but a solid basis for a policy programme that both parties could sign up to. The negotiations that led up to the One Wales agreement with Plaid Cymru were done in exactly the same way. If we need to talk to other people that's where I would want us to start. If we can't reach a policy agreement there's no point in worrying about the political under-pinning for it. But if we can reach a policy agreement then the politics is a matter of will. If you want something to happen you can make it happen. If you want to stop something happening you can always find a reason for it not to happen.'[22]

Early debates within Plaid Cymru concerning the party's participation in coalition government in the Senedd focused primarily on the perceived need to provide a democratic choice to the seeming permanence of Labour or Labour-led governments. This was the argument put forward by *Dewis*, a pressure group within Plaid Cymru in the years leading to the 2007 Assembly election. The group, led by former MPs Cynog Dafis and Dafydd Wigley, adopted the name *Dewis* (Choice) to underline that message. The group put forward an outline for a full-scale manifesto, with a wide-ranging policy agenda that focused on nation-building measures in education, culture, and communications, and proposals for retaining young people in Wales. It prioritised tackling over-reliance on the public sector, promoting an entrepreneurial culture by assisting businesses with the potential

---

22   *Hiraeth* – Wales Politics podcast, 24 March 2021.

to grow, and the formation of a Valleys Regeneration Corporation. It said Plaid Cymru faced a fundamental choice:

> '...whether it wishes to be a party of government in Wales in the near future, and thus influence seriously the course of events, or whether it is content with opposition, free to advance a radically alternative, future oriented, vision of Wales. Whereas we would not question the value of pursuing the second option, we have no doubt that it is the duty of Plaid Cymru to aim to lead the government of Wales.' [23]

A similar case was made during the same period by Adam Price.[24] However, as already stated, these arguments were advanced in a very different political context to the one that applied in the run-up to the 2021 election. In 2007 the Welsh Conservative Party, led by Nick Bourne, was centrist or, in European terms, Christian Democratic and armed with a newly forged Welsh identity. In 2007 the Welsh Liberal Democrats, led by Mike German, were still a relatively significant force in Welsh politics, with six Assembly Members, and had been in coalition with Labour between 2000 and 2003. In the intervening 16 years, the two parties had changed. The Welsh Conservatives, driven by Brexit, had moved to the right, sought to curb the advance of devolution, and had ruled out any arrangement with Plaid Cymru – as had Plaid Cymru with them. Meanwhile the Liberal Democrats were a spent force, unlikely to return more than one member to the 2021-26 Senedd.

Consequently, this left Plaid Cymru as the only available coalition partner for Labour, a prospect that had first emerged during the period following the May 2007 election. At that time Plaid first attempted to forge a Rainbow Alliance with the Conservatives and Liberal Democrats, and when that failed turned to Labour to negotiate the One Wales agreement. By then Adam Price, who was at the centre of the negotiations, strongly favoured what he called

---

23 Dewis, *Deffro Mae'n Ddydd: Plaid Cymru and the Realities of Coalition Politics in 21st Century Wales*, May 2005. The group comprised: Dafydd Wigley, Eurfyl ap Gwilym, Cynog Dafis, Elwyn Vaughan, Phil Cooke, and John Osmond.

24 A. Price, *Comprimiso Historico? Towards a Government of National Solidarity*, paper presented to a joint meeting of the National Executive and the Cardiff Bay and Westminster parliamentary groups, June 2004.

the Red-Green Alliance, calling in aid the Sardinian Marxist thinker Antonio Gramsci:

> 'In seeking to challenge a dominant hegemony there are basically two choices, Gramsci said, either a "war of movement" – a rapid, frontal assault on the citadels of power, or a "war of position" – a slower, broader and less dramatic attempt to appropriate the ruling hegemony for one's own political purposes. A quarter of a century ago Plaid Cymru opted for the latter strategy, positioning itself as a 'socialist' party within the dominant discourse of Welsh politics but seeking at the same time to "burrow into the contradictions" thrown up by the Labour Party's undying support for the unitary British state. The strategy has been electorally and politically successful, gaining Plaid Cymru seats and dragging Labour, however unwillingly, in a nationalist direction.'[25]

This was Adam Price's position on the eve of the May 2021 election, except that by then Labour's 'undying support for the unitary British state' had been considerably modified. Now it was declaring that sovereignty in Wales lay with the Welsh people rather than the Westminster Parliament, and that the relationship between the nations of Britain should be recast into something it called 'radical federalism'.[26] The day after the May 2021 Senedd election, and before the votes had been counted, one of Labour's Special Advisers texted Plaid to say their negotiating team was poised to enter into talks.

---

25 Adam Price (adamprice.org.uk/blog, 25 June 2007).
26 See Welsh Government, '*Reforming Our Union: Shared governance in the UK*', September 2019. A second edition was published in June 2021 (gov.wales/reforming-our-union-shared-governance-in-the-uk-2nd-edition). A group of Labour members, led by Counsel General Mick Antoniw, published *We the People: The Case for Radical Federalism*, in January 2021. The document was referenced in the second edition of *Reforming our Union*.

2

View from the Back Row

Plaid Cymru is a middle-class party. That is to say, the background, education and attitudes of most of its activists, and certainly those of its representatives in the Senedd and at Westminster, are middle class. They are socially progressive on issues such as race and gender and are internationalist, for instance strongly in favour of the European Union. It is also among the reasons why they give such priority to preserving Welsh culture, particularly the Welsh language.

It is something of a paradox, therefore, that the constituencies Plaid represents in its western Wales heartland are among the poorest in the UK, home to working class voters who, it might be thought, would not share these attitudes to the same extent. Plaid Cymru is very much what the American writer Chris Arnade calls a 'front row' party, with its membership composed of upwardly mobile achievers. Yet this puts it at odds with most of its voters, certainly in places where it has attracted much of its support, such as Caernarfon, Meirionnydd and Ceredigion, and intermittently in the Valleys. As Arnade puts it, in his exploration of poverty in the United States:

> 'I spent most of my life focused on getting ahead by education. I left my rural hometown and got into élite schools, which got me into élite jobs, which got me into an élite neighbourhood. I was hardly alone. My office, my neighbourhood, and most of my adult friends were like me, and like the residents of most successful neighbourhoods across the country, ones filled with bankers, professors, and lawyers. Almost all of us had used education to get out of a hometown that we saw as oppressive, intolerant, and judgmental. We were the kids who sat in the front row, eager to learn and make sure the teacher knew we were learning. We wanted to get ahead, and we had.'

Arnade says that, as a result, he and his fellow students in the 'front row' became isolated from the bulk of the country and were left with a narrow view of the world. They valued what they could measure, which meant material wealth. On the other hand, they largely ignored things that couldn't be measured — values such as community, dignity, faith, happiness — because they were hard to see. It didn't occur to them to imagine that the things they valued – as Arnade puts it, 'getting more education and owning more stuff' – weren't necessarily what everyone else wanted. At the same time, while economic growth empowered the corporations that created large franchise companies and stores across the country, these tended to crowd out small locally owned enterprises, shops and restaurants:

> 'While our front row neighbourhoods filled with bespoke and artisanal stores, those left behind, literally and figuratively, were left to cope with the new landscape we had created. If we were the front row, they were the back row. They were the people who couldn't or didn't want to leave their town or their family to get an education at an élite college ... They want to graduate from high school and get a stable job allowing them to raise a family, often in the same community they were born into. Instead, the back row is now left living in a banal world of hyper efficient fast-food franchises, strip malls, discount stores, and government buildings with flickering fluorescent lights and dreary coloured walls. They are left with a world where their sense of home and family and community won't get them anywhere, won't pay the bills. And with a world where their jobs are disappearing.'[1]

Indeed, many parts of Wales are what Chris Arnade would call 'back row' country. His analysis aligns closely with that of David Goodhart who, in his book *The Road to Somewhere* describes Welsh people as typically 'citizens of Somewhere' as opposed to 'Anywhere'. He argues that a key political fault line in both Britain and the United States separates those who come from 'Somewhere' – people who are rooted in a specific place or community, usually a small town or in the countryside, who are socially conservative and often less educated – and those who come from 'Anywhere', who tend to be footloose, often urban, socially liberal and university educated. Goodhart cites polling evidence to show that 'Somewheres' make up roughly half the UK population, with 'Anywheres' accounting for 20% to 25%, and the rest classified as 'Inbetweeners'.

---

1   C. Arnade, *Dignity: Seeking Respect in Back Row America* (Sentinel, 2019, pp. 44-7).

Most Welsh voters tend to be 'Somewheres', people who have lived in one community all their lives. In particular, according to data from UK Understanding Society surveys, Plaid supporters have a higher proportion than those of any other party who still live within 15 minutes of their mother, have not had the opportunity to go to university, voted Brexit, have a strong belief that hard work gives their lives meaning, and have socially conservative views on race and gender. As Goodhart reports:

> 'Looking at political affiliation, nationalist party voters had the highest levels of rootedness: more than 50 per cent of BNP voters live within fifteen minutes of their mother, compared to 42 per cent of UKIP voters, **60 per cent of Plaid Cymru voters** [author's emphasis], 37 per cent of SNP voters (and all the Northern Ireland parties are over 50 per cent). Those least likely to live close to their mothers are Green voters, on 25 per cent, and Liberal Democrats, on 30 per cent.'[2]

An additional element is that for many of these 'Somewhere' identifiers, change is experienced as loss. That is to say, they tend to prefer the familiar, the stable and the routine to novelty and change. All of this is counter to Plaid Cymru's ambition to lead Wales to independence. Early in Adam Price's leadership the need to face this dilemma was recognised. First, it was acknowledged that a substantial majority of the voters the party needed to attract could be described as coming from the 'back row'. Further, we had to admit that beyond Welsh language communities, where 'front row' and 'back row' citizens are united in support for their own culture, we had largely failed to articulate a message that appealed to this very large population elsewhere in Wales.

Highlighting social priorities

These insights influenced a conscious decision to focus the party's attention on social and economic questions. In part this was an effort to counterbalance the undoubted perception that Plaid Cymru is

---

2   D. Goodhart, *The Road to Somewhere: The New Tribes Shaping British Politics* (Penguin Random House, 2017), p.38. The data is taken from 'Understanding Society: Waves 1-5, 2009-2014', 8th Edition, (dx.doi.org/10.5255/UKDA-SN-7111-1)

mainly concerned with the Welsh language and cultural matters. It was also a deliberate strategy to occupy ground that was generally perceived as Labour's territory.

For most of the first quarter of a century of democratic devolution, the Welsh Labour Party has outmanoeuvred Plaid Cymru by the simple tactic of placing its tanks on the nationalist lawn. It has identified itself as *Welsh* Labour, one with which Welsh identifying people could feel comfortable in placing their allegiance. In short, it has projected itself as a soft nationalist party. Welsh Labour self-consciously underlines this tactic by constantly declaring it is 'standing up for Wales'. It has cleverly distanced itself from London Labour, although mainly in terms of political rhetoric. Early on it adopted the rubric 'clear red water' to dissociate itself from unpopular London Labour policies, such as the Private Finance Initiative for investing in public services, and its opposition to the war in Iraq which Rhodri Morgan refused to endorse.

Plaid resolved to counter this by committing itself to policies traditionally associated with the Labour left. The task was to demonstrate not only that Welsh Labour had been indolent and ineffective in implementing policies in these areas, but that Plaid had the energy, urgency and innovative approach to tackle them more successfully.

Renewed attention was given to the growing levels of poverty, and especially child poverty, in Wales. According to Save the Children, a third of children in Wales, more than 200,000, were living in poverty. In the wake of Covid, and with the impact of the UK Government's welfare and taxation changes, those statistics were destined to get worse. In the run-up to the May 2021 Senedd election Plaid determined to orchestrate a campaign for the Welsh Government to do the one thing clearly within its power to bear down on child poverty: to extend free school meals to all primary school pupils in Wales.

In addition, the party would build arguments for other bread and butter issues calculated to appeal to the 'back row' voter, including:

- Reducing inequality, both within Wales, and between Wales and the rest of the UK, by creating good quality jobs throughout Wales, not just in the south-east.
- Dealing with the escalating need for social care for the elderly.
- Tackling homelessness and the lack of affordable housing: local housing provision should reflect local housing need, with priority given to those with strong local connections.

- Giving the same level of support to further education students and apprenticeships as to university under-graduates.
- Emphasising the local, including local government, and the smaller-scale – valley more than county, and county more than region.
- Revitalising town centres and local transport.
- Favouring local firms through localised public procurement.
- Introducing a Welsh Citizens card to provide reduced fares on rail and bus for those most in need, especially the young and the elderly.
- Reforming council tax, with additional bands, so that those in more expensive properties pay proportionately more.

Following the 2021 Senedd election many of these priorities found their way into the Co-operation Agreement. What was largely left out, however, was Plaid's emphasis on the need for an economic programme.

Poor economic outcomes have been a constant feature of the devolution years. There are underlying, structural reasons for that. They include the inheritance of a century's decline of coal and steel; a lack of power over the main economic levers on tax and spending which remain at Westminster; inadequate funding for industrial investment; and, not least, being integrated into a UK economy in which wealth and power are overwhelmingly concentrated in London and south east England. At the same time successive Labour governments in Cardiff Bay have played a difficult hand badly. In particular, they lacked coherence in economic management at the centre, compounded by the own goal of abolishing the major economic tool they had to hand, the Welsh Development Agency.

Economic self-reliance

Addressing 'back row' concerns, Plaid acknowledged Wales's economic and financial weaknesses, summarised as the fiscal gap: the difference between the income from taxes raised in Wales and expenditure on public services, welfare payments and pensions. The deficit is around 18% of Welsh GDP, which in 2018-19 was calculated at about £4,300 per person. Most of Britain is in the same position of having a net deficit, that is nine out of the 12 planning regions, but with the difference that for most of them the deficit is much smaller, an average of just £620 per head. Only London, the South-East and the East of England are net contributors to the UK budget.

To put the problem another way, un-supplemented revenues raised in Wales would be enough to pay for the level of public services offered in a country such as Portugal. Instead, Wales has broadly the same services as Ireland, a richer country on most measures.

As Plaid Cymru saw it, the choice was this: did the party believe that the present system offered a serious prospect of improving Welsh economic performance, which had been sliding backwards relative to the rest of the UK for the past 50 years? Or should the decision be made to change tack and opt for the greater self-reliance and the ability to make key economic decisions to address the fiscal gap that independence would allow?

To opt for the second course was to argue that Wales had failed to make economic progress, not because the country is too small or too poor, but because it is trapped within a wider British economy shaped in the financial interests of the City of London. This flawed model has failed to deliver prosperity for Wales and offers no prospect of doing so. Wales should become an independent country no longer subjected to the fiscal policies determined by a UK government, and no longer subordinated to the economic interests of London and the south east of England.

In the meantime, a more dynamic culture of economic policymaking and implementation should be sought, via the restoration of a national economic development agency fit for the 21st Century. The Welsh economy has chronic structural weaknesses that have persisted for many decades. They include low productivity, a dearth of medium-sized companies, firms that are vulnerable to takeover, a low export propensity, and educational and skills shortcomings. Little wonder then that since the advent of devolution 25 years ago, Welsh GDP per capita has remained stubbornly at around 72% of the UK average.

The Welsh Government's first economic strategy, *A Winning Wales*, published in 2001, aimed to raise Welsh GDP to 90% of the UK average within a decade. However, after three years the target was quietly dropped. At the same time, in 2004, the Welsh Development Agency – responsible for delivering economic policy – was abolished and its functions absorbed into the civil service.

Four subsequent economic strategies – *Wales: A Vibrant Economy* (2005), *Economic Renewal: A New Direction* (2010), *Prosperity for All: Economic Action Plan* (2017), and, finally, *Economic Mission: priorities for a stronger economy* (2023) – all conspicuously omitted any targets or criteria against which success could be measured. Instead, policy became trapped within a risk-averse civil service culture. Economically Wales was going backwards.

This judgement was supported by a paper published by Jonathan Bradbury and Andrew Davies, of Swansea University, in the *National Institute Economic Review* in 2022. Their analysis is all the more noteworthy since Andrew Davies was Economic Development and Transport Minister in the Welsh Government between 2002 and 2007 and, as such, was at the heart of the decision to abolish the WDA. The authors undertook an in-depth analysis of the Welsh Government's successive economic strategies and found they lacked 'a consistent, coherent long-term set of priorities', while being insufficiently focused 'on the means of implementing priorities'. Further, their paper provides a detailed examination of three policy areas they say are central to economic development – transport, renewable energy, and public procurement – and again find a lack of coherence and consistency:

> 'It also reveals a systemic problem of Welsh Government focusing on policy and legislation rather than implementation, leading to a lack of delivery on original ambitions.'[3]

The Welsh Civil Service culture

It is in the nature of bureaucracies to be slow, cumbersome, and focused on compliance rather than action. However, there is evidence, from the observations of a number of commentators, that the Welsh civil service is particularly prone to these characteristics. One close observer, Sir Adrian Webb, former Vice Chancellor of the University of Glamorgan and for ten years a Non-Executive Director on the Welsh Government's Management Board, reported:

> 'Welsh Government is too often slow. Outside organisations are routinely frustrated by the lack of pace. This is inevitably true

---

3   J. Bradbury and A. Davies, 'Regional economic development and the case of Wales: theory and practice and problems of strategy and policy', *National Institute Economic Review*, Vol. 261, (Cambridge University Press, 2022), pp.1-15. See also M. Shipton, 'Top Labour figure says promised economic benefits of devolution remain undelivered (*Nation Cymru*, 19 August 2024), in which Andrew Davies draws attention to the problems of a 'Client State' arising from continuous Labour-run government in Wales.

of government when viewed from a non-public organisation; government has to cover bases which others do not. But there is good reason to believe that Wales is often especially slow. I have worked with a number of Whitehall civil servants who find the context in Wales unbelievably frustrating.'[4]

This was in a document commissioned by Mark Drakeford in 2018 as he prepared to take over the role of First Minister. Webb identified the core problem as being a failure of delivery. He argued that the Welsh Government operates on a 'management model' rather than a 'leadership of joined-up delivery' model, driven by a sense of urgency:

> 'The current mindset puts delivery second best to maintenance of the status quo – especially in the layers of the civil service just below the top. While many (some/a minority of?) civil servants do seek to deliver, civil servants are simply not held *systematically accountable* for delivery or for acting with a sense of urgency.'[5]

Webb reported that, from his direct experience, this cultural 'mindset' operated from the top of the Welsh civil service downwards. He had been involved in UK Cabinet Office appraisals of successive Permanent Secretaries for salary purposes. Yet: 'At no time was delivery against specified goals a consideration.'[6] Webb put this down to a confusion in the Welsh civil service mindset between delivery – which it associated with process and the avoidance of error – and measurable outcomes:

> 'There tends to a box ticking drive to ensure Manifesto and Programme promises can be said to have been met. What I have never seen is an overall attempt to assess whether the desired *outcomes* underlying the Programme for Government and the Manifesto are being advanced. I was a member of the Board for nearly 10 years and I have never been part of a Board with such a lack of measures of progress or outcome success. *The only data routinely seen by the board are budgetary.* Parts of the system do try to use outcome and performance measures, but

---

4 Sir A. Webb, *Machinery of Government* (Unpublished Memorandum, 2018), pp.2-3.
5 Ibid., p.6.
6 Ibid., p.7.

this meets considerable resistance from some (many?) civil servants. The fact that metrics are resisted tells its own tale.'[7]

Another close observer of the implementation of the Welsh Government's economic policy was Graeme Guilford, former senior manager with Amersham International's Cardiff operation. He was also a member of the EU Wales Structural Funds Monitoring Committee and a member of the Welsh Government's Regional Investment for Wales Steering Group. His assessment supported Adrian Webb's judgement about the lack of a 'delivery culture' inside the Welsh Government. Discussing the lessons that needed to be learned to design a post-Brexit regional development policy, he concluded:

> 'This focus on delivery is largely absent within the Structural Funds area. In my experience this is mainly because there has been an assumption that delivery is something that simply "happens" once the project is approved. Indeed, for many projects funding was approved before a project delivery team was in place or even recruited. Within much of the public sector in Wales, project management is seen as a relatively junior administrative function rather than the key, make or break role it occupies in the private sector. This means that the "heroes" in the process are the people who write the successful project application not the people who successfully deliver the project. This lack of focus on delivery was exacerbated by the absence of an effective central support system to help struggling projects particularly in their early stages.'[8]

Professor Gerald Holtham had a close-up view of the operation of the Welsh Government and its civil service when he acted as Special Adviser to Finance Minister Jane Hutt for three years between 2012 and 2014:

> 'My experience was that Ministries acted like semi-independent fiefdoms where the Minister had a policy, which he or she had considerable latitude to change without much Cabinet discussion. Indeed, one Minister was reputed to have never brought a policy

---

7   Ibid., p.8.
8   G. Guilford, *Regional Economic Development in Wales: What does Previous Experience tell us about Future Approaches?* (Regional Investment in Wales Steering Group, 2019).

paper to Cabinet in a long ministerial career. The main limitation on Ministerial discretion seemed to be a belief that things written in the Labour Party Manifesto were commitments that had to be honoured somehow. However, while that belief gave rise to a wish list, it did not impose any priorities. Policy changes may well have been discussed informally and bilaterally with the First Minister but that was not always evident. This ministerial quasi-independence led not only to silo-thinking but limited the ability to think strategically and to reflect that thinking in budgetary allocation. The usual practice seemed to be everyone's budget went up (or down) by a standard amount. The exception was looming crises in the health service might well require extra money and a consequent haircut for everyone else.'[9]

Holtham also observed that silo-thinking by Ministers had a knock-on effect for the Welsh civil service:

'The lack of overarching priorities in government bedevilled work across departments at the official level. Meetings involving officials from several departments operated in slow motion. Because the work was not the "baby" of their own minister it was fitted in with all the other calls on their time. The next meeting was always scheduled on the first day that everyone said they could attend given their other diary commitments. When priorities are uncertain, the diary rules. This meant that cross-departmental work proceeded sluggishly. Because differences were not always thrashed out at Cabinet level, meetings could reflect sharply different degrees of enthusiasm across departments, which ultimately was debilitating and not good for morale. People like to feel they are working for a common purpose, not engaged in a perpetual negotiation.'[10]

In an earlier paper Holtham identified the cause of these and other problems around civil service delivery being a lack of a strong coordinating hand at the centre of the Welsh Government. Indeed, he said Wales had a 'Polo-mint' government, one with a hole in the middle:

'There is no substantial First Minister's department, no strong Cabinet Office and no real Treasury in the Welsh Government. There

---

9   G. Holtham, *Government Process* (Unpublished paper, 2018).
10   *Ibid.*

is no body that is supposed to help frame an overall strategy or to co-ordinate the strategies of different ministries, which all too often operate with detached independence. If the First Minister wants to create an industrial strategy driving the infrastructure plan and to ensure that the policies of all departments are in harmony with it, he will have his work cut out. The institutions to help him are not there. You won't get joined up government if a chunk of the government's central nervous system is missing.'[11]

In the wake of this criticism First Minister Carwyn Jones established an office for himself, in effect a Cabinet Office. Then, following the beginning of devolution of taxation powers by the Wales Act 2014, a Welsh Treasury (actually a small unit responsible for the Welsh Government's minimal tax raising powers) was established within the Finance Department. However, it is not clear what improvement in coordination has resulted from these changes.

Demise of the Welsh Development Agency

Founded in 1975 and abolished in 2004, with its functions absorbed by the civil service, the Welsh Development Agency (WDA) had been first proposed in Plaid Cymru's *Economic Plan*, published in 1970, to:

- Further economic development
- Promote industrial efficiency and competitiveness
- Create and safeguard employment
- Improve the environment

While it sometimes attracted a good deal of controversy and criticism, in general the WDA proved successful.[12] It undertook a large amount of derelict land clearance and pit reclamation, generated £billions

---

11 G. Holtham, 'Industrial Policy and Infrastructure in Wales', in *Debating Industrial Policy in Wales* (Wales TUC, 2016), p.26.
12 In the early 1990s the WDA attracted controversy when its chairman Gwyn Jones, a Gower-based businessman, was appointed to the post after he had met Peter Walker, the Secretary of State for Wales, at a Conservative fund-raising dinner. Jones resigned ahead of the publication of a Public Accounts Committee report which condemned the Agency for a range of irregular payments and appointments. Jones's successor Sir David Rowe-Beddoe instituted a number of reforms including making the Agency conform to Nolan Principles.

of investment and created thousands of jobs. It was credited with bringing major international manufacturing companies into Wales, including Ford, Bosch, Sony, Panasonic, British Airways, Amersham International, and General Electric, plus financial service companies such as Legal and General and Lloyds Bank. It also assisted in the creation of the National Botanic Garden and Llanelli Coastal Park, and contributed to the building of the Millennium (now Principality) Stadium and the Wales Millennium Centre.

All this was achieved in the 20 years between 1980 and 2000 against a backcloth of a large and precipitate decline of the coal and steel industries that had formed the mainstay of the Welsh economy for a century. The comparison with what was achieved in economic and industrial policy during the succeeding period, the 20 years from 2000 to 2020, is sobering.

It is true that the WDA was operating in the years before the opening up of large-scale manufacturing in Eastern Europe and China, which largely replaced Wales as a source of competitive, relatively cheap labour. If it had survived the Welsh Development Agency would have had to find a completely new approach to securing inward investment, but given its track record, its closeness to the private sector, together with the global brand it had established, there is every reason to believe it could have been successful in doing so.

The ostensible reason for the abolition of the WDA in 2004 was to create a more accountable and efficient delivery system. Yet, since the advent of the National Assembly in 1999, the WDA had been held accountable in multiple ways – through an annual remit letter by the Economic Development Minister and, more visibly, through regular public scrutiny by the Assembly's Economic Development Committee. Moreover, there is a wider scrutiny than such formal mechanisms. The WDA had long been held accountable through media attention and the accompanying glare of publicity. However, once its functions were taken in-house, economic policy became less transparent than previously, when the WDA was obliged to publish performance indicators, business plans, and an annual report and accounts.

As to efficiency, the civil service takeover resulted in an inevitable and considerable diminution of commercial nous and agility. This was inevitable because of the civil service culture, which extols process over outcome, and compliance over performance. By its nature the civil service is more risk averse and less innovative than an arms-length, private sector facing body such as the WDA. All this was predicted at the time. Kevin Morgan and Stevie Upton, regional economists at Cardiff University, judged that the merger programme would:

> '...destroy the benefits of the Quangos – their arm's length nature allowing flexibility and responsiveness, plus the scope for a broadly defined accountability – in favour of a system renowned for being risk averse, bureaucratic, and notoriously difficult to scrutinise.'[13]

And they concluded:

> 'On the basis of the evidence to date, it seems that incorporation is being sought not so much for accountability, because that exists in ample form already, as for day-to-day control, the one thing that eludes politicians in the present arm's length system.'[14]

Certainly, there was a frustration amongst Ministers that the WDA operated too independently. Carwyn Jones, made this case in 2003, when he was Minister for Agriculture. He argued that devolution had made many of what were then known as Assembly Sponsored Public Bodies (ASPBs), including the WDA, 'superfluous':

> 'There may be little need now for some bodies to have a separate existence from the Assembly. Much of their work could easily be done by Assembly civil servants, making it more accountable and removing an unnecessary tier of decision-making... The fundamental point remains that the present structure of many ASPBs is superfluous. They should be brought properly under the wing of the elected government elected by the people of Wales to take decisions.'[15]

Doubtless, this was an underlying motivation. At the time, however, there was widespread speculation that the immediate reason was frustration, or perhaps more accurately a fit of pique, by First Minister Rhodri Morgan. This arose following publication of the

---

13   K. Morgan and S. Upton, 'Culling the Quangos' in J. Osmond (Ed.), *Welsh Politics Come of Age – Responses to the Richard Commission* (IWA, 2005), p.98.
14   *Ibid.*, p.96.
15   C. Jones, *The Future of Welsh Labour* (IWA, February 2004).

cross-party Richard Commission report in March 2004 into the powers and electoral arrangements of the National Assembly. Its recommendations entailed radical reforms, including granting full legislative powers, increasing the Assembly's size from 60 to 80 members, and adopting the Single Transferable Vote system of proportional representation.

Initially, there was broad support for these recommendations, including from Rhodri Morgan himself. However, Prime Minister Tony Blair soon made it clear that Westminster would not allow parliamentary time for the necessary legislation. In response, Rhodri Morgan decided that if he could not expand the powers of the National Assembly, he would enhance the role and reach of Government by bringing the WDA inhouse. In his memoirs Morgan points to a spat between himself and the WDA's Chairman Sir David (later Lord) Rowe-Beddoe over control of international investment. As he put it, 'In the end establishing the primacy of the democratically elected body over the appointed boards of the quangos had to be sorted.'[16] He also said that in the marketing of Wales there was a confusion between the brand of the WDA and the essential message of promoting Wales itself, and added:

> 'The second problem was that the WDA was paying its staff 20% more than the equivalent civil servants. The WDA had doubled its number of staff from around 450 to 900 during the life of the Assembly and that, combined with the 20% pay above equivalent civil servants, was a big cost burden. It couldn't continue.'[17]

However, Morgan failed to acknowledge that during this period the WDA absorbed the Development Board for Rural Wales and the Land Authority for Wales, and took on increased functions relating to European programmes, with its combined Welsh Government and European Commission funding rising from some £122m to £250m between 1998 and 2006.[18]

The so-called 'Bonfire of the Quangos' created a mindset among Welsh Government Ministers that, henceforth, policy design should be combined with delivery. They also associated outsourcing

---

16 Rh. Morgan, *Rhodri – A Political Life in Wales and Westminster* (University of Wales Press, 2017), p.275.
17 *Ibid.*, p.276.
18 WDA Annual Reports 1998-9 to 2005-06.

delivery with losing control. Yet such thinking is a fundamental misunderstanding of the role of arms-length agencies that are responsible to Ministers but are not part of the central civil service. As Gerald Holtham put it:

> 'There is an essential role for such agencies in a modern economy, whether it be a venture capital investment fund or a transport authority with statutory powers to deliver the Cardiff city-region Metro, for example. They require technical and commercial expertise and enough distance from government to take risks without being overtaken by party-political sniping. Bringing the Quangos under the arms-length democratic control of an elected Welsh Government or Assembly was essential. Having an indiscriminate bonfire of all of them and transferring the functions into a necessarily cautious, risk-averse and politically hamstrung civil service was just a huge mistake.'[19]

Justifying the decision to bring the WDA in-house the Welsh Government stated that it would 'enhance accountability' and 'create powerful and dedicated "one-stop shop" departments' with 'increased commercial focus'.[20] Such arguments went against the views of most economic commentators. For instance, Leon Gooberman, a Research Fellow at Cardiff University Business School, argued that bringing the quangos in-house actually reduced democratic scrutiny, since they were no longer subjected to detailed questioning by the National Assembly's committees. As to increasing commercial focus, he judged, 'It is difficult to overstate the cultural differences between the civil service and the private sector.' And agreeing with the view of many other commentators, he concluded that the 'Bonfire of the Quangos' was 'caused by a political desire for greater day-to-day control over their activities'.[21]

In 2020 academics at Cardiff Business School reported on interviews about the demise of the Welsh Development Agency with professionals concerned with inward investment into Wales. They were told that the Agency's unified strategy had been diluted by a plethora of separate

---

19 G. Holtham 'Industrial Policy and Infrastructure in Wales', *op. cit.*, p.26.
20 *Western Mail*, 'Why we are scrapping the quangos', 17 July 2004.
21 L. Gooberman, *From Depression to Devolution: Economy and Government in Wales 1934-2006* (University of Wales Press, 2017), pp.196-8.

organisations operating at local, regional and national levels. Many respondents were keen to contrast Wales with Scotland:

> 'We have seen Scottish Development International ramp up their overseas work. They have a very clear goal of where they want to be and how they want to get there. International Business Wales [now part of the civil service inside the Welsh Government] can't compete with them. It is too slow. Everything has to be double checked and put through too many people's desks.'[22]

Indeed, Scotland was accused of copying the Welsh approach to strong regional branding the WDA had developed in the 1980s and 1990s:

> 'Why is Wales in general not attracting as much foreign investment? Short answer, Scotland, long answer, organisation. Scotland is streamlined, they are very efficient.'[23]

An Agency for the 21st Century

Wales is the sole example of a small European country or region abolishing its economic development arm. Comparable countries across Europe have held on to their national economic agencies, in most cases updating their role and extending their reach. An examination of three other agencies operating in similar economies in terms of population size – Scottish Enterprise, Enterprise Ireland, and Business Finland – reveal a number of common themes:

- All have annual targets for job-creation, investment, and innovation, plus a culture of evaluation and learning.
- They operate at arms-length from their respective governments, albeit that these approve their priorities as set out in strategic plans.
- All give a priority to the need to spread investment and activity across their countries, concentrating especially on regions beyond the capital.

---

22 A. Crawley, R. Delbridge, and M. Munday, 'Selling the region: The problems of a multi-agency approach in promoting regional economies', *Regional Science Policy and Practice*, 12 (3), (Wiley-Blackwell, 2020), pp.397-412.
23 Ibid.

- There is a common emphasis on the need to promote high technology, innovation and research and development, and emerging economic sectors.
- All are overseen by management boards comprising between seven and twelve people with a range of experience in business, industry and government. [24]

Plaid Cymru believes there is now an overwhelming case for Wales returning to this tried and tested model. Rather than inward investment, which was a major focus for the 20th Century WDA, the priority now should be promoting indigenous economic development, especially the so-called 'missing middle' of small and medium firms employing between 10 and 250 people.

As shown in shown in the table below, in 2019 these two sectors accounted for 27.6% of private employment and 24.7% of private turnover. However, private employment is dominated by a combination of the micro sector, where the average enterprise employs just 1.6 people, and large firms employing more than 250 people. Between them they accounted for 72.5% of private employment and 75% of turnover.

Table 1: Welsh private business structure: number of enterprises and share of employment and turnover by size band in 2019.[25]

Firms	Number	% Employment Share	% Turnover Share
Micro (0-9) employees	**253,640**	34.9	13
Small 10-49 employees	**9,485**	15.2	11.1
Medium 50-249 employees	**2,215**	12.4	13.7
Large 250+ employees	**1,705**	37.6	62.1

---

24 J. Osmond, *The Case for Enterprise Wales* (Unpublished Plaid Cymru Discussion Paper, 2020).
25 Source: 'Business structure in Wales by size-band and measure', StatsWales: [statswales.gov.wales/Catalogue/Business-Economy-and-Labour-Market/Businesses/Business-Structure/Headline-Data/latestbusinessstructurein wales-by-sizeband-measure].

The small and medium sized business sector is the base on which the future Welsh economy has to be built. The question is how to use policy to create the conditions to enable micro-firms to transition into small businesses, and small businesses to become medium-sized. A major function of a reconstituted Welsh Development Agency should be to map Wales's micro and small businesses, region by region and sector by sector, and then engage with their operations in a granular way to discover what interventions and assistance would encourage them to grow.

As part of this process, an additional function should be to find ways to encourage the ownership of small and medium sized firms to remain in Welsh hands, for example through effective succession planning, management buy-outs, creation of co-operatives, and channelling appropriate investment via the Welsh Development Bank.

An agenda for the future

Creating a 21st Century WDA, with a remit to revive the small business sector and prioritise development along the western seaboard (referred to as Arfor by Plaid Cymru) and in the southern valleys (the Valleys), was at the core of Plaid Cymru's 2021 Senedd election manifesto. However, it was far too transformational for Labour in the talks that led to the Co-operation Agreement.

In the first place, Labour's negotiating team raised what they called 'legacy issues'. By this they meant that any return to the WDA would require a reversal of the 'Bonfire of the Quangos' that had taken place in the early 2000s. There was definitely no appetite for going down that road. Moreover, we were told there were significant problems in creating arms-length bodies. There was the potential for creating conflict with the government if they went off in their own direction. There was also a perceived problem with finding the right people to serve on them.

Labour and Plaid also had opposing views on spatial planning. While Plaid emphasised a north-south vision with a new status for the western seaboard and the southern valleys, Labour thought in east-west terms, giving priority to city regions based around Cardiff and Wrexham. In truth, the two approaches should be compatible, but there were two reasons why they were seen not to be. First was the contrasting political hinterland of the two parties: Plaid's in the western seaboard, and Labour's in the south east, including the southern valleys. Secondly, was Labour's failure to take on board a holistic approach to Welsh planning.

In terms of the contrast explored at the opening of this chapter, Plaid's position could be characterised as a Back Row approach, while Labour's was a view seen from the Front Row. Plaid's thinking was redistributive, seeking to channel resources to the less well-off parts of the country. On the other hand, the effect of Labour's policy was to concentrate on the already more prosperous regions. This was not just a clash of economic priorities. Underlying it was a fundamental divide in identity politics. Labour instinctively adopted a British, east-west alignment in economic planning, linking the east of Wales with neighbouring English population centres, while Plaid's instinct was to prioritise north-south links, putting national unity to the fore.

There would have been no progress in the negotiations had Plaid insisted on pressing this agenda. Labour was intransigent in opposing much of the economic programme advanced by Plaid, for example rejecting, as impractical, its ideas for reconstituting the WDA. So instead, Plaid reverted to a more limited Back Row position, one much more congenial to Labour. This highlighted initiatives within the public rather than the private sector, with the focus put on policies such as free school meals, expanding free childcare, housing, and social care for older people.

For Labour, the gain was a guaranteed majority that would ensure real progress for this agenda. For Plaid, the prize was to advance the cause of Senedd reform as an essential prerequisite for further constitutional progress for Wales and also to be able to present itself as a potential party of government. The overall result was that, however extensive and ambitious its objectives, the Co-operation Agreement remained a policy programme largely confined to the public sector.

Nevertheless, in any potential follow-up to the Agreement in the wake of the 2026 Senedd election, Plaid Cymru planted a signpost for creating an arm's length economic agency. A further indication was a policy statement issued by Jeremy Miles during his bid to become Welsh Labour leader in March 2024. This included a commitment to draw on 'international evidence and experience to consider the case for economic development – focused on sustainable growth, investment, entrepreneurship, productivity support and creating good jobs – to be delivered at arm's length from government.'[26] This could have been lifted from Plaid's 2021 manifesto.

---

26   'Jeremy Miles pledges overnight shift to focus on economy and create new jobs', (*Nation Cymru*, 11 March 2024).

3

The Carmarthenshire Connection

Despite leading parties that are often vehemently opposed, Adam Price and Mark Drakeford have remarkably similar backgrounds. In the first place both are Welsh speakers from Carmarthenshire, from different communities to be sure, but nonetheless places where there is a close connection between urban and rural life. Mark Drakeford was brought up in Carmarthen which is the hub of the county's farming community – indeed, his grandfather was a farmer – and although he was raised in the coal-mining heart of the Amman Valley, Adam Price was always conscious of its location as an interface between industrial and rural Wales.

Both were scholarship boys, the first generation of their families to make their way through university. There is an academic bent to both their characters, a cerebral approach, and a deep interest in ideas as the basis of their politics. At the same time, the left-wing mainspring of their thinking is rooted in their childhood and close family relationships. This is how Adam Price encapsulated it, in his final speech as Plaid leader in the Senedd:

> 'In the middle of the storm you must cling to your anchor, and the crucible moment for me to which I always return is early one morning in 1984 at the side of the road outside Betws New Mine, where I stood at dawn in my school uniform, the rain running down my cheek, arm in arm with my brother and my father, my mother's words of encouragement still ringing in our ears, a picket line which suddenly, instinctively surged forward as one to become a human shield, to defend not ourselves but one another. In a sense my entire political life has been a continual search for that sense of unity and solidarity in the struggle for justice and equality.'[1]

---

1   Senedd Record, Questions to the First Minister, 16 May 2023.

There is a similar account of the personal and the political in an interview Mark Drakeford gave of influences in his childhood:

> 'I have a very early memory of my grandfather calling me out from the farm, telling me to come and see Megan Lloyd George coming canvassing down the road in St. Clears. I remember him telling me that nothing had been the same since Lloyd George was Prime Minister... My father became radicalised by Mrs Thatcher in his later life. He would take me when I was in my teens to eve of poll meetings in Carmarthenshire, from one to the next.'[2]

The shared background of their upbringing, which engendered an appreciation of the essential unity of rural and urban Wales, bred an instinct for consensus and co-operation. Even the sharpest distinction between their two parties, which is on their constitutional aspirations for Wales, became blurred under both Drakeford's and Price's influence. Drakeford has insisted that sovereignty lies not at Westminster but with the Welsh people, and argued that Britain should be reconstituted as a federation.[3] For his part, Adam Price has emphasised that Welsh independence should be mediated by a confederal relationship between England, Scotland and Wales.[4]

The process of negotiating the Co-operation Agreement, followed by the months of collaboration in putting it into effect, gave the two men a greater appreciation of each other's qualities. This is what Price said to Drakeford in his parting comments as he stood down as Plaid leader in May 2023:

> 'We are two socialists from Carmarthenshire, hewn from the same root, on the left wing of both our parties who, through design or default – we will leave it to others to decide – have ended up implementing policies, in many areas, more radical than either

---

[2] Martin Shipton Meets Mark Drakeford (*Wales Online* podcast, 12 January 2018).

[3] See the Welsh Government paper published under his auspices, *Reforming Our Union: Shared Governance in the UK*, September 2019.

[4] A. Price, 'Benelux Britain – Recasting relations in a post-independence era', Speech to the Centre on Constitutional Change, University of Edinburgh, 26 June 2019. The potential for this approach was explored by Plaid Cymru's Independence Commission in *Towards an Independent Wales* (Y Lolfa, 2020), Chapter 7.

of our manifestos. But, beyond us, there is a deeper truth that will outlast us — that in this place what unites most of us is ultimately more important and more enduring than anything that divides us. This Chamber is circular for good reason. Making sense of the Senedd means you must understand that we're not here to create a mini-Westminster, but to build a better Wales, together; to be not an arena of antagonism, but a Senedd in search of a new synthesis, where the different truths we represent are combined anew in pursuit of the common good.'[5]

Mark Drakeford returned the compliment in his own, inimitable, way:

'There is a great deal in what the leader of Plaid Cymru has said this afternoon with which I entirely agree. Of course, he is right: we disagree on many things, and that's the beauty of our democracy, that we can do that, and we can do that while we know that, behind those individual examples of disagreement, there lies an enormous amount of agreement about the purpose of politics here in Wales... Adam Price said that in his politics he was dedicated to finding solutions, and let me say to the Chamber, having spent many hours together finding ways of turning the Co-operation Agreement between our two parties into those practical actions, that is exactly my experience of working with the Leader of Plaid Cymru. I've often thought in politics that there are only two classes of people: there are people who come through the door when there is a problem to be solved whose instinct is to make that problem even bigger, to find even more things that you've now got to address, to find even more angles of difficulty that you haven't yet come across. And then there is another group in politics who, when they come through the door and there is a problem to be solved, their instinct is to find solutions, to look for ways in which common ground can be forged together. And I feel I have been fortunate, during the 18 months I have worked with the Leader of Plaid Cymru in the Co-operation Agreement, that that has always been the way in which he has come to the table.'[6]

---

5   Senedd *Record*, 16 May 2023.
6   *Ibid.*

In June, July and August 2021, as the outlines of the Co-operation Agreement came into focus, it felt as though this was a juncture when the political trajectories of these two Carmarthenshire socialists were destined to cross. Adam Price had cultivated a vision inclined to extend politics beyond the bounds of what conventionally would be thought possible, coupled with an instinct for compromise. For his part, Mark Drakeford had amassed a large amount of political capital. It had been assembled as a result of the calm and methodical way he had led the country through the Covid pandemic. In turn he had equalled Labour's best ever result in a Senedd election. Now he was determined to spend the capital he had accumulated. He, too, was willing to compromise, though there was only so far that he would go. Most of all, he wanted to get things done in the limited time at his disposal, the three years before he had resolved to give way to a new leader of his party. In short, he wanted to be bold. Interviewed in January 2024, in the wake of his announcement that he was stepping down as First Minister, he gave this advice to his successor:

> 'You see the biggest challenge for Welsh Labour when you've been in power, as we have been, for 25 years, is renewal and a determination not just to rest back on the oars of being in government. You could do that, if you're not careful. You're familiar with government, you've been there for a while. I think the challenge for Labour is always to be looking for those radical changes that are necessary. I was once asked what did I regret about being in government, and the answer was that we were not bold enough when we had the chance to be so.'[7]

The making of Adam Price

Adam Price was born in 1968, the year of the New Left's May Day Manifesto, the decade's revolutionary moment when students led demonstrations against the Vietnam War in London, Paris and New York. He grew up in a council house in Tycroes in the Amman Valley. His father Rufus, once a professional boxer and Welsh middleweight champion, was a miner at the nearby Betws New Mine. At the epicentre of the anthracite coalfield, the Amman Valley is a nodal point for Wales's history, culture and politics. Price is highly conscious

---

7   Interview with Mark Drakeford, Institute for Government, London, 25 January 2024.

of that positioning which, he believes, gives him a connection with many of the divisions in Welsh society. As he put it, in his maiden speech in the House of Commons in 2001, his constituency stood on the cusp of rural and industrial Wales:

> 'The interplay and interconnection of the two communities – the coalfield and the milk field – lie at the heart of the special character of my constituency. The markets of the south Wales coalfield helped to build up the dairy sector. Welsh-speaking peasants and farmers, including my grandfather, huddled into the terraced cottages of the pit villages of Amman and Gwendraeth. Where others try to drive a wedge between town and country, we in Carmarthenshire have a bond of solidarity between village and valley, miner and farmer – from the free milk supplied by farmers during the great strike of 1984, to the enormous concern shared by everyone in my constituency at the human cost of the deepening rural depression.'[8]

At the turn of the 20th Century Ammanford was a ferment of anarchists and socialists. George Davidson, the millionaire managing director of Kodak UK, made his White House home in the town an important meeting place that produced a stream of radical leaders. Among them was Jim Griffiths, from Betws, creator of the modern state benefit system as Minister for National Insurance during the 1945 Labour government, and later Secretary of State for Wales in 1964. Another was D.J. Davies from Carmel, one of the most important thinkers on co-operative economics in Plaid Cymru's early history. Later in the 20th Century the Amman Valley produced Adam Price. He absorbed its neighbourliness that quickly transforms strangers into acquaintances. He once conveyed how this works when recalling his parents visiting him in London when he was an MP:

> 'I'd been living in this flat for a few years; by the end of the week, they knew everyone on the street. It was like something out of an Ealing comedy. People were opening their windows in second floor flats and, "Hi Rufus and Angela!" My parents didn't know any other way to

---

[8]   Hansard, 12 July 2001. Reprinted in Adam Price, *Wales: The First and Final Colony*, Y Lolfa, 2018, pp.65-6.

be. It would take us two hours to get from there to the Tube station, because they'd say hullo to everyone. But that's normal, isn't it?'[9]

It's certainly 'normal' in the Amman Valley where political debate was an integral part of his growing up: 'Alongside rugby it was a favourite pastime.' In the Working Man's club in 1970s Ammanford there was a room reserved for political discussion. When he was ten-years-old Price had a chance meeting with Jim Callaghan, the Labour Prime Minister who was visiting Betws colliery:

> 'We bumped into him and his entourage outside the Co-op in Ammanford. The cameras were behind him and he did the usual thing, saying to me, "What do you want to do when you grow up young man?" To much amusement, I said I wanted to be Prime Minister. And he replied, "So you want my job." And I said no, I wanted to be Prime Minister of Wales.'[10]

Not long afterwards he started attending the Gospel Hall, where the Plymouth Brethren evangelical sect held sway. Price's talents as a public speaker were soon recognised and he was dispatched on missionary errands. The Brethren believe that all Christians are ordained by God to serve – so all are ministers – but for Price as a 12-year-old, 'It was quite difficult to talk about your relationship with God outside the Quadrant in the shopping centre in Swansea.' Nonetheless, such experiences honed his confidence as an orator, while his Bible training shaped the patterns of his speech. As he put it, in an interview in 2018:

> 'They were quite traditional in the Gospel Halls so I used to read the King James Bible. But there's some value in that. Much as with William Morgan's Bible in Welsh it has some poetry to it, there is a metre there. Once it's been imbued you never quite forget it. Oratory has waxed and waned over the past few decades, but it has probably come back into fashion, with Obama for example – the great soaring heights of his oratory. Ultimately politics is about moving people. It has to have an emotional intelligence to it and an emotional power. A

---

9 Quoted in R. King, *Brittle with Relics – A History of Wales 1962 to 1997* (Faber, 2022), p. 398.
10 Interview with Nick Robinson, Political Thinking podcast, 21 November 2019.

great political speech has to move you to tears. You can't do it every time, of course. But people want to be taken on a journey. A great speech has an arc. People want to be inspired; they want their hearts to be lifted. That's not that different to the stock in trade of the great speeches of Methodist preachers a generation ago.'[11]

In time Price found that his engagement with religion clashed with his growing political commitments. The Plymouth Brethren believed the kingdom of the spirit was more important than worldly concerns, which was the opposite of political activity. For a while he tried to marry the two, but politics won out:

'For me getting involved and being on the side of your fellow humanity was the very definition of the social gospel. But even though I had a theological parting of the ways I think that early religious experience has left its mark on me, not just in terms of the way I speak publicly but also in the way I see the world. Ultimately, it's rooted in a strong sense of justice but also redemption. Calling out injustice is very, very important but there is also some good news, that actually things don't have to be this way. There is another path that can be followed.'[12]

Although his father and mother spoke Welsh, they decided to raise their children as English speakers. As with many of their generation, they believed English to be the language of advancement. However, Adam's elder brother Adrian decided to learn the language and he handed on his passion to his teenage sibling. Within a year Adam, too, was fluent, which proved a turning point. At the same time, he became absorbed in Welsh history which, together with the language became the bedrock for his outlook on the world. Then, at the very moment of this cultural awakening Wales became gripped by a political drama that would shape the rest of his life. He describes the 1984-5 miners' strike as a 'crucible moment' that to this day defines who he is:

'For me the experience of the Miner's Strike is that defining moment. It spoke to a sense of an injustice felt by a whole community when faced with the power of an unaccountable State determined to push

---
11   'Martin Shipton meets Adam Price' (*WalesOnline* Podcast, 15 May 2018).
12   *Western Mail*, 19 August 2018.

through destructive economic policies whatever the cost. That is everything I'm against. What I'm for is a different kind of future. When you get bogged down in the details and process of day-to-day politics it's so useful to be able to ground yourself back into why you started on this journey and the reason why you want to be a voice for the voiceless.'[13]

For the first time he felt a national sense of solidarity:

'My parents went to stay up near Blaenau Ffestiniog during the strike, as a bit of a respite, and experienced that strong connection with the slate quarrying areas, and those who worked in the nuclear industry in the north-west as well, that was a really strong bond, and that felt new.'[14]

The strike also exposed the complexities of rural industrial relationships:

'There were incredible scenes with the Dyfed Farmers' Action Group, which were another dimension. John Howells was one of Wales's leading Marxist farmers, an incredibly electrifying speaker, making this connection between the struggle of the farmers and the struggle of the miners, with an almost Latin American sense of the politics of the peasantry. In Welsh, 'y werin' doesn't have any of that residue of snobbishness that the term 'peasant' has in English; 'paysan' doesn't have that in any other language, but in English it does. There was a class politics to farming; farmers and miners have had a chequered past in terms of their relationships, as had the language movement and the union movement. History accelerates when these currents come together and, suddenly, you're in a fast-flowing stream and it's difficult quite fully to describe it if you're not in it.'[15]

---

13 'Martin Shipton meets Adam Price', *op. cit.* In 2014 Price won a Bronze Medal at the New York Film and Television Festival for his S4C four-part documentary series on the 1984-85 miners' strike which was also recognised with two BAFTA Cymru Awards.
14 R. King, *Brittle with Relics – A History of Wales 1962 to 1997, op. cit.*, p.307.
15 *Ibid.*, p.305.

The Carmarthenshire Connection

For a teenager beginning to struggle with his sexuality, living through the miners' strike had a more personal impact as well:

'People will have seen the film *Pride*, about London gays and lesbians who supported the miners. They came down to my hometown of Ammanford and were embraced by the local community. It was a very emotional moment for me seeing them in the Working Men's Club because that was the first time I had met anyone who was out and gay. I knew myself that I was gay, but I wasn't out. And to see them welcomed into the heart of my Welsh working-class community planted a seed that it was going to be OK, the future was going to be OK, and at some point, I would be able to come out, and the people that loved me would still love me.'[16]

Another aspect of the strike proved positive as well, when Price ran into other marginalised communities, in London:

'In the summer of the strike I went down to Brixton, that was twinned with the South Wales Area of the NUM. I slept on sofas. It was the best of times and the worst of times in a strange kind of way. I learnt so much. There was an incredible solidarity between the black community which was also oppressed during the 1980s, not long after the riots. There was an immediate meeting of minds. We were two very different communities in some ways but nevertheless found a common core of values. It's always wonderful when that happens. It replenishes your faith in humanity when people can find, across many, many miles and different experiences a central human connection.'[17]

In another interview he added:

'I was a 14-year-old going down to London, sleeping on the floors of SWP members and anarchists and being immersed in it all. I was quite tall, so they thought I was a miner and I'd often have a pint bought for me.'[18]

---

16 Interview with Nick Robinson (Political Thinking podcast, 21 November 2019).
17 *Ibid.*
18 R. King, *Brittle with Relics – A History of Wales 1962 to 1997*, op. cit., p.306.

After attending Ysgol Dyffryn Aman, Price found his way to the School of Geography and Planning at Cardiff University where he took a degree in European Community Studies, a combination of Economics and German. He was much influenced by Kevin Morgan, a lecturer who arrived at about the same time, following a career that had taken him from Rhigos at the top of the Cynon Valley, to Leicester University, McMaster University in Ontario, and the University of Sussex. A Labour supporter, he would go on to chair the Yes for Wales campaign in the 1997 referendum.

After graduating Price joined Morgan's Department of City and Regional Planning as a Research Associate on economic innovation systems in Wales and Baden-Württemberg. He also worked with Morgan and another Cardiff University economist, Phil Cooke, a leading light with Plaid Cymru's magazine *Radical Wales*, on a number of other projects. In 1992 Neath's Labour MP Peter Hain commissioned them to prepare a report for a conference he was organising on 'A new agenda for the Valleys'. Their report, *Rebuilding our Communities,* called for greater solidarity across the Valleys, but for Price the way it was presented left an enduring memory of Labour tribalism:

> 'The experience of the conference was a slightly bitter one for me, because even though I was the co-author of the report, and even though Kevin is a fantastically humble man and even though I was fresh out of university and I was twenty-two, and he insisted I was the co-author and should be treated as such, I was no-platformed at the conference, wasn't even given an opportunity to speak, because I was a member of Plaid Cymru.'[19]

Unquestionably, however, their most important collaboration was *The Other Wales: The Case for Objective 1 Funding Post 1999*, published by the Institute of Welsh Affairs in 1998. This argued for redrawing the European Union's deprivation map of Wales from the conventional north-south division to a new east-west configuration. The distinction was crucial, since to qualify for the Objective 1 funding between 2000 and 2006 and further convergence programmes thereafter, a region had to demonstrate that its gross domestic product was below 75% of the EU average. If Wales's two standard regions for EU funding

---

19   R. King, *Brittle with Relics – A History of Wales 1962 to 1997*, op. cit., p.461.

The Carmarthenshire Connection

purposes were to remain divided between north and south, then this criterion would not be met. If, on the other hand, the division was changed to west and east, then western Wales would easily qualify. The report proved a major contribution to the change in designation that duly took place, resulting in the major EU investment in west Wales and the Valleys that ensued over the following 20 years.

The 'Other Wales' combined the western seaboard of Wales with the southern valleys, bringing together precisely those areas that voted, by a significant majority, in favour of the National Assembly in 1997. It was no coincidence, either, that these areas had provided the core of the historic independent Welsh Princedoms that most resisted the Norman incursion. Political scientists have described them as being two parts of a so-called 'Three Wales Model' in which two-thirds of their population self-identified as being 'Welsh' ahead of being British.[20] As Morgan and Price argued, though different in many ways, the West and the Valleys nonetheless shared many of the same structural problems:

- Socio-economic deprivation because of their historic dependence on coal mining, slate quarrying and agriculture.
- Geographically removed from the major growth poles of the Welsh economy – Cardiff and the M4 corridor, and north-east Wales.
- High levels of out-migration.

The report concluded on a somewhat apocalyptic note, judging that failure to achieve Objective 1 status would:

'...destroy the reputation of the EU in Wales, severely damage the Labour government in one of its electoral heartlands and, as well as overshadowing the launch of the National Assembly, it would seriously compromise the Assembly's economic development strategy for two full terms. It scarcely seems possible that so much rests on a single decision but, in our view, the stakes are indeed that high.'[21]

---

20 See D. Balsom, 'The Three Wales Model' in J. Osmond (Ed.), *The National Question Again* (Gomer, 1985).
21 K. Morgan and A. Price, *The Other Wales: The Case for Objective 1 Funding Post 1999* (IWA, 1998), p.28.

The report was not only influential in ensuring that western Wales and the southern valleys secured major EU convergence funding over two decades, but also provided the essential background for a further policy initiative. This was Price's ground-breaking 2013 publication *Arfor: A Region for the Welsh Speaking West*:

> 'There is now a desperate need for a regional strategy which reflects the reality of our linguistic geography. This should include everything from economic development, linguistic planning, public services, housing and planning, to transport. The main objective should be to revitalise the west in its broadest sense, by merging the economic and linguistic elements together. The only way to achieve this in practical terms is through ensuring that there is a governmental structure which is related to this task. We need to create a region for the west – from Benllech to Burry Port. The four most Welsh-speaking authorities – Môn, Gwynedd, Ceredigion and Carmarthenshire – would be its heart, but without forgetting the Conwy Valley, west Denbighshire and Montgomeryshire, north Pembrokeshire and the Welsh speaking neighbourhoods in Swansea and Neath Port Talbot.'

This was developed through further iterations until the initiative also engaged with the remainder of the 'Other Wales' and advocated a development agency for the southern valleys as well. The two projects were brought together in Plaid Cymru's 2021 Senedd election manifesto, providing it with a cohesive theme.

In the 1992 General Election Price, aged 22, contested Gower and a year later was elected to Plaid's National Executive as Director of Policy. In that role he was instrumental in placing Welsh self-government 'not only back on the agenda, but at the top of the agenda.'[22] He drafted a constitution for an independent Wales, including a Bill of Rights with Wales becoming a republic, duly adopted by the party's annual conference:

> 'Wandering the streets that Sunday the hoardings of Cardiff newsagents carried a three-word poster from *Wales on Sunday*: "Wales a Republic".'[23]

---

22 P. Fletcher, 'Historic Move: Independence and no place for the Queen - Plaid votes for the Republic of Wales' (*Western Mail*, 31 October, 1993).

23 A. Price, *Wales 2030: Seven Steps to Independence* (August 2018).

In the mid 1990s Price left academia to become an Executive Director of the enterprise agency Menter a Busnes, based in Aberystwyth. Later he was managing director of Newidiem, a policy and economics consultancy in Cardiff. Towards the end of the decade, he was selected to fight the newly drawn Carmarthen East and Dinefwr Westminster parliamentary constituency. This followed the incumbent candidate Rhodri Glyn Thomas winning the seat in the first National Assembly election in 1999, creating a vacancy for the 2001 Westminster campaign.

He duly won Carmarthen East with a 7.5% swing, making it among only a handful of seats across the UK that Labour lost. In the House of Commons, he quickly established a distinctive presence. In 2002 he uncovered the Mittal Affair in which the steel magnate Lakshmi Mittal, a Labour Party donor, lobbied Tony Blair to help purchase Romania's steel industry. Then he led an attempt, alongside other Plaid Cymru and SNP members, to impeach the Prime Minister. A trenchant opponent of Blair's role in the Iraq War, he was ejected from the House of Common's chamber in March 2005 for refusing to retract his accusation that Blair had 'misled' Parliament. Returned to the House of Commons in 2005 with an increased majority, the following year he initiated a debate resulting in the establishment of the Chilcot Enquiry into the Iraq War.[24]

Price was Campaign Director in the 2007 National Assembly election, bringing new energy and vision, exemplified by a rebranding of the party, in which a soft-focused, golden Welsh poppy replaced the traditional Triban emblem with its three peaks symbolising the final mountainous stronghold of the independent Welsh rulers. In that election Plaid gained three seats to reach 15, while Labour fell back from 29 to 26. Price took a leading role in the coalition negotiations that ensued, explaining his enthusiasm for the eventual Red-Green Alliance in the following terms:

> 'Plaid and Labour, despite their bitter disagreements over the national question and over much else besides, do still both stem from the Welsh radical tradition with its emphasis on egalitarianism, the values of community, solidarity, progressive universalism and Rawlsian notions of social justice. The reason that many of us (though by no means all) were drawn to Plaid in the first place was not out of an

---

24 See A. Price, *Wales: The First and Final Colony*, op. cit, pp.74-82.

abstract belief in self-government *per se*, but our conviction that only through self-government could these ideals be fulfilled by banishing forever the prospect of a right-wing London government (whether Tory or New Labour) imposing its alien values on Wales. A red-green realignment of the Welsh left – bringing together the traditions of Gwynfor Evans and Jim Griffiths, D.J. Davies and S.O. Davies – is something many have dreamed.'[25]

The following year he expanded this analysis of the relationship between Labour and Plaid, declaring it to be the central narrative in Welsh politics:

'Although no-one should doubt the ferocity of the electoral rivalry, it cannot be characterised solely as one of outright opposition because it has also involved a process of interpellation, a calling-to-account. In this way Plaid has influenced Labour, drawing it in a nationalist direction. Meanwhile Labour, through its unrivalled hegemony from the inter-war period on, pushed Plaid towards its formal adoption of socialism as a philosophy in 1981.'[26]

Interviewed in 2018 Price conceded that he was socialist first and a nationalist second, though there was an intimate connection between the two:

'For me, nationalism is not an end in itself. It is a means. The means is creating a better society. Wales is the perfect size for that kind of project. It is large enough to do something significant but small enough for it to work. There's something about small nations and cities, which make them great testbeds or platforms for innovation. If you think about the Nordic countries, or cities as well, they are great places for innovation because people connect. So, in cities people with different ideas meet, it's as simple as that. Small nations replicate that, but in a different way. It's not that we're all hanging around in somewhere like Shoreditch in London where there are a

---

25 A. Price, 'The red-green grass of home: in support of a Plaid/Labour alliance', *The Welsh Agenda* (IWA, June 2007). Reprinted in A. Price, *Wales: The First and Final Colony, op. cit.*, pp.92-4.

26 A. Price, 'Reinventing Radical Wales', in *Politics in 21st Century Wales* (IWA, November 2008), p.67.

lot of technical start-ups. There's a cognitive proximity that happens in small nations. People speak the same language, sometimes literally but certainly metaphorically. There's a sense of 'Us', there's a sense of actually being connected. Even though we're individuals we have some kind of common bond which is this thing we call a nation. And in small nations in particular that bond is very, very strong, a deep sense of belonging and commitment to something that is bigger than ourselves and that can be channelled into a vision, into projects that are about transforming the country. Small nations all over the world have gone down that route. You can think of Singapore, for instance, that was one of the poorest countries in the world but is now one of the richest in terms of income pe capita.'[27]

After serving two terms at Westminster, Price stood down in 2010, intending to find his way to the Senedd in Cardiff Bay. Meanwhile, he won a Fulbright scholarship to study for a Master's degree in Public Administration in the John F. Kennedy School of Government at Harvard, later gaining a fellowship in its Centre for International Development. As he set off for the USA, he reassured his supporters, 'I am not going to America to escape – but to find new inspiration – a space and time to think.'[28]

While at Harvard he was much influenced by Marshall Ganz, an activist and academic specialising in leadership strategies. He is credited with devising the successful grassroots organising model for Barack Obama's successful 2008 presidential campaign. Ganz argues that leaders must build a three-part narrative explaining their calling: why they feel inspired to act (story of self), how the resultant action relates to their audience (story of us), and what urgent challenge the overall activity seeks to address (story of now).

How does this apply to Price? His 'story of self' goes back to the miners' strike, when his Amman Valley family shifted from Labour to Plaid. It was a crisis moment for his family but also a pivotal moment in the history of the nation. As we've seen, his experience of living through that moment is fundamental to his politics.

His 'story of us' relates directly to the nation as a whole. It is about demonstrating that the Welsh level of government is the most

---

[27] 'Martin Shipton meets Adam Price', *op. cit.*
[28] A. Price, *Wales: The First and Final Colony*, *op. cit.*, p.84.

effective for bringing about political change to create a fairer and more prosperous society. As he explains:

> 'That sense of 'Us' can be harnessed to create the good society. Now why can't that be done at the British scale, why not channel your energies there? For me the problem with that is that the British nation is a manufactured construct. It's created out of institutions like the Royal Family, and Pomp and Circumstance and all that. But if you look beyond that, I don't think there's a deep and prevailing idea of what that nation constitutes. Because, of course, it isn't a nation. It's a composite of four. Also, within the British State there are deep structures of conservatism which have stayed the same by changing. And that's, of course, the mystery of the British constitution which is in a constant state of evolution. If you're in the business of radical change you could waste a lot of time by trying to shift the British State. It's a super-tanker that doesn't shift easily. Whereas the flotilla of small nations is much more agile and much more responsive to waves of change.'[29]

Price's 'story of now' is for Plaid Cymru. It is about concentrating the energies of the party on being an instrument for making transformative change happen in the here and now. He says we need a decade-long process of change in which Plaid Cymru has a leading role:

> 'At the end of that decade we can turn round and, based on a record of success, we can say to the Welsh electorate: "It doesn't have to be this way. We don't have to be at the bottom of the league in terms of world education rankings, we don't have to be in this constantly creaking system of poorly resourced public services, we can place ourselves on a path to progress." At that point we can have a meaningful discussion with the Welsh people and say: "We've shown what we can do within the structures of the Westminster straitjacket. Imagine what we could do if we empowered ourselves completely.'[30]

The future, he says, will be determined by the experience the people of Wales have in seeing the Senedd and Welsh Government make a

---

29 'Martin Shipton meets Adam Price', *op. cit.*
30 *Ibid.*

tangible difference to their lives. He is fond of paraphrasing the 19th Century Italian statesman Massimo d'Azeglio who in 1861, at the first meeting of the newly unified nation's parliament, declared, 'We have made Italy. Now we must make Italians.' As Price has it, 'We have created a Welsh state, now we have to create Welsh citizens.'

Mark Drakeford's positioning of Welsh Labour

In January 2022 *The Sunday Times* nominated First Minister Mark Drakeford as the most popular political leader in Britain, some way ahead of both Boris Johnson and Nicola Sturgeon. This was because of his distinctive approach to handling the Covid pandemic. Indeed, the newspaper judged that it meant that 'the Welsh border, which has been mostly ignored since the two nations were unified under Henry VIII in 1536, has begun to matter again.'[31]

There is little doubt that the cautious path Drakeford steered through the pandemic, often resulting in his adopting an adversarial stance against the Westminster Government, resulted in the cementing of support for devolution. Certainly, it demonstrated – for the first time for many people – that Wales had its own government capable of making its own decisions.

Mark Drakeford was not the most obvious candidate for leading such a shift in Welsh opinion. In the first place, at the start of the pandemic in the early Spring of 2020, although he had been First Minister for more than a year, he was still relatively unknown. He was a somewhat retiring figure, reluctant to engage in the cut and thrust of political infighting. Moreover, he was far from a leading proponent of greater autonomy for Wales, preferring to emphasise the benefits to be had from the collective social and economic insurance provided by British unity.

His personality has a lighter side that many might find surprising. An ardent reader of P.G. Wodehouse, he has a soft spot for Jeeves and Bertie Wooster. His subject at university was Latin. He tends an allotment, plays the ukulele and clarinet, is an opera and poetry lover, and has been a member of Glamorgan County Cricket Club for more than 50 years. Yet underlying all this is a determined flintiness, evidenced by an unwavering commitment to democratic socialism.

---

31 *The Sunday Times*, 16 January 2022.

He was the only member of the Welsh Cabinet to support Jeremy Corbyn when he first contested the Labour leadership.

Born in 1954, Mark Drakeford was barely a teenager in Carmarthen when Welsh nationalism was on the march. At the town's Queen Elizabeth Grammar School, he was surrounded by ardent nationalists. He recalled attending the Urdd Eisteddfod in Carmarthen and hearing Gwynfor Evans speak. That was in 1966, shortly after Evans had won the Carmarthen by-election that marked the beginning of the modern movement towards devolution:

> 'Gwynfor wasn't always a hugely inspiring speaker. But that afternoon he was on the platform saying to an enthusiastic audience that was very much on his side, that the tide of nationalism in Wales was like a tide beating on the shore. "It's coming in, it's coming in, it's coming in," he cried. And by God, by the time he got to the third utterance, the whole tent was on its feet.'[32]

Drakeford himself, however, was unmoved. By then he had joined Labour and had already been canvassing for the party. As he put it:

> 'For me it was always Labour, and consciously Labour, because in the end the thing that really shapes people's lives is not the accident of geography, it's not where you happen to be born, but your relationship with the economy. So, people's chances in life are economically determined. And the chances of someone living in the Ely estate in Cardiff are more shaped by the same forces that shape someone living on an estate that's like it across our border than they are by the fact that they happen to have been born in Wales rather than England. Being Welsh matters a lot to me. I'm pleased to be able to speak Welsh as much as I am able. I've put my own political career very much into trying to do as much as possible in Wales. But in the end, it's economics that shapes people's lives. And that's a Labour analysis rather than a nationalist analysis.'[33]

Drakeford studied at the University of Kent in Canterbury, a place he chose because he wanted to go to a newly established university

---

[32] 'Martin Shipton Meets Mark Drakeford' (*WalesOnline* podcast, 12 January 2018).
[33] Ibid.

where there would be a radical edge, but also because the city possessed a county cricket ground. As he said, 'I was still in that era when people thought that going to university was about getting an education rather than preparing you for work.'[34] During his third year he responded to an advertisement in *The Guardian* inviting applications to train as a probation officer. He moved to Cardiff in 1979 and worked as a probation officer and youth justice worker in the Ely and Caerau communities. In the late 1980s he helped establish the Welsh youth homelessness charity Llamau.

From 1991 to 1995, Drakeford was a lecturer in applied social studies at Swansea University. He then moved to Cardiff University as a lecturer at the School of Social and Administration Studies, becoming a senior lecturer in 1999, and appointed Professor of Social Policy and Applied Social Sciences in 2003. He retained his academic post until he became a Welsh Government Minister in 2013.

Between 1985 and 1993 Drakeford represented Pontcanna on the old South Glamorgan County Council, alongside Julie Morgan, Jane Hutt, Sue Essex and Jane Davidson. Later all five joined the Welsh Cabinet. Together with Rhodri Morgan, who became MP for Cardiff West in 1987 and later, of course, First Minister, the six Cardiff activists formed a close bond on the pro-devolution wing of the Welsh Labour Party during the 1990s.

Drakeford actively supported devolution through the 1990s and had a leading role during the 1997 referendum. He stood in Cardiff Central in the first National Assembly elections in 1999 and was bitterly disappointed to lose to the Liberal Democrats. Keen to be involved in the early years of establishing the Assembly, he jumped at Rhodri Morgan's offer for him to become his Special Adviser in 2000. As Drakeford put it, 'This was a different way of getting back into that early story.'[35] And it was mission critical for the very survival of the fledgling institution. The National Assembly faced a combination of only marginal approval in the referendum, and deep hostility from much of the Labour Party establishment. The fact that it survived those early years Drakeford put down to the Rhodri Morgan's leadership:

---

34   Ibid.
35   Ibid.

'When I arrived in the Assembly in the beginning of May 2000, I thought the institution might not last. People were exhausted, at the end of their tether and operating hand to mouth. I thought that unless we managed to turn this around, we might all conclude in short order that this was just a bad mistake and it couldn't be made to work. I always felt that the tide turned during that Autumn. Primarily it was because we got the stability to be able to have a government that could make its writ run on the floor of the Assembly. But then a series of events happened. Foot-and-mouth, flooding, the fuel crisis, and suddenly there was a sense of when something went wrong in Wales, where do people look?

In those beginning days, I think you might have said that the Assembly politicians in the Labour Party were fruitless. You had MPs who were very clearly the political aristocracy. You had Labour local government leaders who were powerful people and at the end of the fiefdom approach to Labour. And then there was the Assembly. By 2007 when Labour Party members were faced by a choice between what leading politicians at the Assembly were suggesting to them – over the coalition with Plaid Cymru – and what leading people in London were saying to them, they decided it was the Assembly's voice that they would listen to. That's pretty remarkable, isn't it? Who else but Rhodri could have managed to pull that off?[36]

Until he became First Minister, Drakeford's main contribution to the development of devolution was as Welsh Labour's ideologue. He was the mind behind Rhodri Morgan's 'clear red water' philosophy, set out in a speech at Swansea University in December 2002. Contrasting

---

36 A. Eirug and J. Williams, *The Impact of Devolution in Wales: Social Democracy with a Welsh Stripe* (University of Wales Press, 2022), pp.10-11. The quotation is taken from M. Sullivan, 'Interview with Mark Drakeford', The *Sullivan Dialogues*, 2017-19 (unpublished manuscript). Whilst Professor of Social Policy at Swansea University, Mike Sullivan – who died in 2018 – was active within the Welsh Labour Party and chaired the first exercise to identify and select Labour candidates for the inaugural National Assembly election in 1999. He served as a specialist adviser to Rhodri Morgan on health policy between 2007 and 2011 and was influential in the creation of the coalition between Labour and Plaid Cymru and the formation of the One Wales administration. On his return to academic life after 2011, his experience of the One Wales coalition led him to join Plaid Cymru.

Welsh Labour values with those of Tony Blair's New Labour at Westminster, it proved to be the party's most significant political positioning during the first quarter of a century of devolution.

The origins of the speech lay in a reaction to New Labour's social policies, combined with a desire to mark out a distinctive position ahead of the 2003 Assembly election. In his biography Rhodri Morgan declared that this would be 'neither Old Labour, nor New Labour, but Welsh Labour!'[37] As Drakeford recalled, Morgan was determined to sustain an identification between Labour and Wales: 'He didn't want cede Welsh identity to the nationalist cause. Keeping Welsh and Labour close together in people's minds was always really important to him.'[38] The way Rhodri Morgan summarised this political approach was as a move away from New Labour's 'quasi-market and pseudo choice, to Welsh Labour's we're all in this together':

> 'The *citizen* amounted to much more than a *consumer* exercising choice: the citizen was also the taxpayer and voter who had communally created the services in the first place and was the ultimate owner of the public service facilities. Whereas the consumer in England, especially in southern England, might have the means to choose between a private school and a state school, the same was far less likely in Wales.'[39]

In the first part of his 'clear red water' speech, Rhodri Morgan traced three major trends in the development of Welsh society during the previous century. The first was the shift in employment patterns, the second the rapid growth of Welsh industrial communities, and the third the way political devolution was offering opportunities for finding new ways to manage these changes. The early noughties were proving an era of low unemployment in which it was difficult to recruit people for the caring professions, especially nurses and care workers. It was noteworthy also that the speech was delivered between 1999 and the 2007-08 financial crash, when budgets were increasing substantially, enabling 'clear red water' largesse. At the same time, a society that was beginning to mirror the more affluent

---

37 Rh. Morgan, *Rhodri – A Political Life in Wales and Westminster*, op. cit., p.250.
38 'Martin Shipton Meets Mark Drakeford', *op. cit.*
39 Rh. Morgan, *Rhodri – A Political Life in Wales and Westminster*, op. cit., p.250.

areas of southern England was also facing large-scale structural transformation:

'We have seen communities grow in Wales – in many cases from nothing at all a hundred and fifty years ago – to become significant centres of population with all the institutions and systems necessary to provide the complex network of local political and service organisations. We have also seen the same communities severely challenged by recent changes in fuel use, the switch from coal to oil to gas and the huge productivity gains in steel. This is the fabric of Welsh life with which we are all very familiar. This is the sometimes proud, sometimes agonising history of a nation built very largely on the efforts of working people in hard surroundings. This is the raw material, the social heritage out of which Welsh devolution has been created.'[40]

Moreover, devolution was now providing a test bed for large-scale experimentation in the delivery of public services, a 'living laboratory' in which different approaches to problems could be worked out and applied:

'The development of Glas Cymru (Welsh Water) for example, shows that exactly. The water supply industry has always been close to public consciousness in Wales. A not-for-profit company, run in the public interest, rather than in the interest of private shareholders, although with operations and customer services outsourced, has provided a solution which is both practical and which chimes with the community's sense of how such a basic necessity of daily life ought to be organised and provided. It is a step back from conventional privatisation. It is a historic compromise. It is a Welsh version of the so-called post-war consensus in the British body politic on the welfare state, a consensus which now seems such a distant memory.'[41]

---

40 Rh. Morgan, 'Clear Red Water', speech to the National Centre for Public Policy, Swansea University, 11 December 2002: [sochealth.co.uk/the-socialist-health-association/sha-country-and-branch-organisation/sha-wales/clear-red-water/].
41 Ibid.

The meaning of 'clear red water' was to apply this historic compromise to the provision of public services which in England were being subject to competition and consumer choice. Instead, in Wales they were to be regarded as citizenship rights, free at the point of use, universal and unconditional. Examples included:

- Free school milk for youngest children.
- A free nursery place for every three-year-old.
- Free prescriptions for young people aged 16-25.
- Free local bus travel for pensioners and disabled people.
- Free entry to museums and galleries for all citizens.

Free services bound society together, making everybody feel they were stakeholders in it:

> 'That is why my administration has been determined to ensure a continuing stake in social welfare services for the widest possible range of our citizens. Universal services mean that we all have a reason for making such services as good as possible. Free access to social welfare services means that they become genuinely available to the full range of people in Wales, not simply those able to afford them.'[42]

Three years later, in a paper presented to a seminar at Glasgow University, Mark Drakeford attached six principles to 'clear red water' that, taken together, he described as progressive universalism.[43] The first principle was to assert the virtue of government as a source for good, in contrast with the Tories who constantly sought to diminish the role of the state.

The second was a belief in universal rather than means-tested services, because 'services which are reserved for poor people very quickly become poor services.' The third principle was that co-operation is better than competition, closely associated with the

---

42 Ibid.
43 M. Drakeford, *Progressive Universalism*, presented to an Economic and Social Research Council seminar, Glasgow University, March 2006, and published in the Winter 2006-07 issue of *Agenda*, the journal of the Institute of Welsh Affairs. It was republished in J. Osmond (Ed.), *Unpacking the Progressive Consensus* (IWA, November 2008), in which it was subjected to critique and debate by Gerry Holtham, David Marquand, Peter Stead, John Kay, and Will Hutton.

fourth principle, participation. That entails a preference for improving the collective voice rather relying solely on individual choice.

Fifth is a reliance on high trust relationships in the delivery of public services. Users and providers should be regarded as being engaged in a joint enterprise. This idea rules out, for example, injecting a market relationship into the functioning of the health service, or introducing league tables into education.

The sixth and most ambitious principle behind progressive universalism, is an insistence on equality of outcome rather than equality of opportunity. This stresses the virtues of social solidarity, pointing to evidence that, for example, although often less rich overall, more equal societies produce improved health gains and often have higher life expectancies. So, although they may spend less on health services, they reap social dividends delivered by less unequal and more cohesive community structures.

All this was a somewhat theoretical perspective, as seen by a Special Adviser who still had one foot firmly entrenched in academia. More than a decade later, after years of hard-won experience in the political trenches as initially Health Minister and then in charge of the Finance Ministry, Drakeford viewed progressive universalism rather more prosaically. Now it was fundamentally about putting money in people's pockets. As he explained:

> 'Successively over the period of devolution, Labour Governments have used our budgets in a way that leaves money in people's pockets, that across the border people have to find themselves. So, if you have free prescriptions, if you're someone who works 16 hours a week in a minimum wage occupation and you need a couple of prescriptions every week for a chronic condition, that's £16 every single week that you have to pay across the border that you don't pay here. That money stays in your pocket and you can use it to manage other difficult things...
>
> Barbara Castle, one of my political heroes, used to call this the social wage, the things that governments can do that leaves money in people's pockets. Families that are living at the margins in Wales, just about managing, have probably got about £1,000 a year in their pockets as a result of things that the Welsh Government have done compared with families that are living somewhere else in the UK. A £1,000 a year is £20 a week. If you're really struggling that's the

difference between putting food on the table. In my surgery in Ely I see people who come through my door on a Saturday who haven't eaten since Wednesday. And it's often women who are feeding children and who are not eating. The social wage is about trying to do what we can with our budget to push back on those incredibly difficult sets of circumstances.[44]

Less than a year into his period as First Minister Mark Drakeford published a wide-ranging, radical document on the future of the United Kingdom. While being supportive of the continuance of the union, the document's analysis of its character and recommendations for reform were in sharp contrast to the views of both the Westminster government and those previously held by the Welsh Labour Party. It opened with the following declaration:

> 'Whatever its historical origins, the United Kingdom is best seen now as a voluntary association of nations taking the form of a multi-national state, whose members share and redistribute resources and risks amongst themselves to advance their common interests. Wales is committed to this association, which must be based on the recognition of popular sovereignty in each part of the UK; Parliamentary sovereignty as traditionally understood no longer provides a sound foundation for this evolving constitution.'[45]

The document went on to suggest a federal approach, and included the following recommendations:

- The House of Lords to be replaced by a new Upper House whose membership would reflect the multinational nature of the UK rather than be population-based and which would ensure that the position of the devolved institutions is properly considered in the UK parliament's legislation.
- Strengthening the voice of the devolved administrations in international discussions.
- Ensuring that funding be distributed among the territories in a fair, needs-based manner and that decisions on the funding of

---

44 'Martin Shipton Meets Mark Drakeford', *op. cit.*
45 *Reforming Our Union: Shared Governance in the UK* (Welsh Government, September 2019).

the devolved administrations should be made by a public agency which would be responsible to the four administrations jointly.
- Devolution of policing and justice to Wales.
- A Constitutional Convention to consider future constitutional developments.

These proposals went with the grain of ideas that had been set out by Drakeford's predecessor Carwyn Jones, but struck a much more assertive note. Brexit had emboldened the Westminster government to seek to undermine and even roll back devolution. A few months earlier, in a speech to the Institute of Government, Drakeford said that as a result of Westminster's 'muscular unionism', there was a possibility of the UK breaking up. Scotland might vote for independence and Northern Ireland could seek unification with the Republic: 'For the first time in my political life, there is a real prospect of the UK not surviving as a four-way nation.' Brexit was the reason:

> 'My experience of being in the room now with many Conservative Cabinet Ministers is that there remains a considerable number for whom Brexit is an opportunity to return the UK to the place it was in 1973, in which the dreadful mistake of devolution can somehow be brushed under the carpet... The UK government has a deep and profound ambivalence about devolution. Their attitude towards devolution is a grace and favour approach. Devolution has been given to us. Indeed, a Cabinet Minister said exactly that to me: "We gave you devolution", as though it was entirely their gift. And the corollary of that, of course, is a deep belief that what has been given can be taken away. Devolution is fine so long as those people who have been given devolved powers behave themselves properly and do the things that the UK government are happy to see done. If we do that, if we behave ourselves properly, in this grace and favour model then out of the goodness of its own heart the UK government allows some powers of self-government, provided that they are carefully limited, provided that they are provisional.' [46]

---

46 M. Drakeford, 'The future of devolution: the UK after Brexit', speech to the Institute for Government, 9 May 2019.

Two years later, in June 2021, a second edition of *Reforming Our Union* was published with Mark Drakeford writing a new, more pessimistic, introduction:

'... it has become harder and harder to make the case for the Union, and the threat to it has never been greater during my lifetime... where the UK Government acts in an aggressively unilateral way on behalf of the whole UK, without regard for the status of the nations and the democratic mandates of their governments, this inevitably creates anger and alienation.'[47]

A few months before this, Drakeford had struck a similarly pessimistic note, this time in evidence to the Welsh Affairs Select Committee:

'There is no institutional architecture to make the United Kingdom work. It is all *ad hoc*, random and made up as we go along. I am afraid that that really is not a satisfactory basis to sustain the future of the United Kingdom... At the moment we have a Prime Minister [Boris Johnson] who, I would say, clearly displays outright hostility to the fact of devolution. We heard what he told a group of Conservative Members of Parliament, that he thought devolution was Tony Blair's biggest mistake. I am afraid that while there is a mindset of that sort at the centre of the Government, the break-up of the United Kingdom comes closer every day.'[48]

Undoubtedly Mark Drakeford's aspirations for reforming the Union in a federal direction has support in Wales, but to what extent is that mirrored in Scotland and England? On the one hand, a significant proportion of Scottish opinion, if not yet a sustained majority, is set on re-joining the European Union as an independent country. On the other, despite the growing patchwork of city region government, there seems little appetite in England to undertake the constitutional engineering that would be necessary if Drakeford's vision were to be realised.

---

47 Welsh Government, *Reforming Our Union: Shared Governance in the UK*, 2nd Edition, June 2021.
48 M. Drakeford, evidence to the Welsh Affairs Committee, *Hansard*, 4 March 2021.

It is true that shortly after he became Labour leader, Sir Keir Starmer made a commitment to a federal approach, telling Scotland's *Daily Record*:

> 'I want to build a future on the principle of federalism. We will establish a constitutional convention in opposition that applies that principle of federalism and a new settlement for the UK.'[49]

That commitment did not materialise. Instead, in September 2021 Starmer appointed former Prime Minister Gordon Brown to chair a Commission tasked with 'settling the future of the union', as he put it.[50] Yet, when the Commission's report appeared, in November 2022, its proposals for constitutional change were underwhelming.[51] So far as further devolution was concerned there was nothing to give Wales and Scotland more secure access to the proceeds of any higher tax rates they set, and no more than 'consultation' over enhancing their borrowing capacity. The Senedd and Scottish Parliament would gain the right to enter into international agreements in their areas of competence, which might ease the consequences of Brexit. Wales was offered devolution of youth justice and the probation service but not overall control of the justice system with the creation of a distinctive legal jurisdiction, as is the case with Scotland and Northern Ireland.

To be sure, there were proposals for an 'Assembly of the Nations and Regions' to replace the House of Lords, but the report was silent on whether there should be weighted representation for Wales and Scotland, merely committing to 200 members 'elected on a regional basis', which might or might not entail a proportional system. The new Assembly would have a role in supervising intergovernmental arrangements, including a 'Council of the Nations and Regions' with an independent secretariat. In addition, the Sewel Convention – which prevents Westminster from legislating on devolved matters

---

49 *Daily Record*, 6 April 2020. It is noteworthy that the commitment was limited to these two sentences. It is noteworthy, too that they were made in the Scottish press – doubtless as an attempt to strengthen Scottish Labour's hand against the SNP.
50 Keir Starmer, speech to Labour's annual conference (*Glasgow Herald*, 29 September 2021).
51 Labour Party, *Report of the Commission on the UK's Future - A New Britain: Renewing our Democracy and Rebuilding our Economy*, November 2022.

without devolved consent – would 'not be restricted to applying "normally" but should be binding in all circumstances.'[52]

Overall, however, the Brown Commission proposals amounted to a minimal commitment to moving Britain in a federal direction. Starmer himself was vague about whether any of the proposals would be included in Labour's manifesto for the next election, or, if so, whether they would be considered in the first term of a Labour government.

Meanwhile, the effect of the Westminster Government's drive towards 'muscular unionism' or what Ciaran Martin, a former leading civil servant in the UK Cabinet Office, has called 'know your place unionism', is to drain emotional attachment from allegiance to the UK.[53] Instead, it becomes ever more regarded as a contractual relationship. Its benefits are seen as merely economic and providing an insurance system in which social security provision – pensions and so on – are shared. Once that is acknowledged, it is but a short step towards a recognition that for many the union is also highly conditional. So, for example, if Scotland were to secede from the union and Wales was left in a sole relationship with England, many Welsh people would feel deeply uncomfortable. Many would regard the position as unsustainable.

Such considerations are compounded by the relatively weak position of Wales within the United Kingdom. This was illustrated by Mark Drakeford himself when, towards the end of a presentation he gave to the Institute for Government in May 2019, he was asked what political leverage he had in negotiations with the UK Government

---

52 *Ibid*, p.103. The report adds: 'Of course it would then be in principle possible for an administration to legislate simply to disapply this provision in relation to any particular legislation. That leads to a second recommendation, which is that the legislation giving effect to the Sewel Convention should be one of the protected constitutional laws which require the consent not just of the House of Commons but of the reformed second chamber also. This entrenches the convention as part of the UK's territorial constitution. It will succeed where the present legislation has failed in ensuring that the powers of the devolved legislatures cannot simply be overridden by the Government of the day. This form of entrenchment of the devolution settlements provides protection for them analogous to a written constitution.'

53 See C. Martin, 'Can the UK Survive Muscular Unionism' (*Political Insight*, December 2021).

compared with Northern Ireland and Scotland. His answer was disarmingly frank:

> 'With Northern Ireland the peace process and the need to sustain peace on the island of Ireland is a huge default leverage. Scotland has leverage. A second referendum and the possibility of Scotland leaving the United Kingdom is a big piece of political leverage. Wales has neither of those things. And in the Brexit context we don't have the fact that Wales voted to stay in the European Union, either, whereas both Northern Ireland and Scotland are able to advance that. Our position is always different. What we rely on are two things. One is the force of the arguments that we are able to make. We have published a whole series of papers setting out what we believe are credible and constructive policy proposals on the big issues that Brexit throws up. We put a lot of effort and energy into trying to make the quality of those arguments as good as we possibly can. The second thing that we rely on is that we are the only devolved administration that unambiguously believes in the future of the United Kingdom. That gives us some leverage and political space because no other devolved administration speaks with the same clarity on that issue.'[54]

These are brave assertions. However, the blunt political reality is that, compared with the position of the Scottish and Northern Ireland governments, in negotiations with the UK government the Welsh Government has very little political leverage at all. Mark Drakeford illuminated this point himself in the written evidence he gave to the Covid Inquiry in December 2023, and on which he was interrogated in March 2024. At the end of a long statement, he turned to the lessons he had learned. He offered a criticism and two recommendations:

> 'I reject the suggestions I have seen by some UK Ministers that a newly centralised approach, over-riding devolved responsibilities, would improve the response to any future pandemic. It is not simply that the suggestion comes so improbably from those whose actions so comprehensively undermined the confidence of citizens in the UK's response to Covid-19, but it entirely overlooks the fundamental issue of trust in persuading individuals to take actions necessary to protect

---

54 M. Drakeford, 'The future of devolution: the UK after Brexit', *op. cit.*

their own lives and those of others. The empirical data collected during the pandemic demonstrates, beyond doubt I believe, that trust is best engendered and preserved when decisions are made as close to the lived circumstances of those affected by them as possible.

My own recommendation would lie much more in a reform of the practice of intergovernmental relations, so that in any future pandemic there is, already in existence, a predictable, well understood, well-used pattern of interaction between the four nations, in which participants are ready to share information and to explore together the responsibilities which each, separately, will discharge.

My second recommendation lies in the field of finance. I believe that the single most damaging decision during the whole Covid-19 experience, was the explicit refusal of the Treasury to make funds available to Wales when public health conditions here required action to be taken. It might be argued that, in doing so, the Treasury was simply enforcing a rigid interpretation of the Barnett formula approach to devolved funding. In that case, my recommendation would be that a future pandemic must adopt a different approach. If any component nation of the United Kingdom concludes that action is needed to address a public health emergency, and that such action can only be taken if centrally funded, that nation should be able to make its case to the Treasury against a set of common criteria. I do not argue, at all, that all this should not be rooted in proper process, including robust scrutiny by the Treasury. My point is that all nations must be treated equally, each able to make a case for funding on the same basis as any other. Only in that way can the Treasury genuinely act as a Treasury for the whole of the United Kingdom rather than, as was transparently the case during the Covid pandemic, a Treasury for England, with all other nations funded as a consequence of those made-for-England determinations.[55]

Where Plaid and Welsh Labour meet

Mark Drakeford has moved a long way from the view of his mentor Rhodri Morgan, set out in 2008:

---

55 M. Drakeford, Witness Statement to the UK Covid-19 Public Inquiry, 13 December 2023, paras. 297-99.

> 'Devolution – as opposed to unionism, federalism or nationalism – offers the people of Wales the best of both worlds. We are able increasingly to take control of our own domestic affairs, while retaining the benefits which flow from being part of Britain.'[56]

With the benefit of hindsight, there was some irony when Morgan chose to highlight the impact of a future pandemic as an illustration of the benefits of being part of Britain:

> 'When – not "if" – a new global influenza pandemic does break out, our resilience in face of that risk will rely, crucially, on being able to draw on being part of a wider network of services, both public and private.'[57]

As we have seen, when that eventuality did materialise 12 years later in the form of Covid, Mark Drakeford's actual experience of solidarity across Britain was not quite as Morgan had predicted. But there are more straightforward objections to his claim that devolution gives Wales the best of both worlds. In the first place, it reduces the solidarity he praises to a transactional matter of self-advantage. More fundamentally, it was a sleight of hand to try and distinguish devolution *from* unionism, because in reality devolution *is* a form of unionism.

So it is of some significance that Mark Drakeford moved away from a unionist interpretation of devolution, declaring that sovereignty lies with the people in Wales and not with the Crown in Westminster. Moreover, and, contrary to Rhodri Morgan, he has adopted federalism as opposed to devolution as Welsh Labour's constitutional objective. And as we shall see in Chapter 7, the Constitutional Commission set up as part of the Co-operation Agreement stress-tested federalism and found that, although theoretically viable, it was most likely unworkable in the British context. The result was to push Drakeford's thinking further, so that in in the Senedd debate on the Commission's report, in March 2024, he spoke warmly of Dominion Status as an

---

56   Rh. Morgan, 'Welsh Labour's Future', in J. Osmond (Ed.), *Politics in 21ˢᵗ Century Wales* (IWA, 2008), p.20.
57   *Ibid.*, p.19.

option for Wales.[58] Significantly, that was Plaid Cymru's policy in the 1930s.

One consequence of the Co-operation Agreement is a blurring of the previously sharp difference between Plaid and Welsh Labour's constitutional objectives. Which raises the question of what really separates the two parties. Fundamentally, it is ideological, in the sense that Welsh Labour emerged from a collectivist trade union tradition that is statist and top down, for all its egalitarianism. In contrast Plaid Cymru has quite different roots, in the ideas of individual freedom and responsibility that can only be realised through collective involvement in community. Welsh Labour's is a democratic collectivist tradition, while Plaid Cymru's can be best described as democratic republican.[59]

Of course, these traditions overlap. Increasingly, elements of each can be found in the thinking of both parties. Certainly, Adam Price and Mark Drakeford were sensitive to the overlap, which was a further reason why they were able to work together in forging the Co-operative Agreement. Nonetheless, the ideological demarcation is part of the reason why Plaid Cymru is relatively strong in the west and north-west of Wales, while Labour dominates in the more urban centres of the south-east and north-east. Together with proportional representation, now becoming more deeply embedded due to Senedd

---

58 See pages 241-3 for a discussion of the case for Dominion Status.

59 These categories form part of the intellectual framework for David Marquand's *Britain Since 2018: The Strange Career of British Democracy* (Weidenfield & Nicholson, 2008). Born in Cardiff, David Marquand (1934-2024) was Labour MP for Ashfield between 1966 and 1977, having first fought Barry in 1964. He resigned from the House of Commons to work with Roy Jenkins when he became President of the European Commission. Marquand then combined with Jenkins and the other members of the 'Gang of Four' – David Owen, Shirley Williams and Bill Rodgers – in founding the Social Democratic Party in 1981. He re-joined the Labour Party in 1995, admiring Tony Blair's early leadership, but left once more in 2003, this time in protest at the Iraq War. He was Professor of Politics at Salford and Sheffield universities before becoming Principal of Mansfield College, Oxford 1996-2002. In 2016, partly in response to Brexit, he returned from Oxford to live in Wales and joined Plaid Cymru. He described republicanism as 'not so much a doctrine as a cast of mind'. As he put it, 'Central to the republican ideal is the proposition that the people should take control of their own destinies by and through democratic activity.' (*Renewal*, 'Progressive dilemmas after the election: David Marquand interviewed by Ben Jackson', April 2010.)

reform, these are the structural reasons why some formation of Plaid/Labour cross-party governance is likely to continue in Wales.

But personalities matter as well. Any future collaboration in government between Plaid and Welsh Labour will depend as much on the successors to Adam Price and Mark Drakeford as the nature and relative strength of their parties.

Part II

The First 100 Days of Plaid's New Leader

A Diary

The 100 Days

Plaid Cymru rules on leadership elections allowed for a contest to be held the summer preceding the October 2018 National Conference in Cardigan. In practice this was the last opportunity for a contest before the 2021 Senedd election. The challenge that materialised to Leanne Wood's leadership was prompted by a lack of policy direction and by Plaid's lack of progress in successive elections. More immediately, Brexit had profoundly disturbed the party's equilibrium. It had been strongly in favour of Remain in the 2016 referendum and there was a desire to keep the European flame alive, not least by supporting the campaign for a further referendum. However, Leanne Wood, whose Rhondda constituency had voted to leave, was less than enthusiastic in stressing Plaid's pro-European stance.

Ynys Môn MS Rhun ap Iorwerth was the first to announce he would be a candidate, immediately followed by Adam Price. On the first round of voting Price won 49.7% (2,863 votes), ap Iorwerth was second with 28% (1,613), and Wood third with 22.3% (1,286). In the second round, after Wood had been eliminated and her second preference votes redistributed, Price won 3,481 votes to ap Iorwerth's 1,961. For Leanne Wood, who had gained a good deal of popularity due to her performance in the 2015 general election TV leadership debates, her poor result was unexpected. Certainly, it was not conducive to creating unity within the Plaid Group in Cardiff Bay.

Moreover, at that point the Group was in disarray for other reasons. Due to a defection and an expulsion, its membership had fallen from 12 to ten. First to leave had been Dafydd Elis-Thomas, disenchanted since the Plaid leadership election in 2012 when he came third behind Leanne Wood and Elin Jones. He had disagreed with Wood's oppositionist approach to Labour and had more recently been pointedly removed by Wood as a Plaid-nominated Chair of an Assembly Committee. Elis-Thomas left the Group in October 2016 to become an independent backbencher and a year later joined the Welsh Government as Deputy Minister for Culture, Sport and Tourism. In January 2018, South Wales Central List member Neil McEvoy was expelled from the Group following allegations of bullying made by a colleague. Then in July 2018 Plaid's AM for Mid and West Wales, Simon Thomas, resigned after his arrest on suspicion of possessing indecent images of children, and was replaced by Helen Mary Jones. Thomas subsequently pleaded guilty in court and was convicted.

Consequently, when he became leader, Adam Price's first task was to provide Plaid's Assembly Members with unity and a sense of direction. He immediately set himself the challenge of accomplishing these objectives within 100 days, recalling American President, Franklin Delano Roosevelt, who adopted the same horizon in tackling the Great Depression in the 1930s.

What follows is a weekly contemporaneous account of those 100 days, between early October 2018 and the party's Spring conference in late March 2019. During this period, we believed a momentum was gathering pace that might herald an historic change in the party's fortunes. The hope was that, when the 2021 election to the renamed Senedd came, the stars might align in such a way to give Plaid Cymru a chance to be in government.

Week 1: 15 October 2018
Touching base

I arrived at the Senedd at just gone nine on Monday, complete with laptop. Giving me a temporary pass, Mabli Jones, the Group's Chief of Staff, led me through a maze of corridors to the large open-plan Plaid office on the second floor. It's lined on either side with smaller offices for the Members. However, Adam has decamped from his, and put himself among the researchers, exposed to the swirl of conversation and opinions. This seems like Harvard management-speak, but it probably works. Later I discover that Adam hardly ever sits at his desk anyway. Coffee in hand, he's constantly on the move.

I attend a staff meeting at 10am. It's held in what used to be Leanne's leader's office. This has now become a common meeting room, to be booked by whoever needs it, part of a pattern of change that signifies Adam's arrival as leader, though so far this morning he hasn't appeared. In fact, most of the AMs only arrive in time for plenary on Tuesday.

An exception is Steffan Lewis, our South East Wales List MS, Leanne's former point man, finetuned to the political winds that blow through these corridors. He is acerbic, intelligent, and... stricken with cancer. He turns up, ashen faced, when he feels up to it, perhaps for half-a-day.

The main impression of the staff meeting is a sea of young faces I don't know. And if I wasn't there, they'd be speaking in Welsh.

Nearly everyone apart from Leanne Wood speaks Welsh fluently, and uses it in preference to English. That becomes apparent the following day, at the 11am regular Tuesday Group Meeting. This is held – for the last time – in a committee room on the Senedd's ground floor, with the translators holed up in their cubicles behind a large sheet of glass. All our Senedd members are here together with most of their researchers and other staff, including election supremo Geraint Day from Plaid's headquarters, Tŷ Gwynfor.

The staff sit behind the MSs on chairs against the surrounding walls. I'm the only one to sit at the oblong benches with the MSs, and that's because the translation equipment is here. I note that only Leanne and myself are making use of it. I wonder how she must have felt as Leader, being in this sense an outsider. Of course, it's one of the structural problems Plaid has in getting through to the majority Anglophone population. I tell myself that part of my role is to be a constant reminder of this bleak reality. As if to underline the point, at the end of the meeting Elin Jones, the Presiding Officer, who is sitting next to me glances across and remarks, 'Goodness, didn't realise you were here! I've heard something about your new role...' or words to that effect.

Afterwards I get taken up with First Minister's Questions and start researching what Labour's three leadership candidates to succeed Carwyn Jones have been saying on the hustings about their party's policy. Adam is looking for conflicting points of view. And soon enough we find some, on Brexit. Vaughan Gething and Eluned Morgan are speaking ardently in favour of a People's Vote on Brexit (though they voted against a Plaid motion to that effect in the Chamber last week). Meanwhile, Mark Drakeford is cautious, worried that it might result in another No vote. He's sticking to the Corbyn line of wanting a General Election instead.

Brexit has led to another innovation. At 12 noon there's the inaugural meeting of Grŵp Brexit. It comprised Plaid's MPs, Adam, Steffan Lewis (responsible for External Affairs), various Westminster staffers, including Head of Comms Ben O'Keeffe and Head of Research Heledd Brooks-Jones, and me. Moreover, three of our four MPs at Westminster attend in person – Jonathan Edwards, Liz Saville Roberts, and Hywel Williams (Ben Lake is holding the fort in the Commons, dealing with farming questions) – along with Jill Evans MEP, and (Lord) Dafydd Wigley. Apparently, it's the first occasion there's been such a meeting of MEP and MPs with AMs in Tŷ Hywel: another Adam first.

The meeting turns out to be fascinating, with Jonathan Edwards guiding us through the machinations of various scenarios surrounding the forthcoming key parliamentary Brexit votes. Adam points out that a Sinn Féin delegation is meeting with Prime Minister Theresa May in Number 10 this very day. He says, 'If they can get their foot in the door, with none of their MPs taking up seats at Westminster, why shouldn't we?'

I notice that Ben O'Keeffe is immediately texting on his phone. Within a few minutes he interjects. 'Number Ten are interested, in fact they're very interested. They want to know if it would be a serious meeting?'

Adam looks across, 'Tell them, yes'. This provokes a swirl of comment. There's talk of how we cannot afford to sell out, we have our red lines and so on. But Wigley supports Adam. 'No harm in talking,' he says. 'We might get something.'

The meeting ends with general agreement that it's been worthwhile. Liz insists it must become a regular event. Adam adds that it must be face to face. Phones down the line are no good, except for the odd participant. It's agreed that the meetings will occur fortnightly, either in London or Cardiff, for as long as the Brexit crisis continues, and after that as well, though not so regularly. They also set up a Grŵp Brexit on WhatsApp, which persuades me I need to buy a smart phone.

During the week I only have a few snatched conversations with Adam, except when we meet over lunch on Wednesday for a rare chewing of the fat. I bring out a list of things I've compiled, about meetings we need to set up outside Wales, the launch of Adam's forthcoming book,[1] policy questions and priorities. Here is my list:

- What policies are owned by Plaid in the way Labour owns health, and the Tories defence? The only clear answer is the Welsh language. This has both positives and negatives: it's positive in that it bolsters our core support – 70% of Welsh speakers who vote, vote Plaid; but negative in that English-speakers tend not to identify with Plaid.

---

1 A. Price, *Wales: First and Final Colony, op. cit.*

- In comparative surveys of party association with policy issues, Plaid generally scores relatively highly, but depending on the issue tends to be trumped by another party – except for the language.
- In general, therefore, we are regarded in a broadly benign way, but not as a party that attracts priority support for voters on any central concern – apart from the language.
- Answer: choose and accentuate Plaid attachment to a small number of key policy areas. Suggest: the economy, transport, and environment.

Adam accepts all this. The priority, we agree, is the economy and establishing a strong Economic Policy Group. Meanwhile, my main task for the rest of the week is to draft a speech he's been committed to give in Crymych since before the leadership campaign. This proves reasonably straightforward as I've already done most of the research for my book about Preseli – the chapters on Waldo and D.J. Williams come in especially handy.[2]

Week 2: 22 October 2018
The Shadow Cabinet

On Tuesday I attend my first meeting of the Shadow Cabinet. The portfolios were announced at the end of last week after what seemed like days of protracted negotiations – Adam talking on the hoof with one MS after another, in their offices, in corridors, amidst the open plan office.

Shadow Cabinet meets for the first time in the office meeting room on the second floor. Previously it's been downstairs in one of the committee rooms, to enable simultaneous translation. But Adam has asked for a translation booth to be set up in our office. It creates the intended, more autonomous feel of Plaid's Shadow Cabinet in session on its own terms. It's another, subtle declaration that under the new regime things are going to be different.

---

[2] J. Osmond, *Real Preseli* (Seren, 2019). Brought up in Mynachlog-ddu and Llandissilio, the mystical poet Waldo Williams (1904-1971) was Plaid Cymru's first candidate in Pembrokeshire in the 1959 general election. His friend and fellow writer D.J. Williams, one of the founders of Plaid Cymru, lived for much of his life in Fishguard.

But the atmosphere is frosty. Adam sits at one end, in a chairing role, one that he soon realises he must give up. At the other end, is Rhun ap Iorwerth, alongside Leanne. She sits rigidly. A strained discussion takes place around two points. The first is whether the two-year budget agreement with Labour should be continued (it has so far lasted one year) in the light of the latest announced cuts to education and local government, with an easy bung being thrown at health.

Leanne immediately objects. After all it's her deal (which Adam negotiated). She asks how Plaid's word on any future relationship or deal could be trusted. Rhun follows, raising doubts. As does Steffan Lewis, in his usual pointed way. Helen Mary interjects to complain that she hadn't been forewarned of this possibility and had just taken the weekly press conference where the question had been raised, which she had flatly denied. The matter is left unresolved.

The other discussion surrounds a Plaid plenary debate later in the week on nuclear energy. Neil McEvoy, our dissident South Wales Central former colleague, has put down an amendment designed to exploit the differences in the Group over this neuralgic question. Despite this being acknowledged we proceed to rake over the differences. Llyr Huws Gruffydd, our environment spokesman, insists that our anti-nuclear position has been endorsed time and time again by countless conference decisions. Rhun defends the right of local parties – and in particular, his Ynys Môn constituency where a new nuclear power station is planned – to go their own decentralised way. Adam backs the party line, defends the current compromise approach, and suggests the further compromise that we abstain on McEvoy's motion. At the same time, he says that we're going to have to adopt a more robust stance in future.

Altogether it's a tense meeting. Leanne complains that in a paper detailing additional briefs that accompany the cabinet portfolio positions, she is shown as taking responsibility for the Leadership Academy. She points out that Siân Gwenllian's Deputy Leadership role entails overseeing co-ordination across the party structures, so she should do it. Adam acknowledges this and apologises for the lines still being included in the paper.

It was an oversight, a mistake, but it brings into the open how rankled Leanne feels and creates an unpleasant air of disunity as the meeting breaks up. How can all this be resolved?

We're immediately plunged into preparations for First Minister's Questions (FMQs). We've decided to go on the M4 Relief Road. I've prepared questions aimed at Carwyn Jones' prevarications, asking when the Planning Inspector's report, known to have been with Ministers since early September, will be published. Is Carwyn minded to leave the decision to his successor, Mark Drakeford, who takes over in a matter of months and is known to be lukewarm? However, all this is thrown into confusion when it transpires that on this occasion the Leader of the House, instead of the First Minister, is taking FMQs.

Adam declares that, following procedure he recalls from Westminster, his deputy Rhun should lead on FMQs, and promptly disappears to address a Brexit rally on the steps of the Senedd. I then scramble to redraft the Plaid questions, discovering that the Leader of the House, Swansea West MS Julie James, has already announced a date for a M4 debate in December. Rhun comes over and sits alongside me, helpful and supportive in rejigging the whole thing.

Then it transpires that the Assembly's conventions are different to Westminster and Adam will be leading after all. In the subsequent exchange on the floor of the Senedd we get a surprising concession – for that is how it seems – that the vote on the Relief Road will be binding when it comes in December. This holds out the prospect of exposing Labour's divisions on the decision and makes a story on the BBC website. Adam is pleased. It's a result, and he wants results from FMQs.

I fail to see how it is that significant. I assume that Carwyn's road will be approved one way or another, but the main feeling I get from the episode is that Rhun is fundamentally on side. This is good news. Adam has made him his deputy and he's going to need solid support. I see Rhun as being for Adam what John Swinney has been for Alex Salmond and Nicola Sturgeon in the Scottish Parliament. He's been the dependable person in charge of keeping the engine room of government ticking over efficiently, while Alex and Nicola keep the Front of House on the road. Something like this is going to have to happen for us as well, if our plans for getting into government are going to work out.

My favourable impression of Rhun gets another boost on Wednesday when he, Adam, myself and Eurfyl ap Gwilym, Plaid's economics adviser, meet to discuss the Economic Policy Group I've been working on. Eurfyl has agreed to chair it, but this is the first that Rhun, our new Economic Development spokesperson, has heard of it. However, he does not cavil, but contributes enthusiastically to the discussion. Adam is quite astute in the way he leaves much of the initiative to Rhun, giving him a sense that he has ownership. It's another, small but significant, sign of his political skills.

Later Adam and I have lunch outside the Senedd in Côte Brasserie, across the way from the Millennium Centre. These Wednesday lunches look like becoming a weekly appointment. I go through another list of issues I've made: including the importance of a new Comms appointment, upcoming engagements in Brussels and Dublin, launch events for Adam's book, and the St. Davids Festival of Ideas.[3]

So far, we don't seem to have disagreed about any major question. Adam emphasises how important he sees the Economic Policy Group, and how he hopes it will prove a template for similar groups in other key policy areas, especially renewable energy. Then he launches into an analysis of the Shadow Cabinet meeting. Confesses he felt nervous and was somewhat at a loss to know how to deal with Leanne. Rhun was a different matter. They'd been out for a few beers the previous evening and settled things. I suggest that he ask Siân Gwenllian to mediate with Leanne. Then he rushes off to some meeting leaving me to pick up the tab. 'I'll do it next week,' he calls over his shoulder.

Later that evening we resume our conversation in the Wahaca Mexican restaurant near the Central Library. We're there for a leaving do for Elin Roberts. It's the first time I've met her. She has been our Head of Comms but has now left to do the same job for Presiding Officer Elin Jones. I buy a drink for Mabli who appears awfully young to be Chief of Staff. But then, so do all the staff, most of whom are in their twenties. I sense she harbours loyalty to Leanne but is coming round. She tells me she was brought up in Grangetown and has moved back there. Went to the University of Bristol but also a Welsh-

---

[3] Inspired by Almedalan Week, held in July on the Swedish island of Gotland – one of the most important forums in Swedish politics – Adam despatched me to St. Davids in October 2018 to drum up support for a similar festival there. After many meetings, involving local organisations and activists, we held the inaugural festival online in March 2021 in the midst of the Covid pandemic, followed by the first in-person festival in March 2022. This attracted an audience of more than 100 and a wide range of speakers, plus the promise of steady future development. Another successful festival was held in 2023. In March 2024 the festival evolved into Tir a Môr: Festival of Land and Sea.

medium school in Cardiff which, of course, explains things. I find her impressive, quietly efficient, gets things done.

It's noteworthy that the only MSs to turn up are Adam and Helen Mary Jones, one of whose characteristics is the time and care she takes with the staff – time well spent. Also present is Carl Harris, and I realise again how essential he is to Adam's operation. He's been at his side in Carmarthen East for ten years. Now he's moving into a more central role in the party head office. He whispers in Adam's ear that he should say a few words, and suggests some lines.

A while later I hear Adam repeat them. Elin Roberts is moving from Plaid's office on the second floor of Tŷ Hywel to the fourth floor to work for the Presiding Officer. But he looks forward to the day, not long now, in 2021, when we can all come together again, in government on the fifth floor. It's a light piece of banter, but well judged, gives a surge of morale: the leader's role. Afterwards Adam gives me a glass of red wine and asks how I like coming out of retirement. We reminisce over the first few weeks. 'You know I'm hoping you might consider staying on beyond December,' he says, referring to my initial commitment for a trial period in the job until Christmas.

Week 3: 29 October 2018
Adam meets Theresa

It's half term so the Assembly is in recess. No FMQs this week – they're already becoming something of a trial for me. At the same time, I think Adam has a love-hate attitude towards them. Puts him on his mettle. Likes the cut and thrust, looking for new angles, catching people out, the potential media coverage.

This week the main event is in London. Today is the UK budget and Adam has gone up for the debate, treading familiar Westminster corridors, seeking out old friends, ready for a soundbite in front of the camera on College Green opposite the Houses of Parliament.

On Tuesday morning I'm patched in to a telephone conference call from Grŵp Brexit. In my study at home in Penarth, overlooking the Senedd and the Bay, I put the phone on loudspeaker and listen. We're discussing tomorrow's event, the meeting with Theresa May. There's anxiety, especially from the MPs, that we could buckle and accept some kind of compromise on Brexit in return for doubtful promises of 'doing something for Wales'.

Adam listens and is conciliatory. He acknowledges that the chances of a deal are remote. But hey, we've got a foot in the door. We're suddenly relevant in a way the Welsh Government and Carwyn Jones are not. Make the most of it. This is real politics and so on. He's already buoyed up by a pre-meeting with the Welsh Secretary Alun Cairns, who's clearly been sent out to find out what our agenda is... are we up for a serious discussion?

We agree that our main requirements at this stage are:

1. Extending the transition period during which the UK remains a member of the Single Market and Customs Union. Critical for us is the length of the transition period – we're looking for it to take us beyond the general election, assumed to be in 2022, with the hope that a change of government might offer the chance of a reversal of Brexit.
2. If a degree of flexibility is afforded to Northern Ireland in relation to its participation within European frameworks (especially, Customs Union and Single Market) then we want Wales to be offered the same opportunity.

And if its coverage we want, we get it. There's a page in the *Western Mail* before and afterwards. Meanwhile, Welsh TV camera teams relish their moment on the steps of Number 10. Adam comes out with Liz Saville Roberts and, as the trade saying has it, the optics are good. As Adam told the *Western Mail*, 'We're not tribal in our politics. We actually want to do a positive job for the people of Wales and that does sometimes mean trying to find common ground even with people in other political parties.'[4] That's a strikingly different tone from Leanne, for those who want to prick up their ears and listen.

Week 4: 5 November 2018
Economy front and centre

Unlike most of the other MSs, Adam is intent on appearing in the Senedd early on Monday morning to put his stamp on things. We meet in his office to discuss this week's FMQs, but soon turn to more interesting matters. Adam is much exercised by Gerry Holtham's critique of his *Ten Point Plan for the Economy*. I asked Gerry to pen a

---

4   *Western Mail*, 1 November 2018.

few thoughts and I've sent them to Adam ahead of a meeting of the Economic Policy Group later this week.

Adam's Ten Point Plan was published as part of his campaign for the leadership. In his critique Holtham, an economist and former Director of the IPPR think tank, wrote, 'This reminds me of Lloyd George's advice to a Parliamentary tyro (I forget who). He remarked his speech had made a number of points, fine for an economic journal article but too many for a Parliamentary speech. He should make just one point and hammer it home. There is just too much in this so the reader ends up feeling it's one bloody thing after another and begins to doubt the practicality. I lost count, for example of the number of new bodies or institutions to be established. You end up asking not so much where the money is coming from but where are all the knowledgeable responsible people coming from....'

Adam is concerned that I've also sent Gerry's paper to Rhun ap Iorwerth, and that they will play into his conservative instincts. 'The one thing we don't want at this stage is to close down ideas,' he says, and elaborates: 'I see policy making like a diamond. You need to diverge before you converge. It's important not to evaluate too early, to converge too early. Let's get everything on the table.'

What is the objective? Adam asks the question, then provides an answer. 'Our level of GDP per head is currently in the low seventies compared with the UK average. It should be realistic to get into the low eighties by the end of two terms. To get there we'll need to get our income per capita rising by 2.5% to 3% a year. That's an increase of at least 1% GDP on recent experience. Cumulatively it would represent accelerating growth. What are the policies that would best achieve that? I've put mine on the table. If you reject them, what do you put in their place?'

He goes on to muse that policy development must be a combination of top down and bottom up. By top down he means him. Bottom up is whoever else we can get to participate from the wider party. He reflects back on the previous Senedd election in 2016, and how preparing the manifesto was placed in his lap in the January before the poll. He had just three months, writing more or less from scratch. It has to be different this time.

The Shadow Cabinet meeting on Tuesday is less fraught than the inaugural meeting a fortnight before. It helps that Siân Gwenllian is chairing. This removes Adam from the immediate front line. However, Leanne still sits at the far end of the table, avoiding eye contact. A major item on the agenda is a paper that Adam and his researcher Steffan Bryn have prepared, on our policy development strategy for the 2021 election. The first I'd heard of this was yesterday, and set eyes on it a half hour before the meeting. However, I'm reassured. Most of it revolves round the creation of policy development groups along the lines of the Economic Policy Group I've initiated. The main purpose appears to get buy-in from the MSs.

I note that in the section on communication there's a reference to another paper I'm preparing, 'A radical new *Welsh Nation* publication to be published by Nova Cambria', a think tank Adam has been trying to create, and also to the St. Davids Festival of Ideas. But my main reaction comes from its reference to a new position I haven't clocked: a Senior Policy Officer who will co-ordinate all the work. Who is this? I panic for a moment, thinking it might be me. But I'm reassured when an embarrassed Steffan tells me it's the lead policy officer in Tŷ Gwynfor. But how can that work? It used to be Emily Edwards, but she went on maternity leave ten days ago, after having her baby, a boy, two months early while on a weekend break in Venice. She's still there.

Meanwhile, her deputy, Fflur Elin, who has taken her place, is attending Shadow Cabinet. I signal to her towards the end of the meeting that we should have a chat. She's young, early twenties, and her current policy officer position is her first job. And it's not really a policy job, more organising events, specifically the annual conference. Nevertheless, I'm impressed. She's bright, from Tonyrefail in the Rhondda, read history at Bangor. We go over a few things. I ask her whether she's heard of the Rhondda writer Gwyn Thomas. She shakes her head. I tell her that he used to say there's only one way out of Tonyrefail – by vertical take-off! But she doesn't appear to appreciate the reference or the joke. Makes me feel my age. Then I suggest that it will be impossible for her to carry out the role envisaged in the Policy Development Strategy paper based in Tŷ Gwynfor. She'll have to move to the Senedd.

She sees the sense of this, but then raises the issue of the Fiscal Commission the party is committed to creating, following a motion passed at conference. Could this be folded into the Economic Policy Group? I agree and say I'll sort it with Adam.

Later in the morning I catch him in his office intending to raise this and a few other things. But he's unusually agitated, not to say angry. It seems the advert for the Communications Director post went out without the caveat he had asked for – that a line be put in to the effect that a higher salary than £40K could be negotiated for an 'exceptional candidate'. Chief Executive Gareth Clubb's hand is in this. The upshot is that there have only been four applicants. Adam complains, 'When you get into power – and I suppose you could say that as Leader I'm in a position of power of sorts – you're supposed to be able to pull levers. I pull levers and nothing happens. It's as though there's no wire attached to them.'

I change the subject. The day before I'd run into Dafydd Elis-Thomas and we'd had a chat. He hadn't heard of my new role as Adam's Special Advisor and was amused. He vouchsafed to me, in his conspiratorial manner, that he's minded to vote against Labour's Black Route proposed for the M4 Relief Road. 'How can we be expected to vote for it without seeing the Inquiry report,' he asks, with a certain amount of confected anger. I allude to collective Cabinet responsibility, and he smiles, 'Well, yes, quite so.' But he insists that he will still vote against it. He then tells me he's had a message from Adam suggesting a drink but is not inclined to respond very soon.

I tell Adam all this and he's suddenly animated. It appears he's thinking in terms of trying to entice Dafydd back in to the Group. He had a long conversation with Dafydd Wigley about it last week, over dinner in London. The purpose in the first instance would be to get Elis-Thomas' vote when the Assembly comes to elect the First Minister on 11 December (when Mark Drakeford replaces Carwyn Jones). There could be the possibility of a deadlock, even leading to the forcing of an election. Wigley's advice was that Dafydd El might be persuaded if he was allowed a run at standing again in Meirionnydd in 2021.

I find this astonishing, not to say absurd. The party wouldn't wear it. 'What about the MSs here?' I ask mildly. Adam admits there are downsides, but the potential upsides could override them. It would signal the party coming together, a new unity. Public would like it, and so on. It's how his political mind works. His first thought is not ideological, but how a gearshift can get you to a different place. Anyway, he suggests I have a conversation with Dafydd El and just see if he's interested in having a conversation. I agree to try but am not hopeful.

On Wednesday night I'm supposed to be meeting at Eurfyl's place with Adam and Rhun, for an exploratory get together to discuss how the Economic Development Group is going to work. But late in the afternoon, staring at the screen, I experience a sudden turn. I feel sick, clammy, unsteady on my feet. I decide I must get home, and if I walk it might clear my head. I stagger across the barrage and collapse into the house. It's an attack of labyrinthitis. I had one back in 2010. Something goes wrong with the inner ear – the cause is not clear, maybe a viral infection – but it affects your balance.

I stay at home for the rest of the week: working away, on the proofs of Adam's book, writing a script for a five-minute Channel 4 film Adam is doing next week, and working up a first draft of the speech he'll be making in Brussels. Am pleased to hear that the Economic Group evening went OK. They were there until nearly midnight, anyway.

Week 5: 12 November
Nuclear options

The week begins with a classic example of the often circular, mind-numbing, time-wasting character of professional politics. At 11am on Monday Grŵp Brexit meets in the Senedd in an atmosphere of crisis. MPs Jonathan Edwards and Hywel Williams plus Dafydd Wigley are present, along with Jill Evans, Adam, Steffan Bryn, Ben O'Keefe, and myself. Down the line in Westminster are Liz Savile Roberts, Ben Lake and Heledd Brooks-Jones.

On the agenda is the imminent publication of the EU Withdrawal Agreement on Tuesday, and the rumour that the Government is pushing for an immediate 'meaningful vote' on Wednesday. All this comes from 'reliable sources' which invariably turn out to be unreliable. Nonetheless, it prompts a long, circuitous, and anxious discussion about lines to take, relationships with other parties, especially the SNP, sequencing of possible amendments and votes. Of course, it all turns out to be so much humid air. But it gets Adam tuned up. He demands the production of various briefing papers on different aspects of policy.

The Shadow Cabinet follows and we get bogged down (again) in an argument over nuclear power. There's an energy debate on the floor next week and McEvoy has again put down an amendment opposing nuclear power, calculated to cause division within the Group. Predictably it does. Earlier I had spoken with Llyr Huws Gruffydd who said he was going to argue that we should support the amendment. Sitting on the fence was becoming unsustainable, and he was going to have a conversation with Rhun ap Iorwerth to tell him so.

An acrimonious debate in Shadow Cabinet ensues. Rhun says he's being placed in an impossible position on Ynys Môn. There would be resignations and so forth. Helen Mary points to our national policy, as does Leanne, and of course Llyr.

Eventually Adam sums up. He's trapped by the commitment he made during the leadership campaign, that our position on nuclear would no longer be dodged. But he does accept that in the past we've always come up with a formula whereby local parties and councils have a form of decentralised freedom to go their own way... our version of subsidiarity.

It's left that we will draft our own amendment, and Rhun and Llyr agree to come up with a form of words. It's a classic example of how parties can divide on what appears to be – and, of course, is – an issue of principle, but about which there is no prospect of having to make an immediate choice or, indeed, over which they don't have any real influence since nuclear power decisions are retained at Westminster.

The following day, after FMQs, I sit over a coffee with Adam in the staff canteen. He's at a low point, compounded by lack of sleep, it seems to me. He confides that the previous evening he'd had a tense, hour long, conversation with Liz Saville Roberts over, guess what, nuclear power. She'd got wind of an imminent new statement to be made in the Senedd, and was in high dudgeon. What would be her position in Meirionnydd, where she is backing a new initiative at the Trawsfynydd nuclear power station? 'Talked about having to resign', Adam said.

It occurs to me again how gratuitous this whole argument is. I expostulate with Adam. Tell him that people outside the bubble are not even thinking about nuclear power, certainly not at the moment. They're preoccupied with all manner of other, more prosaic problems, like rail fares, prices in the shops, finding a job, exam results... the list is endless, but certainly doesn't include a nuclear power station on Ynys Môn or in Meirionnydd. If we split over that there'd be incomprehension. Adam agrees but says his integrity as a leader is at stake. I say, park it, save it for some other day when a real choice has to be made.

A meeting we have on Friday in Aberystwyth then comes up. It's an away day for our elected members to meet with the former SNP Parliamentary leader Angus Robertson. He's reviewing Plaid's organisation and electoral strategy. Adam has to give a presentation to open the event. He confesses he hasn't got a clue what he's going to say. I offer to put something together for him. He's relieved and we agree to meet on Thursday morning to go over a draft.

Walking home, the long way round the Bay since the barrage is closed, I realise I haven't a clue what to say either. It's partly because it's not clear precisely what the meeting is about, what form it will take, who will be there. Overnight I literally dream the speech, which I envisage in three parts – (i) Changing Plaid; (ii) Changing Wales; and (iii) Changing Britain, which collectively give me the title.

It takes me the best part of a day to put together, just over 2,000 words: 20 minutes to deliver and, at the risk of sounding smug, I'm quite pleased with the result. I'm stepping back, trying to think about where we've come from in the past few months, and where we're going. I e-mail it across to Adam, and also Carl Harris, our Head of Strategy. Next morning I'm in the office by 10am and Adam signals that he, Carl and I should meet somewhere else. We repair to the café in the Senedd entrance area, which serves very good coffee.

Adam is re-energised, suddenly enthusiastic once more. He has a printed version of my speech in his hand, but doesn't refer to it. Instead, he extemporises, talks about what we've achieved, the trajectory we're on, where we're going, all the things we have to do, the underlying excitement of it all. I take notes while Carl goes for more coffee, comes back and tells me he can send me a list he's put together of what we've done. I agree to go away and redraft, but realise time is running out. We'll be setting off for Aberystwyth the following morning.

Back at home I hit the keyboard, writing over the speech I've already written, some of which is retained, but most of which is replaced by the new approach, the fresh way of looking at the problem that Adam has put in my mind. The title is now *Forming the Government in 2021*. It's about the same length, and the opening and closing sections come out like this:

> Friends, I am very proud of the leadership campaign we conducted a few months ago. We had a constructive and civilised debate. We came through the process stronger as a party. There is no doubt our members have become energised. And, indeed, many more have joined us – more than 3,000 at the last count.

The First 100 Days of Plaid's New Leader

Our members told us they wanted a change in the party leadership because they wanted change in Wales. We here, in this room, have the best chance in a generation to make this change. People in this room can form the next government of Wales.

In my reckoning, we have just enough time. But equally, there is no time to waste.

We are here this afternoon to share together our thinking on how we can make most use of the time we have between now and the election in 2021.

I am very grateful that we have Angus Robertson from the SNP to help us. It's great he is here. His review is going to guide us on putting the best structures and strategies in place. Our discussion this afternoon will feed into his review.

But we can't stand still while waiting for his recommendations. It's a case of advance on all fronts. I see the time between now and the 2021 election as dividing into three phases:

Phase 1
This the period we are now in, lasting six months to March next year. This is the **Foundation Phase**, when we put in place the new people and structures we will need to take the campaign forward. I'll come on to what we currently have underway.

Phase 2
This is the period between next Spring and the end of 2020. This is the time when we gear up the target constituencies we will need to win, put in place a campaign strategy, and take forward a conversation with the Welsh people about the policies of the next Welsh Government

Phase 3
This is the five-month campaign period between January 2021 and the election in May 2021. This is the time when we focus our key messages and pledge cards, when we target our voters, and motivate them to vote.

Throughout these three phases we need to keep in our minds what I regard as the three Ps of politics –
- **Party** – by which I mean our organisation and campaigning.
- **Programme** - our policy development.
- **Performance** –which builds on our communication with the electorate in its broadest sense.

The speech goes on to deal with these, and then ends:

> Of course, our goal is independence for Wales. In the short term, this means forming the next government of Wales.
>
> But we must not lose sight of our longer-term vision. One idea I want to put in hand is the creation of a constitution for an independent Wales.
>
> This process will enable people to imagine what an independent Wales should look like.
>
> For example, what should be our rights, and also our obligations, as Welsh citizens? What language and community rights could we enshrine in the constitution? What obligations could there be for ensuring Wales makes its contribution to climate change mitigation?
>
> We also need to explore our future relationships with our neighbours across the British Isles and the rest of the European Union.
>
> This is why I am planning a series of speeches over the coming months – in Brussels, Dublin, Edinburgh, Manchester, and London – setting out how I think Wales's interactions with our close neighbours can be made to work for our mutual benefit.
>
> These interventions will be a striking testimony to the way Plaid Cymru and its thinking are changing. They will demonstrate to our friends – and, I hope, our enemies – that we are serious in our intentions for Wales to make a great leap forward in the 2020s.
>
> They will be an indication of the potential Wales has for influencing the forthcoming debates about the future of democracy and

co-operation, not only across Britain and Ireland, but within the European Union as well.

But we will not be able to make an impact on this wider stage unless we first make an impact within Wales itself. This is why our forming the next Welsh government in 2021 is so important.

This afternoon is a step on that road. Friends, we're building the road as we travel.

There are some elements of my original speech left, but only traces. I realise that my efforts to start a process of thinking about how we're going to 'remake' Britain are premature for where Adam currently finds himself. He's not against the sentiment. He's made it himself – notably to the SNP conference a few days after he was elected leader. But it's too early for him to want to devote much thought to it. Instead, he wants to reiterate his commitment to independence, his signature policy in the leadership election.

In place of my original draft comes a different kind of energy, a more forceful sense of direction. I realise that speechwriting is going to involve a lot of this kind of iteration. It's heavy lifting and entails a lot of effort, but hopefully what comes out will reflect what's put in.

I send it across at the end of the afternoon, and later get enthusiastic e-mails from Adam and Carl. Adam e-mailed back to me and Carl (at 8.27pm), following a meeting he'd had in Cathays Park with Lord Thomas of Cwmgiedd, former Lord Chief Justice, who is chairing the Welsh Government's Commission on the devolution of justice powers to Wales:

> 'This is excellent and exciting. Well done both!
> Had an excellent session with Lord Thomas of Cwmgiedd. Walking through the corridors of Cathays Park I had an overwhelming feeling that we can and will win - if we implement the kind of vision set out here.'

Messages like this, however optimistic, make the effort worthwhile. However, the enthusiasm was deflated the next day. Driving to Aberystwyth I was held up for an hour by an accident on the M4 north of Swansea, and arrived to find Adam on his feet. The meeting was in the council chamber of the National Library. I'd never been in it before but the oblong shape, and high ceiling somehow seemed to take the oxygen out of the room.

I was struck too by the smallness of the audience. The four MPs were there, also Jill Evans, but only a scattering of MSs, though including – surprisingly, I thought – Leanne. Who else? Rhun, Helen Mary, Siân Gwenllian (of course), Elin Jones but no one else. Staff from the Senedd and Tŷ Gwynfor made up the numbers.

For the first time I've seen him speak, Adam was struggling, not on top of his game. But he managed. Then Angus Robertson spoke about his review and the SNP's experience. He was good, invigorating. But when he said, 'You've made the first, most important step, you're talking about being in government in 2021' it somehow fell flat.

Afterwards we separated into groups to discuss ways of engaging the electorate. A wave of tiredness swept the room. They'd all been round this track many times before. There was no magic bullet. Leanne voiced this view. 'It's just a matter of consistently talking with people, day in day out.' No one could disagree. Seemingly there was no alternative.

However, Helen Mary, trouper as she is, kept the thing going by orchestrating the feedback. And so the time went. During the coffee break Adam took me to one side. 'That was the most difficult talk I think I've given,' he told me. 'I was getting nothing back.'

The atmosphere lifted when we went to the Marine Hotel for a drink with Angus, Adam, Carl and Ben. We swapped reminiscences about past conferences, personalities, and Adam visibly cheered up. They went on to dinner, and I went to stay with Cynog and Llinos Dafis (Plaid's former Ceredigion MP and his wife).

The next day, Saturday, Adam attended his second NEC as leader, with the aim of pushing through the two key appointments he wants to make – Head of Communications in the Senedd (with a salary above the £40K we're currently advertising) and a Head of Strategy in Tŷ Gwynfor. He tells me later that he had a hard time persuading people during the morning. But over lunch he collared Alun Cox, a Rhondda activist and fervent Leanne supporter, and the Chair Alun Ffred Jones, and managed to win them over. So much so that the afternoon was a breeze. He got both through.

Week 6: 19 November 2018
Party, Programme and Performance

In an effort to give our campaign some momentum, at the start of this week I came up with the idea for a top-level meeting to focus on the progress we were making. What have we achieved and where have we fallen short? What are main upcoming milestones? We organised it on Wednesday morning, and dubbed it 'Stocktake'. Adam was enthusiastic. As well as ourselves, we pinpointed Carl Harris, Steffan Bryn, Siân Gwenllian and Geraint Day as the people to be involved.

I'd prepared an agenda, utilising Adam's three Ps – Party, Programme and Performance – and placed at the beginning, a moment for Adam to make some opening remarks. But, rather than do it himself, he indicated that I should. I was taken aback. So, without having given any previous thought to what I might say, I launched into a raw, emotional speech about where we'd been at the start, how far we'd come, the importance of taking an overview of what we were doing, and not becoming trapped by the overwhelming demands of fire fighting in the Senedd.... there was an inherent danger of being dragged into the mire of serving the Senedd, when we should be using it as a base for campaigning in the country... that kind of thing. Anyway, it won a plaudit from Siân who said we needed to be reminded of our higher purpose from time to time, though I noticed Adam looked amused at my exuberance.

Nonetheless, he soon got down to business, producing a 5,000-word document he'd 'prepared earlier' – actually much of it during the summer, when he was thinking about his leadership campaign. Entitled *Lean Campaigning – a ten-point plan to victory* it had the following headings:

1. Concentrate on our existing supporters – not on persuading the floating voter
2. Use targeted online advertising
3. Renew our use of political technology
4. Find our story
5. Adopt a new data-driven approach to messaging
6. Build the 'voluntariat'
7. Up our performance in traditional media
8. Invest in Brand Adam

9. Become a permanent, effective and universal campaigning organisation
10. Raise £1million

He canters through all ten headings. This is a complete 21st Century compendium of political campaigning, drawing most of its lessons from the United States. I'm most intrigued by three of the headings, the ones I suppose register most personally with me – the first, fourth and eighth.

On the first, the core vote, he writes:

> Political parties often choose between a core vote or a floating voter strategy.
>
> Plaid in Wales, in contrast say to the Liberal Democrats, does have a core vote. We have consistently polled around 10% in Westminster elections and 20% in the National Assembly over the last two decades of elections.
>
> It may be better to speak of a latent core vote.
>
> This is because though we consistently achieve broadly the same result we have weak levels of people who say they identify with us. This feeds through to weaker consistent support.
>
> The party has been following a partial core vote strategy in that our Treeware operation has tactically prioritised Get Out The Vote engagement over persuasion of non-supporters.[5]
>
> However, our messaging has been aimed at the floating voter or switch voters, largely from Labour. Our focus group activity has revealed a lot, for example, on the barriers that prevent those who do not vote for us from doing so, rather than seeking to identify the principal motivations of those who do.

---

5   Treeware is a computer-based system for categorizing details of voter attitudes and support gathered while canvassing.

The First 100 Days of Plaid's New Leader

Who are our Core Vote? Our base consists of a hard core of around 200,000 who support us regularly and a soft core of another 100,000 who are more irregular.

We think that people identify with a party because they share its values e.g. Left, Right or Centre. But values-based identification is not the only way that parties build core votes. People also identify with parties they think represents the group to which they belong. It is this second type of identification that is strongest in the case of Plaid. So-called Welsh-identifiers support us in far greater numbers across the Left-Right spectrum.

Advertising and direct contact – mail, phone calls, canvassing – which seeks to persuade 'floating' voters to change their vote has zero effect. It is time, money and effort wasted.

We need to focus all of our effort on identifying and mobilising our existing base of support.

We should focus our efforts on rousing the enthusiasm of existing supporters instead of reaching across party lines to win over new supporters. We need to start from – and then maintain – a clear sense of what the party is about. Emphasising independence and nation-building is central to that strategy.

On finding our story:

A simple, consistent and motivating narrative is essential; narratives – containing facts and events – are retained longer than rational information, are difficult to change once lodged, and can be executed in a number of different ways without getting tired.

Let's think of a number of key elections in the last ten years. In the US in 2008 Obama's narrative was 'from rootless to rooted'; the story – a twist on the classic American Dream – told of a man who had grown up without a stable family, or a father in the house, or a community to be part of, and went on to achieve great things and became a symbol of achievement, familial stability and success.

Bernie Sanders' story in 2016 was being someone who is unfailingly consistent and 'gives a shit about you', while Donald Trump's narrative was 'Stop laughing at us'.

The similarity between Trump's underlining narrative and that of the Brexiteers was uncanny; when Trump and Farage met up in November to celebrate their collective victories, their narratives reached a joint conclusion: 'Look who's laughing now.'

As well as having a narrative it's important to tell it consistently, but also constantly; nature abhors a vacuum and if you're not telling your story, then somebody else will.

And on Brand Adam:

Leadership matters. All the great election success stories of the last few years have had a single theme. Popular outsider candidates with a simple message of hope mobilise a grassroots movement backed by digital marketing to defeat 'the establishment': eg Obama, Macron, Trump, Corbyn, Christoph Lindner (German FDP). The personal narrative and personal popularity of the leader is critically important. The television debates will be crucial.

Actions:
- Develop comprehensive brand strategy for leader
- Appoint personal coach for leader
- Tailor media training for leader
- Appoint Digital Comms Manager for leader

Most of the discussion is taken up with issues around putting in place people and structures for the Party. But, briefly towards the end, we get on to the Programme. Adam makes it clear that despite the policy groups we're putting in place, he intends to be across the whole policy range, and at the end of the day: He will decide.... He will write the manifesto. Carl protests, not so much against the imposition, but the opportunity cost – it could draw him away from campaigning, getting round the country and so on. Adam overrides him, says he'll be on top of things, and on all fronts (which is typical). Then he adds that he needs to be across all the policy agenda anyway, so that he's up to speed for debates and interviews. It's his way of doing his homework.

That was brought into sharp focus the following day when we spent the morning and afternoon filming a three-minute Channel 4 political slot with a crew that came down from London. We had to provide the script, locations and logistics. They – a producer and camera/sound operator – were the technical support.

I produced the script, which I'm pleased to hear the producer, a woman from Juniper Films in London, report that the C4 Commissioning Editor described it as, 'The first half-decent script we've had'. It took me back to my television days in the 1980s and 1990s. The best thing was the weather, a gloriously blue day, but very cold.

We started filming in Penarth above the marina, with the Cardiff Bay skyline as the backdrop, then along the barrage, into Mermaid Quay and on to the steps of the Senedd. I hired a boat, *The Daffodil*, which gave some extra shots on the go, and we also filmed outside the Coal Exchange, now a hotel, where the world's first £1m cheque was signed. Adam was superb. I'd provided him with crib cards for the lines and he used them diligently, all the time getting colder and colder as we traversed the Bay. The script was just 400 or so words, but wrapped up in some stunning footage, dictated by pace, place and weather. I was struck, too, how accommodating and considerate he was with the film crew. A professional.

Week 7: 26 November 2018
Brussels

This proved to be the most exhilarating, exhausting, interesting, and worthwhile week so far.

It began for me on Sunday. We returned home at lunchtime from a weekend wedding in Hampshire, with the upshot that I was pretty well washed out.... The previous Friday I'd written a draft of a speech Adam is due to make this coming Thursday, at the European Policy Centre in Brussels and sent it to Hywel Ceri Jones. A former Director General in the European Commission and former chair of the Policy Centre, he has been instrumental in getting us the platform. Although Adam had professed himself happy with the speech, Hywel was critical. It was far too 'Welsh', too introspective, not enough about the current Brexit crisis, and insensitive to the Brussels audience.

I took this on board, went to see Hywel, who lives around the corner, and started redrafting. This took me past midnight.

On Monday morning I went through the speech briefly with Adam, then returned home to do an afternoon's work on it. Hywel came round to go through it again with me. I'm impressed by how keen he is to contribute to anything that might have the slightest chance of influencing events. He is, of course, an ardent Welsh European. Brexit threatens his life's work. It transpires Hywel doesn't operate a computer, but drafts in secretarial support! I'm not the oldest generation involved in all this.

In the evening we went to the launch of Adam's book *Wales: The First and Final Colony* at Insole Court in Llandaf. I'm relieved to see there's a respectable audience of more than a hundred, and amused that Carl Harris had overridden other staff and laid on wine. Adam was 'in conversation', and performed well, at the top of his game. The audience was mainly Plaid but not altogether, some new faces. It was a good start for the Wales tour he's embarking on to promote the book. Tomorrow it's Neath, next week Llanelli and Arfon, and other places in the New Year.

I spent Tuesday doing more work on the speech, getting useful input from Eurfyl ap Gwilym, and some hyper-critical comments from David Marquand[6], but all useful. This was turning into a marathon.

On Wednesday we set off, on a tour of three capitals, as Adam put it. First up is Cardiff, and then at ten o'clock we set off for London. On the train I read an excerpt from the *Guardian*, a story by its 'Welsh and West of England' correspondent Steven Morris about how 'Rhuthun feels left out of the prime minister's plans…'

> Cefyn Burgess, who weaves Welsh tapestry blankets, quilts, throws and cushions, was distinctly unimpressed by Theresa May's trip to his beloved homeland [she had been visiting Wales and Northern Ireland the previous day to sell her Brussels deal].
>
> 'To be honest, I think it's insulting to us that she's come here. She visits on her walking holidays but I really don't think she or her government care about Wales. We're a non-entity to her, invisible.'
>
> Burgess, who was to be found yesterday behind the counter of his eponymous shop at the craft centre in Rhuthun, north Wales, said he

---

6   See footnote 59 in Chapter 3.

considered himself Welsh and European, not British. He believed May had not taken Wales into account during the Brexit negotiations.

'She has ignored Scotland, paid off Northern Ireland and is indifferent to Wales,' said Burgess, who has joined the nationalist party Plaid Cymru because he trusts its stance over Brexit.

Adam is delighted: 'He's obviously read our lines to take.' We arrive in Paddington at lunchtime and head straight for Westminster. Here we have a scheduled meeting of Grŵp Brexit – the four MPs, Wigley and staff, with Steffan Lewis and Jill Evans down the line.

It's the most dynamic of the meetings we've had so far. Following a focused discussion Adam firmly sets out our line. After the defeat of the Withdrawal Agreement, we should press for Britain staying in an EFTA [European Free Trade Association] single market arrangement, with a Customs Union added, and put that to a referendum, with Remain as the alternative option. He thinks we could get a cross-party movement to row behind the thrust of that. Anyway, he says we should put it out there to ensure we're ahead of the curve. Only Steffan Lewis dissents: he thinks putting what are, in effect, two forms of 'Remain' on the ballot paper would be seen by Leavers as underhand and hostile, calculated to split the country even more and alienate potential voters.

All this is typical of the kind of discussions going on across the Westminster bubble. All of them are pretty inconsequential. Nobody knows what will be the sequence of events, let alone the dynamics that will be thrown up as a result of May losing. Even so, these conversations serve some purpose in educating and clarifying minds.

There's half-an-hour before we're scheduled to meet Jeremy Corbyn in his office, a couple of blocks away in the rather bleak Norman Shaw building. The staff have prepared an *aide memoire* which tries to unpick Corbyn's position on Brexit. It suggests that while John McDonnell, Labour's Shadow Chancellor, is moving towards supporting a People's Vote, that decision will only be when all other options are exhausted. The *aide memoir* then goes on to say there is a split between Keir Starmer and Corbyn about the revocability of Brexit, which indicates an internal compromise between Labour left-wing Eurosceptics and pro-EU centrists on the following basis:

- Defeating Tory deal
- Prioritising a general election
- Moving towards a People's Vote

Controversially, there's a heading: *Cooperation if a General Election is called*: 'Plaid Cymru must have assurances of remaining in the Single Market and Customs Union, along with a commitment from Labour Party that they will not campaign in key Plaid Cymru seats.'

At 4pm we get inside Corbyn's office, a smallish room behind a much larger one, full of people peering at computer screens. We sit around a coffee table with cups, coffee, teapot, a water jug and glasses. Alongside Corbyn is his minder Seumas Milne and another adviser, an 'expert on Europe who used to work in the Commission' but who says nothing.

On our side are Adam, Liz Savile Roberts, Ben O'Keeffe and myself. Corbyn greets Adam as a long-lost soul – they clasp together in a male hug and reminisce about their times together on the backbenches. This takes ten minutes of our half hour. Then Corbyn asks about views on Brexit in the Welsh constituencies that voted Leave. Are they changing? Adam says he thinks a minority of Leavers have switched sides, but the majority have dug in deeper against. Corbyn nods sagely.

Only in the last part of the meeting do we turn to realpolitik, the nature and sequencing of parliamentary votes. The conversation turns to votes of confidence and Corbyn says something along the lines that we'll have to be careful, because we've only got one go at it. Whereupon Seumas Milne chips in, 'Jeremy, I think you mean the Tories have only one go at forcing May out.'

I glance at Ben O'Keeffe and he raises his eyes.

Generally, Corbyn seems to think that the determining factor will be the arithmetic. If May loses by around 25 or 30 votes, she will be able to come back with an alternative proposal of some kind. If she loses by 100 or more, she'll have to go. Depending on what happens Labour will make its move. Adam suggests gently that it would be a good idea to have various strategies, based on eventualities. It's now 4.30pm and Liz says we have a train to catch (she doesn't say that Adam has TV interviews to do on College Green as well).

Seumas Milne says, 'Well, you can't miss your train.'

I make my only intervention, suggesting that we send them a note on the conversation, with suggestions on how we can take it forward.

Corbyn greets this enthusiastically. On the way out we all line up to shake hands. As I pass, Corbyn takes my hand, leans forward and says, 'Don't forget the note.'

An hour later and we are queuing in St. Pancras Station, having crossed London on the tube, as though being carried in a sardine tin. The Eurostar takes two hours to Brussels; we gain an hour on the way, so arrive at nine pm. On the train Adam buys Liz and me a drink at the bar. The conversation is mainly about how hopeless Labour is in getting its act together.

In Brussels we walk to the hotel, which takes 20 minutes. Then, after half-an-hour we're out again, walking to the Grande Place. It's lit up, changing colour from pink to blue to red to purple, and beautiful, despite the rain. Adam knows a place, Bar Cuba, down a side street and we all gather there, including the Westminster team. Liz buys a round of Mojitos. It's years since I've had one of these.

Soon a terrific band starts playing – keyboards, bass guitar and trumpet. The keyboard player is huge, with vast hands. His fingers remind me of a Ceri Richards painting. It's a miracle they don't cover more than one key. I get into a conversation with Liz, who tells me she was brought up in England, with English parents, but discovered Wales, studied Welsh at Aberystwyth ... and the rest is history. Has twin daughters, one of whom works on a tugboat in Milford Haven. I say I sailed on one in the summer, while researching my Preseli book.

It's 1.30am by the time we get back to the hotel.

Next morning we're up early to get to the European Parliament for 9am, where Michel Barnier, the EU's chief Brexit negotiator, is reporting on the Withdrawal Agreement, which was signed by the 27 Member States in Brussels four days earlier.

The Parliament is a massive building and architecturally impressive, at least inside. The last time I was at this spot, in the 1990s, it was a building site. Now I learn it's beginning to crumble. No hot water is allowed since the pipes are infected with Legionnaires Disease. Apparently, it would be cheaper to knock the whole thing down and start again, but no one appears to be suggesting that.

The chamber is vast and mainly empty. We spot Jill Evans, Plaid's MEP, in her seat, surrounded by empty ones. She waves. Farage is lounging at the front, a grin on his face that can be seen even from our distance. But I have to disappear to the Plaid office – festooned with posters and flags – to work on Adam's speech. He needs it printed in 16 point and single-sided. The Parliament's printers are defaulted to printing double-sided, so we have to print it out, page by painful page.

At 10.30am we have a meeting with the Catalan Government's Representation to the EU. The lead representative is Meritxell Serret, who is an exile in Brussels. If she returns to Barcelona she'll be arrested. She seems a slight and modest figure, charming. Jill hugs her in a greeting that appears as if they're family who haven't met for decades. A conversation ensues about the Catalan situation.

At 11.15am we move on for a meeting with the European Free Alliance (EFA), a taxi ride away.[7] Their office is on a fourth floor, reached by a perilous small lift, and a flight of very narrow winding stairs. I remark to Syd Morgan, Jill Evans's partner, that they remind me of those that led up to the Plaid office in Cardiff's Queen Street in the 1970s. He agrees and laughs.

Inside, however, it's spacious. We sit at a long table which has their flag, and of course, ours. This is the important meeting of the day, to discuss Adam's potential participation in the *Spitzenkandidat* ('lead candidate') process, introduced at the European Parliament elections in 2014, whereby those who had run as the lead for their respective political group in the European Parliament are accepted as nominees for the President of the European Commission by the European Parliament. If Adam's name is put forward, he will be the lead for the European Free Alliance in a matter of months. It all seems a bit improbable. Why should a Plaid nominee, who is not in the European Parliament, and whose country is planning to leave the EU, be a candidate to lead an alliance of European parties? But this doesn't seem to phase our hosts. It's enough that we're members of the Alliance.

Across the table from us is Günther Dauwen, EFA Director, an impressive character, Flemish, with excellent English. Equally impressive is EFA's Political Adviser Eva Bidania Ibargutxi, from the Basque Country. And alongside her is EFA's Italian Legal Adviser, Gio Paolo Baglioni.

After the pleasantries Adam explains Plaid Cymru's current strategy in the lead up to the 2021 election. Then I launch in,

---

7   The European Free Alliance, of which Plaid is a member, is an umbrella organization for 49 civic nationalist, regionalist and autonomist parties within the European Union, representing stateless nations, emerging new States, regions and minorities in Europe.

The First 100 Days of Plaid's New Leader

judging that it is better that I be the sceptical voice, rather than Adam himself. I lay out our position bluntly. I say that we're concerned that Adam's candidature might be regarded as frivolous, ridiculous even. The upside is exposure, coverage for our views and so on. However, the judgement is whether standing would help or hinder our 2021 campaign.

Dauwen is not at all put out. He completely agrees with our criteria. Anyway, EFA has yet to decide whether it will participate at all. It's a tough call for them. There are financial implications, quite apart from an ideological issue over the wisdom of giving the EU and the Commission democratic cover for the Presidency appointment.

If it happens, the campaign itself will he held during May. There will be rallies involving sister parties in Catalunya and the Basque Country, in Brittany, Germany, Greece and Latvia. Funding will come from the European Parliament, in the region of 250,000 Euros. The candidature will be announced at a European Free Alliance conference in Brussels on 7 March. It all sounds rather heady. If it were to happen it would take over our lives.

After an hour's solid discussion, we repair for lunch to a rather good restaurant a short walk away. Adam looks at his speech and starts to panic at the length. 'I won't be able to get through all this in half-an-hour.' I take it from him, sit down and start making cuts, blocking off about a dozen paragraphs. All that precious prose....

However, left in is my reference to Raymond Williams' involvement in liberating Brussels in 1944:

> 'I am a Welsh European, proud to be a European citizen. I have complementary identities. Living with them has made me realise how each one informs and changes the other. In thinking of myself as a Welsh European I remember that it was Raymond Williams, one of my party's leading intellectuals, who first linked these identities together in this way.
>
> Raymond came from working class roots in the Welsh border country. In the late 1930s he went to Cambridge University. The Second World War interrupted his studies. He was a tank commander who landed in Normandy and followed General Montgomery across France to the Rhine and beyond.

He was with Allied forces when they marched into Brussels. This is how Williams recalled that experience, in the first issue of *TwentyOne*, the Army newspaper he edited in Germany from June 1945:

> 'As we entered Brussels in September '44, the delirious welcome of the people seemed to become more feverish in every street. Thus, while in Chaussée Ninove they had been content to throw lilac blooms, in the Boulevard Nord they began to throw bottles. There were bottles of champagne, straw flasks of chianti, flagons of beer and long tapering decanters of Benedictine.'

Indeed, Raymond was hit by a champagne bottle that forced him to retreat beneath the tank's turret. *Then he recounts how he saw through the driver's periscope a pair of dangling female legs.*

But the point of this story is, surely, how it reminds us of the origin and *raison d'être* of the European Union, its early highly charged purpose.

Adam has run a pen through the sentence I've highlighted in italics, sensitive to its incipient sexism.
    At lunch I'm sitting next to Iva Petković, project manager with the Coppieters Foundation, a think tank associated with EFA, and we fall into a discussion. It seems they have access to a good deal of European Parliament funding and can use it to support organisations that are members of the EFA. It seems also, that my scheme for the party's English language paper *Welsh Nation* might fit their criteria. In the middle of our conversation Adam comes over and suggests we should discuss this very thing. I tell him I'm, so to speak, on the case. Iva and I exchange e-mail addresses.
    Jill has provided the wine, and I'm just about relaxing into the lunch when it's time for us to leave. Taxis are waiting outside to take us to the European Policy Centre. When we arrive, we find about 20 students from the University of Kiel in Schleswig-Holstein crowded in the lobby. They're visiting Brussels and for some reason have decided to attend Adam's lecture. I'm glad to see them – at least they'll swell the numbers. The EPC turns out to have a fine suite of offices, with a large lecture room where Adam will speak. But first he undertakes an interview with a freelance journalist.

Then he's on stage, with the EPC Director Fabian Zuleeg introducing him. The set-up is a bit disconcerting. A small raised platform, two chairs, but no podium. Adam has to stand, clutching his notes. But he projects well, starting with some words in German, thanking Fabian. The audience is respectable, about 150, though not quite filling the room, but still very good it seems to me for a Thursday afternoon.

Adam largely follows my speech and it's strange to hear the words being spoken. I realise this is the speechwriter's worst moment. How will it go? It seems to be alright. There are plenty of relevant questions. At the end I turn and see that Günther Dauwen is sitting behind me. He nods enthusiastically. 'He performs well,' he tells me. It turns out that Günther was in the audience when Adam spoke at the SNP conference, the same weekend he was elected leader. 'It was an electrifying experience,' Günther says. 'People were sitting on the edge of their chairs.' That's when he clocked Adam as a possible *Spitzenkandidat*.

Hywel Ceri Jones' son Gwilym appears, unmistakeably with the same looks, though slighter in build. Generally, however, he is gloomy about the prospects for Brexit. Afterwards we emerge from the building and walk a few yards to a café where we meet with David Tripp, head of the Welsh Government's Brussels Office. He is keen to discuss what the office should be doing after Britain leaves, which he assumes will happen. My main thought is how rare it is we get the chance to meet with civil servants, and how, if we do get into government after 2021, they're going to be a huge challenge.

Then Adam and I get into a taxi and head for the hotel, though we're immediately stuck in rush hour traffic. I mention my thoughts about the civil service, but for a while Adam is slumped, the adrenalin rush evaporated. Then, rarely, our conversation turns to personal matters, how the constant demands of political life impact on home and family. I deliver a homily about my own life's experience, how when my older children were small, I hardly saw them, working for a morning newspaper 12 hours a day and often at weekends as well. I go on to say that when my younger daughter came along, 20 years ago, when I was around 50, I was determined to do things differently. Adam sees the point I'm making, and begins talking about Swami and Ilar, his partner and young son, and their relationship. He then reveals they're planning to have another child, quite soon within a year or so. 'We realise that when Ilar grows up, we'll be getting on,' he says. 'We want him to have a sibling.'

We have a short time at the hotel, before it's out once more, to meet the others at an Italian restaurant, somewhere near the Grande Place. That turns out to be quite far, and we walk the streets, Adam attempting to guide us with his mobile phone. I haven't had the presence of mind to arrange for my phone to get a signal abroad, so I've left it in the hotel. This makes me realise how phone dependent everyone around me is. Phones are a constant presence, on the table in front of everyone at meetings, constantly pinging, offering some kind of parallel virtual existence.

A guest at dinner, in a restaurant about a 20-minute walk from the hotel, is a long-standing friend of Adam's, the SNP's Alyn Smyth, one of their MEPs. We have a long conversation about SNP internal politics. He's impressive, a lawyer, mid-40s, multi-lingual, very much based in Brussels where I judge he'll stay if Britain leaves. He's guarded about the future of his political career.[8]

Later we walk through the streets once more, eventually landing up in Le Dolores bar. One beer leads to another and I eventually fall into a long, diffuse conversation with Syd Morgan, about Ireland. He's 74 today but doesn't look it. He's been researching the early history of Plaid's relations with nationalist figures in Ireland in the 1920s and '30s – there was much more contact than I realised. I speculate about a confederation between Wales, the Republic, the north of Ireland, and maybe Scotland, in order to keep us inside the EU. I say we could send representatives to Seanad Éireann, the Upper House of the Oireachtas (the Irish legislature). Syd laughs, but then ponders the idea seriously.

I look at my watch and see it's 2am. I've had enough, lurch out of the bar, and then lurch back in, realising I've no idea where I am. Ben O'Keefe takes me in hand, leads me out again to find a taxi. He puts me in one and names our hotel. The driver shrugs and points round the corner. It's only yards away.

The next morning, I worry that Adam is not getting up, but eventually he appears, and we get a taxi to the station. For most of the journey on the Eurostar we're unusually quiet. Once through the tunnel my mobile comes to life. At St. Pancras we take our leave,

---

8   Just over a year later, in the December 2019 general election, Alyn Smith was elected MP for Stirling

shaking hands. Adam is heading north to Caernarfon where tonight he's slotting back into his book tour of Wales. 'I'm beginning to enjoy this,' he says.

Week 8: 3 December 2018
Black and Blue on the M4

As at the start of every week in this political world, First Minister's Questions take centre stage. Actually, very often they come into view over the weekend, which was the case this week. I found myself, at 8am, listening to Vaughan Roderick's BBC Wales Sunday politics programme, *Sunday Supplement*. Vaughan is one of the few commentators left in the Welsh media who has a political memory.

One topic of discussion was the proposed 14-mile M4 Relief Road, which has been debated for some 20 years to sort out the congestion that continually happens at the Bryn Glas tunnels on the northern edge of Newport. It was proposed and rejected by the first Labour administration in the Assembly. It was proposed and rejected by the One Wales coalition government when former Plaid leader Ieuan Wyn Jones was Transport Minister. Now it's being proposed again, and has been the subject of an expensive Public Inquiry.

The M4 is topical this week, since we've been led to believe it's the moment when the Welsh Government will come to a decision. But will Carwyn Jones do so, particularly when he's just days away from standing down and passing the First Minister's baton to Mark Drakeford who is known to be sceptical about the road?

All this adds a certain frisson and encourages us to make it the issue for FMQs. Moreover, I have a direct interest in this since one of my last acts as Director of the IWA was to edit a report by Professor Stuart Cole, making the case for a less expensive, and less environmentally intrusive, so-called 'Blue' alternative to the 'Black' route being promoted by the Welsh Government. The costs of the latter have risen steadily from around £1 billion to £1.7 billion, and who knows how much more if it were ever to go ahead. The 'Blue' route, which is broadly Plaid's position, would cost about half, though its costs are rising, too.

The environmentalists, of course, are against the whole thing. They're against all new roads. They argue, and I tend to agree, that new roads just attract more traffic and that the proposed 'South Wales Metro' public transport system should take the strain. Anyway on Vaughan Roderick's show, Stuart Cole is making this case once again. Idly flicking through the Sunday papers, I prick up my ears when I hear him refer to some distant economic impact study that revealed that much of the benefit of the M4 Relief Road would accrue in England. 'That's a line,' I think, and so does Adam, who is also listening, in Carmarthenshire. Later that evening I get an e-mail from him on the subject.

This is a regular Sunday evening occurrence, a jolt that next week's work is beginning. FMQs are a necessary theatre, part of the ritual of holding government to account. But few people like them, including Adam himself. 'I hate FMQs', he tells me again this week, in a rare aside about his 'Performance' role when we're in the middle of working out the precise wording. And I agree, they're a ritual joust, like Prime Minister's Questions in the House of Commons. Nevertheless, they concentrate the mind. They make you decide what are the most pressing concerns that week, that day. Ideally, they force you to up your game.

This week I do some research, following up Stuart Cole's reference to the economic impact study. I phone him about it, but he's vague. 'Quite a while ago,' he says. 'Five or six years, you'll have to look up the Public Inquiry website.' I do, and after some scrolling about, find the report and the figures.

At the last minute we're given pause to think about the M4 as a topic when we learn that Carwyn Jones won't be taking the questions. Apparently, he's unwell. Some say it's stress due to the Carl Sargeant inquiry.[9] The Leader of the House, Swansea West MS Julie James, is standing in for him. As it happens, this helps us because a month ago it was she who said that the Assembly would be making a 'binding' decision on the Relief Road this week.

Brexit absorbs the rest of the week. Adam has been invited on to the Jeremy Vine BBC Radio 2 programme on Wednesday lunchtime, a real opportunity since it's a chance to reach millions of people across the UK, and consequently a lot in Wales who don't normally

---

9   Carl Sargeant, AM for Alyn and Deeside since 2003, was Minister for Communities and Children. Following allegations about inappropriate sexual behaviour towards a number of women, which he denied, he was suspended from the Welsh Government on 3 November 2017. Four days later he was found dead in his Connah's Quay home. Later an inquest ruled his death a suicide.

tune in to politics. However, the sequence only lasts half-an-hour and Adam will be sharing it with other 'small' parties – the Lib Dems (Vince Cable), the SNP and the DUP... plus, *inter alia*, several pop songs. Also, he has to choose whether to go to London to be in the studio or do it down the line from Cardiff.

Adam argues the case for going to London: 'It's always better when you're in the studio, you get the vibes, the body language works better.' I agree, but tell him he can't possibly justify going to London for such a minimalist slot. Adam goes to London. Vine is patronising, saying he'll give Adam priority since he's taken a three-hour train journey to come on the show. Hilariously, the DUP only show up halfway through, having got lost trying to find the studio. Adam gets a few points across, but it hardly seems worth it.

One of the reasons Adam goes to London is that he's been invited to speak at a pro-Remain rally in London on Sunday, ahead of the big forthcoming vote in Parliament on Prime Minister May's Withdrawal Agreement. Meanwhile, on the Thursday I go to St. Davids in pursuit of the Festival of Ideas, and then spend a congenial night with friends in Solva. On Friday there's a chance for a leisurely morning driving back. I stop in Narberth for a coffee, read the papers, and then wander around the shops. However, in the car on the M4 I get a call from Heledd Brooks-Jones in our Westminster Office. Adam wants me to draft something for his speech on Sunday. But it can't be more than 250 words, and they want it as soon as possible.

Heledd is upbeat. She tells me it's going to be a huge rally, at the ICC Auditorium in London's Docklands, organised by Best for Britain, with an audience of more than 3,000. Other speakers include the Conservative MPs Anna Soubry and Philip Lee, Labour's Mary Creagh and Luciana Berger, the Greens' Caroline Lucas, Liberal Democrat leader Vince Cable, and Michael Heseltine, plus actors such as Charles Dance. 'It's a great opportunity,' she enthuses.

Yes, but 250 words? At home I ring Adam for a line to take but he's not picking up, so instead dash off the following:

> If there's one thing the past week of manoeuvres and argument has shown it's simply this: there is no Brexit deal that can beat the flexible deal we already have inside the EU.
> Tuesday's vote in the House of Commons presents a stark choice. Either:

> To take us OUT of the EU, with no control over the rules that govern most of our trading relationships.
>
> Or:
>
> To change course towards a second referendum, and the opportunity to stay IN the EU, with control – with a say and a vote.
>
> Friends, when it comes, the People's Vote will NOT be a re-run of the last referendum.
>
> In 2016 the question was theoretical, inviting all manner of false promises.
>
> In 2019 the People's Vote will be concrete. It will be a real choice. Between:
>
> A messy, sub-standard divorce, and LOSING control.
>
> Or:
>
> Building a better economic and democratic future with our European partners and KEEPING control.
>
> But our position CANNOT just be to Remain in Europe, as it was before 2016.
>
> That meant remaining with spending cuts to our hospitals and schools. It meant remaining with falling living standards.
>
> Who would want to remain with that?
>
> This time our watchword must be CHANGE.
>
> We must campaign to STAY in the EU, but with the steadfast purpose of Reform.
>
> REFORM for quality jobs for our poorer communities.
>
> REFORM for more democracy, for the peoples of Europe, for Wales, Scotland, and the neglected regions of the north of England.
>
> We must campaign to be Welsh, Scottish and, YES, English Europeans.

I'm quite pleased with these (actually) 256 words and later get an email from Adam – 'Cheers'. But next day, he writes something emotionally different, and better:

> We're about to witness a parliamentary tug of war perched on the edge of a precipice.
>
> Mrs May wants us to abseil to a ledge half-way down where we spend the next ten years in a sleeping bag tethered to the cliff face.
>
> Others want to recreate Boris Johnson's famous zipwire moment but this time without the helmet, without the harness, even without the

zipwire – just two plastic Union Jacks fluttering in our hands as we plummet to our destiny.
There's no majority for either of these. Not in the House of Commons, not in the Welsh or Scottish Parliaments, nor among the people.
They're asking for the chance to step back from the abyss – not a re-run of the last referendum.
In 2016 the question was based on a fantasy of false promises and contradictory demands. In 2019 it will be a real choice.
But our position CANNOT just be to Remain.
Who wants to remain in poverty, in austerity and injustice?
This time we must be the movement for CHANGE.
A vote to re-main has to be a vote to re-form, re-new and re-generate.
It cannot be simply a vote for the Europe that **is**, but for the Europe that **can be**.
Social, democratic, decentralised and diverse.
We will win the argument not just because the facts are on our side, but because we have the better dream. For a new society, for a new politics, for a new Europe, a new Wales, a new England, a new world.

It's an example of what looks like becoming a pattern. I write something, which serves merely as a stimulus for him to write something else, in his own style and much better. But I suppose they also serve who write the first draft of the speech.

Week 9: 10 December 2018
Carwyn

The week begins in the mezzanine coffee bar in the public area near the front of the Senedd. Adam likes to meet here. It's away from the office, relatively anonymous and, above all, the coffee is good. This morning he needs it. He's been up since 4am, he tells me, the result of life with a small baby.

Steffan Bryn finds me peering at my laptop in the office – I still haven't logged into the Senedd's computer system – and says Adam wants to mull things over. He leads the way through the corridors to the café where we find Adam on his second cup of black coffee. I order another round.

Adam has jotted down a list, but first he rises and greets me like a long-lost friend. We haven't seen each other since the previous Wednesday when he headed off to London. He remarks that the long gap seems odd, but quickly goes on to gossip about the previous day's People's Vote rally. He remarks on the star quality of the faces in the Green Room – actors Charles Dance and Michael Sheen, ageing politicos Peter Mandelson and Michael Heseltine, the original spin doctor Alistair Campbell. It's clear Adam is still flushed with the way he was fêted amongst this crowd, how well his speech had gone down. 'I think we did a bit of good,' he says, then goes on to remark how overwhelmingly white and middle class the whole event was.

'What do you expect?' I answer.

But we quickly turn to business, which this week is the handover of First Minister. With his unerring feel for the choreography of politics Adam senses the significance of the moment and wants to prepare.

First, we deal with the handover itself and whether there is any combination in which Plaid could emerge as a competitor. Adam grabs a sheet of paper and does the maths, adding up those for and against. But this is not the same as when Leanne was put up at the beginning of the session, won the unsolicited support of Tories and UKIP, and tied in the vote with Labour.

Now we've lost two members, Neil McEvoy and Dafydd Elis-Thomas, and as a result the Tories are the second party and nominating their own leader, Paul Davies. Adam says he had a conversation the previous evening with Dafydd El which had been amicable but, all the same, he will be voting for 'stability'. Labour also has Kirsty Williams on board and she will be continuing as Education Minister under Drakeford, signalling again the 'strange death of Liberal Wales'.

Why are we even considering all this? Perhaps we're foreshadowing the situation in a few years' time. But now is not that time. Adam crumples the scrap of paper, and places it carefully in his pocket. We move on.

He's interested in my views about Mark Drakeford who has just been elected Labour's leader. Previously he'd looked forward to Drakeford becoming First Minister, regarding him an easy target as the continuity candidate, responsible for much of the inactivity over the past 20 years. Now he's not so sure. Recognises that his intellectual engagement might give Labour some new momentum. He asks me to produce a paper. 'Let's call it *Dealing with Drakeford*'.

Next on our list is Carwyn. Today will be his last FMQs. After that there'll have to be the eulogy, which I have to write.

The FMQs suggest themselves. Earlier at the Monday staff meeting I'd asked for the manifesto Carwyn drew up when he'd stood for the leadership nine years ago to be fished out. It's a simple matter to scan through and pick out some commitments he made then and measure them against what has been achieved. I start with the economy, Carwyn's commitment to 'an investment rather than grants culture'. Then again, he had pledged to reduce child poverty, which has gone up; to a 'green transport policy', when actually his signature initiative was the M4 Relief Road. When all these are put to him Carwyn bats them away with his usual relaxed composure.

I find it harder when it comes to the eulogy. My thoughts go back to an IWA seminar I'd organised for Carwyn at Gregynog in 2003. The publication that came out of it, *The Future of Welsh Labour* had helped advance his leadership prospects. He'd committed to full legislative powers for the Assembly, taxation powers, and abolition of the Welsh Development Agency and other Quangos. In the process he'd put himself at the head of the soft nationalist wing of Welsh Labour. I recall that at one point during the seminar Carwyn had referred to Plaid being Labour's main competitor, but that with Adam Price in the ascendant and with his emphasis on Independence, Welsh Labour would simply 'clean up'.

A few days later I'm intrigued to see that in his *Western Mail* piece looking back at Carwyn's career, headlined 'Ardent apostle of devolution overtaken by political events', the paper's political columnist Martin Shipton refers to the same seminar, in which he had been a participant.[10] Martin judges that, 'Based on his Gregynog Paper and the discussion that preceded its publication, I believe he genuinely wanted to move devolution forward.' I'm of the same view in my draft of Adam's speech:

> First Minister, you will be the first to agree, I am sure, that over the years we have had our differences. Yet I have never doubted that at every point during the period you have held high office you have had the interests of our country foremost in your thoughts.
>
> When you took office, you were the only second First Minister in our history. In many ways one of your major responsibilities was to build on the achievement of your predecessor Rhodri Morgan, to establish

---

10   *Western Mail*, 12 December 2018.

our fledgling National Assembly firmly in the affections of the people of Wales. Working with the coalition that was then in place with my party, you took that responsibility seriously. Most notably, you did so by pressing ahead with the referendum we had agreed should happen, to provide this place with the primary law-making powers it now enjoys.

That was a major achievement and I want to put that on record today. In collaboration with ourselves, in Plaid Cymru, you oversaw that successful referendum in 2011 which was an historic milestone in the development of our country's institutions.

Your articulation of the constitutional framework Wales needs to become a more successful country will, I believe, come to be seen as your most important contribution. As well as developing our law-making powers, during your period of office we have acquired the beginnings of the tax varying responsibilities that will be necessary for creating a more fully rounded economic policy. You have also argued the case for a distinctive legal jurisdiction for Wales and set in train the Commission on Justice which I am sure will take that agenda forward.

Not only that, you have made a number of interventions on the British stage more widely, calling for greater co-operation between the devolved administrations and the UK government at Westminster. You have called for a federal structure for the United Kingdom, with the devolved nations and English regions being represented in a reformed upper chamber. This has pointed the way towards the next stage in the evolution of our relationships in these islands which I am sure will happen in the next decade.

During this time, closer to home at the Despatch Box in this chamber, you have generally sustained a quiet dignity in your dealings with colleagues. You have overseen a very wide brief with masterly composure. I for one have found you a tough opponent to disrupt. Shall we just say, it is hard to ruffle your feathers.

Those outside the immediate cut and thrust of political life will find it hard to understand the stresses and strains that inevitably affect us all, and not least the families on which we depend. As well as paying tribute to you personally, therefore, I think it fitting that we should also acknowledge the support you have received from your wife Lisa, and your children Seren and Ruairí.

Carwyn, through all your period in office you have demonstrated notable resilience, a quality I am sure will be necessary for your successor, whoever that turns out to be.

I watch the TV monitor impassively as Adam delivers the script. Maybe that's because he delivers most of it in Welsh (having translated it) and I struggle to follow. In any event, I'm pleasantly surprised when Adam emerges from the chamber and tells me he felt overcome with emotion when he was on his feet.

It's an odd moment, but on reflection I think it reveals that deep down most Labour members in the Senedd have come to share our vision of a (Welsh) national interest. It's a feeling that cannot be extended to the Conservatives, or at least only to a handful of them, David Melding being one along with, possibly, Glyn Davies in Montgomeryshire and Paul Davies in Pembrokeshire.

In the midst of this, Adam and I meet with Michelle O'Neill MLA, Vice President of Sinn Féin and Leader of the Sinn Féin Group in the Northern Ireland Assembly. She's giving the Wales Governance Centre's annual lecture, with Brexit as the chosen subject. She's down to earth and genial. It's hard to credit that her father, Brendan Doris, was a Provisional IRA prisoner; her uncle, Paul Doris, is a former national president of the Irish Northern Aid Committee in the United States; a cousin, Tony Doris, was one of three IRA members shot dead by the SAS in 1991; and another cousin, IRA volunteer Gareth Malachy, was shot and wounded during the 1997 Coalisland attack on an Ulster Constabulary and British Army base.

We exchange pleasantries. Michelle says how appreciative people in Northern Ireland were of the visit the previous week of our Westminster leader Liz Saville Roberts to a Gaelic cultural centre in Derry. At this point Blaenau Gwent Labour AM Alun Davies joined us by prior arrangement. He takes a keen interest in Northern Irish politics and launches a tirade at the intransigence of the DUP. Michelle says it's noteworthy how over Brexit they're losing much of their core support amongst the business community. We meet for an hour and towards the end Adam suggests we must forge closer links as parties, mentioning that he'll be in Dublin in January.

The Politics of Co-Opposition

'Maybe I could get an invitation to speak at their *Ard Fheis*,' he says to me afterwards. 'Why not? After all, it's years since the troubles have been over.'

On Thursday we have a follow up to the Stocktake meeting I had organised three weeks earlier. We had intended this would occur two weeks ago. However, the pressure of events has prevented us being able to reconvene until now. The main item on the agenda is a paper that Carl Harris and Geraint Day have put together. It has no title but I quickly realise that Adam has commissioned it and sees it as the beginning of what he refers to as 'our Bible', our strategy for winning in 2021. It's also going to be the basis of our submission to the Angus Robertson review.[11] But our general discussion is pre-empted by some paragraphs in the paper under the heading 'Membership and Activism':

> In recent years the party has had a steady membership of around 8,000. Since the election of Adam Price as Leader at the end of September 2018 we have seen over 3,000 people take advantage of the free membership, bringing our total membership to over 11,000.
>
> But the process adopted by the central party was flawed, seeing potential new members directed to a standard 'sign-up' page on the party website, instead of them being asked to complete a Direct Debit mandate to secure their membership contributions from 2019 onwards.
>
> As a result, a disproportionate amount of party resources and staff time have been spent on a project to try and turn the 3,000 people into fully paid-up members. To date only 100 of the 3,000 have done so.
>
> There is a serious risk that we have lost the momentum of electing a new leader to capitalise on attracting new members.

Adam says the thing is a disaster, could threaten his whole campaign. 'My enemies in the party will seize on this,' he says. 'It's just the

---

11 Immediately on becoming leader Adam Price commissioned Angus Robertson, former SNP leader in the House of Commons, to undertake a root and branch review of Plaid Cymru's organization and strategy.

ammunition they're looking for, to confirm all their prejudices against what I'm trying to do.' He goes on in this vein for some time. Emergency action is needed. Christmas will have to be cancelled as we work the phones contacting people to get them to renew.

Geraint Day tries to soften the blow. The 100 figure is by now nearly 300, he says. Also, renewals are only due from the beginning of January. After Christmas will be the time to get on the phone.

That evening Adam is in Aberystwyth as part of his book tour, this time being interviewed by Cynog Dafis, who next day e-mails me a reassuring message:

> 'Adam's session in Aber last night was excellent - everyone delighted and queuing up for the book and the signature. There were about 100, of whom only four needed simultaneous translation. I think we may have picked up the membership of an erstwhile LibDem activist – a very bright young woman who's the moving spirit behind the Aber 'Wales in Europe' group. Adam's very appreciative of your service and says he feels that he's settling in, feeling now that 'I can do this!' It's an awful thought that he had to drive himself all the way from Cardiff to Aber just for this event. Plaid needs to look after this invaluable asset that it has been given.'

Despite all this, Brexit has dominated most of this week. Looking at my diary I see that Grŵp Brexit meetings, held between the MPs and staff at Westminster, and ourselves in the Senedd, have been held on every day, apart from Friday. It's an indication of the way the question dominates, invading all our other, generally more important activities.

Of course, this week the 'Meaningful Vote' was due to be held on Tuesday, though that was pulled early on Monday. Yet this anti-climax only accentuates the sense of feverish engagement. Each day, it seems that important decisions need to be made, on which might hang important consequences. Yet, as one day turns into another, the important decisions of the previous meeting dissolve, and the caravan moves on to the next conundrum. It leads to a kind of nervous exhaustion, made worse because nothing is achieved.

It also occurs to me that, if this is the effect upon one tiny Cardiff adjunct, how much more must the phenomenon affect the Westminster/Whitehall machine itself. The opportunity cost is enormous.

At one of this week's meetings, at 9am on Thursday, following the staff Christmas party the evening before, I arrive in the office to find it deserted. I am the only voice down the line in the group telephone call. In London Dafydd Wigley voices displeasure. But we press on. At the end, nearly an hour later, I say I'll make a note of what we've discussed and share it with colleagues. It turns out like this and is of interest because of the apparent import of what was discussed.

Grŵp Brexit Meeting 9am, 13.12.18 (Draft Note)

Overnight our Westminster team has been circulating an Early Day Motion, stating:

> That this House declines to approve the Withdrawal Agreement and the Framework for the Future Relationship negotiated between the EU and the UK.

The six lead names on the motion are crucial, and have been obtained in the following order:

> Liz Saville Roberts MP, Westminster Leader, Plaid Cymru
> Jeremy Corbyn MP, Leader, Labour Party
> Vince Cable MP, Leader, Liberal Democrats
> Ian Blackford MP, Westminster Leader, SNP
> Nigel Dodds MP, Shadow DUP Brexit Spokesperson
> Caroline Lucas MP, Leader, Green Party

It was felt a priority to have representatives from the Opposition parties in the top six. Conservative names can come immediately below, with the objective of obtaining Steve Baker MP of the European Research Group (ERG) and Anna Soubry MP for the new Remain group. It is noteworthy that other parties were content to see Plaid leading on this, to make it easier for them to row behind.

With the party Whips now working for the motion it looks likely that the numbers signing will grow rapidly through the day. The question then is when will be the optimum moment for publicising the motion – before the weekend or on Monday? It is likely that the initiative will develop its own momentum

In short order the Motion should result in demonstrating that the Government has no majority in the Commons for its Withdrawal Agreement, and lead to a debate on the floor of the House.

Following a Commons debate we are once more into anticipating the choreography and sequencing of motions and amendments. Questions that arise:

- Will Labour commit to a No Confidence Motion, or indicate it would support one from a smaller party?
- What will be the Government's response?

On the latter, early intelligence is indicating that the Government is willing to contemplate a Norway-plus option to avoid a No Deal.

Surprisingly, the ERG appears to be moving in this direction also, since Norway-plus would better allow later stepping out of the EU orbit, rather than the Government's present deal, plus the Northern Ireland Backstop.

The Norway-plus model would probably have to become a bespoke arrangement for the UK, since an attempt to join EFTA is likely to meet with resistance.

Plaid Cymru would want a Norway-plus option (entailing Britain remaining within the Single Market and Customs Union) being linked with a confirmatory referendum – with the choice being Norway or Remain. However, depending on the sequencing of motions and amendments this may not be an option for us. In these circumstances we would vote for Norway-plus as being preferable to leaving with No Deal.

Jill Evans reported that she has picked up that the European Council is actively considering allowing Article 50 to be suspended beyond 29 March to allow a UK referendum to be held. The time being contemplated is three months, to July 2019. In these circumstances the European Parliament elections would go ahead in May, with a proviso that the UK elections to the Parliament would be held later in the year if a referendum approved UK remaining in the EU.

as agreed that Grŵp Brexit should reconvene on Monday 17 ember, at a time to be confirmed.

Of course, none of this comes to pass, apart from the reconvened meeting. The various signatories to the Early Day Motion (EDM) are indeed lined up at various times, but not all in tandem. Corbyn will only sign if all the rest are signed-up. The DUP prove to be the most elusive. First of all they agree, but then hold back until we can persuade a prominent Leave Tory. Eventually the ERG Group twig that they need to be cautious, because if May's deal falls then the whole Brexit project might fall as well. It's a demonstration that the Prime Minister's tactic of continuously kicking the can down the road, until the road reaches close to the precipice, when hard choices will have to be made, might be working for her.

Week 10: 17 December 2018
Something out of nothing

The last week before what feels like the end of term and the Christmas break really begins, starts with a late morning meeting of Grŵp Brexit. The next day we reconvene our Stocktake meeting. It's just Adam, Carl, Steffan, Geraint and myself. Mabli is on leave, while Siân Gwenllian is in the north where she's come down with shingles. I raise *Welsh Nation* and say we have to make a decision if we want it to appear by the Spring conference in the new format we've been discussing. I also say that if it's to happen I've concluded that I'll have to edit the thing myself, to ensure it gets out, though I don't much want to.

A long discussion ensues, as if this is the first time we've considered this. The Welsh language raises its head. Carl predicts a blowback. 'That's why we're getting Nova Cambria to be the publisher', I remind everybody. 'There'll still be blowback,' Carl says. Adam then rehearses the arguments as though speaking to himself. 'We'll just have to say that we're putting the new *Welsh Nation* first. Yes, let's call it that, *New Welsh Nation*. A new format for *Y Ddraig Goch* can follow sometime later. We'll advertise for volunteers.'

Carl and Steffan continue to look dubious, but the decision appears to have been made. I immediately start thinking about ideas for articles while the meeting continues. I've already stapled together some mock-up pages, anticipating this moment.

The First 100 Days of Plaid's New Leader

We move on to the 'Bible', the emerging campaign strategy which we're calling 'Project 21' (to win 21 seats in 2021). Adam says we'll need some big picture stuff, a narrative, and glances at me. I say we ought to get together soon after Christmas, before the whole dynamic kicks-in once again, to take time to reflect on where we're going. Adam's eyes light up. 'Good idea', he says.

Then there's a party political broadcast to consider. We discover it's being made on 4 January. Tŷ Gwynfor has handled it with very little consultation. I'm amazed to learn that £10,000 is set aside for a three-to-four-minute slot, going out during January and February on the BBC and S4C.

We discuss themes. Tŷ Gwynfor's proposal, in connection with the production company they've hired, is 'An Introduction to Adam' set in Ammanford. 'That's OK,' I say, 'But this will be in the middle of the Brexit crisis, the Meaningful Vote, approaching the cliff-edge and so on.... Surely, we can't just ignore that?' Adam nods thoughtfully.

Suddenly I have an idea. 'Why not do something in the Rhondda, with Leanne? Why these people voted Leave. What they think now. Plaid's answer, Remain but Reform...'

Adam's imagination is caught by the idea. It's risky but interesting. He ponders the risk of Leanne simply refusing, and what that would do to their relations. 'Let's think on it overnight,' he says. Meanwhile, I say I'll get hold of the producer and talk to him.

After this Adam disappears, but a few hours later he's back for an emergency meeting he's called, with the phone lines open to the Westminster team, on planning for a snap Election. He's already put the party on a formal election alert. Now we're looking at the logistics.

Ben O'Keeffe is first up with why and when we might expect an election. The scenario is simple: May loses her vote on the Withdrawal Agreement in mid-January. Then, faced with the options of a calamitous No Deal Brexit, or a party-splitting referendum, opts instead for a dissolution of Parliament, and a snap election, called to get backing for her deal. It sounds implausible, but it's as implausible as most other scenarios we can think of, so we'd better be prepared.

Voices from the party machine round the table are pessimistic. This will be a defensive campaign. The main objective will be to hang on to our four seats. Arfon will be particularly vulnerable...

Adam responds in typical fashion. Far from being in a defensive mode we must immediately go on the attack. He's already heard Wigley saying the moment reminds him of the crisis election in February 1974, when Edward Heath called his 'Who Governs?' election amidst the miners' strike and the three-day week. The answer Heath was given was – 'Not you!' That was the moment of Plaid's breakthrough when we won Arfon and Meirionnydd for the first time and came within three votes of regaining Carmarthen.

Adam sees the parallel and starts making the argument. It'll be something along the lines: 'Don't vote for either of the Westminster parties that have made such a mess of Brexit.... Vote for ourselves, for Wales!'

He hints that we might have a few powerful candidates up our sleeve – for Ynys Môn and Llanelli. Then there's the prospect of a hung Parliament, and who knows, our handful of MPs might be in pole position to secure an enticing wish list for Wales:

1. A referendum with Remain on the ballot paper.
2. Additional money for Wales in the form of an enhanced regional development package – our share would be at least £5 billion.
3. A new constitutional deal for the UK – a new Wales in a new Britain.

Thus, on the basis of pure speculation, Adam turns around the mood of the meeting from pessimism to hopeful optimism about the prospects that might, however improbably, lie before us. It's a case of conjuring something out of nothing.

Week 11: 29 December 2018
Scenario gazing

This point, near the end of the year feels like halfway through Adam's 100 days. And, indeed, my active involvement has been around 50 days.

It's a Saturday – a grim, dank, wet day – and I'm heading west down the M4 to a meeting of Adam's closest advisers at his home near Nantgaredig, to review the 'Bible', our campaign strategy.

Joni Eds is there – he was an hour early by mistake – as is Carl Harris who has just returned from the constituency office with freshly printed copies of the document we've all been working on over the previous few days. Steffan Bryn is down from Anglesey, where he's been spending Christmas with his family, and Geraint Day has travelled from Pontypridd. Adam then appears, after popping out to to buy (decaffeinated) coffee.

As well as the 'Bible', we have to consider an associated paper dashed off by Adam himself, containing 53 separate points. The first four of these is his assessment of the situation we're likely to face following the election in May 2021. They dominate the first hour or so of our conversation and read as follows:

1. Our aim is to lead the Government in 2021 and to be re-elected in 2026, and then to call and win a successful independence referendum by 2030. We will win on a relatively narrow base in 2021, necessitating an arrangement with the Conservatives. By 2026 our record in government should have raised our levels of support though we are still unlikely to achieve a majority. Calling a referendum will probably require a full coalition at this point though it is not clear at this stage with which party/ies as there will likely be additional seats and additional parties represented in a larger Senedd.
2. Looking at the range of likely outcomes for the party currently in terms of seats, it can be summarised that anything below 15 makes it highly unlikely that we will be in a position to lead a government; 15-17 makes it possible though difficult; 18-20 probable; 21 and above, almost certain. The median figure in the range – eighteen seats – is a critical one and should form the basis for planning. What is the lowest percentage share that could reasonably give us 18 seats?
3. In all these scenarios we will be a minority administration. Only when we get to 21 seats do we have any hope of being in a position of plurality (that is, having more seats than Labour, as the SNP achieved in 2007). Even in this position, however, we would need to secure the stability of our government by seeking, at a minimum, a confidence and supply agreement with another party. It is difficult to imagine any circumstances in which Labour, having just been ousted as lead party, would want to enter into a 'grand coalition' as junior partner. This is even less likely where Labour will remain the biggest party.
4. As no single party will be able to determine the outcome of the crucial First Minister's vote, the reality is that seeking the

Conservative Party's support will be essential in forming a government. This is most likely to involve actively securing a positive vote for Adam Price in the First Minister vote. In this vote it will be necessary for the combined votes of Plaid and the Conservatives to outnumber the combined votes of the Labour Group and any Liberal Democrat member (on the assumption, which is highly likely, that the single Liberal Democrat, if returned, will remain wedded to Labour). As a minimum this would have to equal 30 seats, though 31 seats constitute an effective majority. The consequence of this is that we must factor into our targeting of seats, making our gains at the expense of Labour rather than the Conservatives.

Of course, all this – though a pretty accurate assessment of the possibilities – raises the toxic question of a relationship with the Tories. It's the issue that dominated the leadership election campaign, with Leanne's USP being to rule out a coalition with the Tories under any circumstances. This forced Adam to do the same, though in a more modulated way. One reality is that if we did try to force the question, following the election, three of the Plaid Group would probably peel off – Leanne herself, Helen Mary Jones, and Bethan Sayed. That would undermine the whole project.

The dilemma is: when do we confront this, before or after the election? And if before, when? There's no clear answer to this. The instinct in the room is to let it go for a while, perhaps a year, or even more. But Adam says, rightly I think, that the longer we leave it the more difficult it will be. If we have the row now it will be nasty, but settled. The closer to the election, the more difficult, and potentially more destabilising it will be.

'Welsh society changes in a glacial way,' Adam says. 'We don't do revolutions. In 2021 success will simply be leading the government, however that turns out.' He mentions the French leader Emmanuel Macron whose biography he has been reading over Christmas. 'He won the first round of the French Presidential election with only 24% of the vote, but that was enough. In 2021 Labour are going to win the vote but lose the government. If we think in landslide mode, we are not allowing ourselves to think in terms of what real victory will look like.' Macron won the second round of the election in May 2017 with 66% of the vote. That, Adam implies will happen with us in *our* second round, in 2026. 'That's the revolution,' he says.

Of course, there's a long way to go before we get there. To do so we're going to have to pivot from leaning towards a 'progressive alliance' with Labour to equidistance between Labour and the Conservatives.

Week 12: 7 January 2019
Dublin

To all intents and purposes this week and our political New Year begins in Cardiff Airport shortly after 6am on Wednesday. Adam, Steffan Bryn and I are catching the 7am flight to Dublin.

The evening before I'd organised a presentation for the Plaid Group in the Senedd on opinion poll evidence around identity questions across the UK, given by Richard Wyn Jones, Director of the Wales Governance Centre. When we were underway, I was surprised to see that Adam was not there – he's intensely interested in the topic. Mabli tells me the reason is that he's gone to see Steffan Lewis, our South-East Wales AM.

Now I'm sitting in the airport, across from Adam, listening, while choked with emotion, he tells me about the previous evening. Steffan is coming to the end – he's been gravely ill for the past year with cancer. He emerged from drifting sleep yesterday afternoon and asked his mother to call for Adam. So he went, immediately, to the hospital in Ystrad Mynach. It seems he had a good conversation with Steffan for three-quarters of an hour. Then spent another couple of hours with the family.

The conversation with Steffan was wide ranging. It was plain he knew he didn't have long. They spoke about Ireland and our trip. Steffan has long been a Hibernophile – he prefers Ireland to Scotland. If well he would certainly have been on our trip. They spoke about shared memories. But most of all, it seems Steffan wanted to implant in Adam's mind his confidence that independence was coming, in the reasonably near future, and that he was only sorry he would not be there to see it.

It turns out that though Steffan is not actually with us, his presence accompanies us for the three days of our visit and frames the whole experience.

On the first evening we're in the bar of the hotel having a pint of Guinness, preparing to go out for dinner, when Adam's phone goes. It's Math Wiliam, Steffan's researcher. He says that Steffan is not expected to last the night and that we need to put together an appreciation. He's sending through a draft.

Adam cracks, his eyes fill. For a moment he is incapable of responding, but gradually we go through a form of words, with Steffan Bryn typing on his laptop. The process seems to help.

I feel it, too, but vicariously. I don't know Steffan personally, who of course is of a completely different generation. Since I've been working with Adam, he's come into the Senedd most weeks, though only for short periods. But he was there for the critical vote before Christmas, on Brexit, in which he oversaw Plaid's successful amendment to Labour's weak, incoherent, motion on leaving the EU. That was a crowning achievement and must have taken a huge effort.

Though he's only 34, so young, he has achieved a good deal in his short time in politics. He was Leanne's speech writer, got in the Assembly himself in 2016, and swiftly made his mark with the European question and our cross-party response to Brexit. All this goes into Adam's eulogy.

The next few days pass in a rush, with a multitude of meetings. We see members of the Dáil, the Irish Parliament, from Fianna Fáil, Fine Gael, and Sinn Féin. The meeting with Mary Lou McDonald, President of Sinn Féin, is a highlight. She's impressive, business like, empathetic, across all the issues, especially Brexit and its impact on the north. We agree that she will accept an invitation to speak to our conference in the Autumn.

On Thursday morning we visit the Institute of Public Administration in Lansdowne Road where we are hosted by its Director General Dr Marion O'Sullivan. The Institute, an independent organisation, is Ireland's national centre for education and research in governance. Adam is interested because he has a long-term interest in establishing what he calls a School for Government in Wales, modelled on the Kennedy School at Harvard where he's studied.[12]

Later Adam gives a lunchtime keynote speech at the Institute of International and European Affairs, which I'm pleased goes down well, eliciting a lot of relevant questions. I spent the best part of three

---

12 The idea found its way into the Co-operation Agreement with the commitment to, 'Explore how setting up a National School for Government might contribute to the principle of a One Wales Public Service.'

days sweating over it. It prompts a number of television and radio interviews.

By this time Rhun ap Iorwerth has joined us, coming across on the ferry from Holyhead. Adam seizes a moment, following the end of his speech when we're waiting for a taxi, to engage Rhun in a conversation about some internal party matters. We retreat to the room where we had lunch earlier, to have a coffee by ourselves. I'm struck how Adam makes use of the moment, instantly diving into difficult questions, almost self-consciously drawing Rhun into his private domain.

Later we go out for dinner, and it's a relaxed affair, but Rhun declines to come on with us afterwards. He stays in the hotel, while Adam and Steffan Bryn take me to an Irish bar they say I shouldn't miss. It's O'Donoghues, a noisy atmospheric place with a traditional Irish band – accordion, banjo, fiddle and drum playing, with a couple of clog dancers amidst the throng.

After a while we assemble outside, holding another Guinness, and Adam reminisces about his time in Aberystwyth – I guess when he was working with Menter a Busnes in the early 1990s. He says he could leave Aberystwyth at 4.30pm on a Friday afternoon, drive to Holyhead, catch the fast ferry and be in Dublin in time for a pint that evening.

The next morning, we spend a useful hour at the Investment and Development Agency of Ireland, equivalent to the Welsh Development Agency we've lost, and which we're determined to bring back. We meet Mary Buckley, Executive Director, quietly efficient, and James Farrell, Head of Strategic Policy, brimming with confidence. We learn that since the Brexit vote they've brought 50 businesses from the UK into Dublin, mainly financial services, pharmaceutical and life science companies. They say they haven't actively sought them: 'They've come knocking on our door'.

Rhun is absorbed by the meeting, takes notes, and asks questions. Ireland is due to increase its population by a million over the next 20 years or so. They're planning for a good deal of decentralisation, to regional centres built around places like Cork, Limerick and Galway. Adam is also engaged with this. If only we had these problems.

Our schedule ends with meeting Helen McEntee, the Fine Gael Minister for European Affairs, responsible for Brexit. She seems icily efficient, blue dress and long flowing blonde hair. Calm, giving nothing away, she listens intently. Brexit is plainly their number one, most difficult issue. What will happen in the next few weeks? Nobody knows for sure.

We have lunch in a pub close by, amidst breaking news that Ford at Bridgend is under threat, potentially losing 1,000 jobs, a body blow. I'm impressed by the way Rhun responds. He quickly drafts a statement, then gets Steffan Bryn to go outside with him to make a video. He shows it to us when they return. It looks professional, quite steady with Rhun well-framed, and shot against a neutral parkland background. 'Broadcast quality,' Rhun mutters as he sends it to the news outlets back home who have asked for his reaction.

We part at the hotel. Rhun is catching the ferry back to Holyhead later in the evening. Then, before we know where we are we're in a taxi heading for the airport, and a text comes through. Steffan Lewis has died. We get a message from Carl Harris that Adam must put out a tweet. He looks at me wryly. 'There's no escape,' he says. Adam has 15,000 followers and the objective is to increase these substantially, but he's not keen on the medium. It's too terse and compressed for his temperament. Nonetheless he bows to the inevitable.

At Cardiff Airport, not much more than an hour or so later we spent what seems an endless moment composing the required short text for Twitter, in Welsh and English. Then we vanish, in another taxi, into the night.

Week 13: 14 January 2019
The nation's perfect son

This was the week of the ambush, when Adam was inveigled by Drakeford to present a united front with him alongside the Tory leader on combatting a no-deal Brexit. In the wider political world, it was the week when Theresa May's Brexit Deal went down to a crushing 230-vote defeat in the House of Commons, on the evening of Tuesday 15 January. The small-scale ambush we fell into was directly related.

On the evening of the Commons vote Mark Drakeford's office contacted us to ask if Adam would attend a meeting with him at 9.30am the following morning, together with the leader of the Welsh Conservatives Paul Davies. They want to discuss what collaborative moves might be considered to deal with the looming Brexit crisis. We replied that we were happy to meet with Drakeford, but on a one-to-one basis. We didn't see why the Tories, the architects of the crisis, should be involved.

It then transpired that Drakeford's commitments meant he couldn't make a 9.30am meeting after all. We heard that he had been called to Bridgend to discuss the redundancies at Ford, but it later emerged he was meeting the Presiding Officer Elin Jones at 9am. In any event, later in the morning we had a fresh message from his office that Drakeford was now meeting with Paul Davies at 12.30pm and would Adam come along?

Adam, Steffan Bryn and I considered this over a coffee in the canteen on the floor below our office at around 11am. My instinct was for him not to go. However, Adam eventually decided that it would appear churlish if he refused to meet with the First Minister. It was decided that he should go, accompanied by myself and Steffan.

When we arrived in Drakeford's office on the fifth floor we immediately realised we'd been set up. Sitting at a large table was a smiling Paul Davies. There were also a few officials. Drakeford looked alarmed to see me, muttered to Adam and indicated that I and Steffan should go. I noticed that Steff was in agitated discussion with one of the officials and then saw the film crew. The whole purpose was to get Drakeford in the same room with Adam and Paul Davies, so he could be seen reaching out across the parties to address the crisis. I thought the best thing was for me and Steffan to leave. Adam was left shaking hands in front of Union Jack, and the pictures duly appeared in the news bulletins that evening.

As we left, Steffan was shaking with anger. He felt traduced, and responsible. He was certainly traduced but I told him he wasn't responsible. I felt mildly surprised that Drakeford would indulge in such tactics. I suspected it was his media people, rather than him, but that was to give him the benefit of the doubt.

The subject matter of the discussions led me further to believe my own interpretation. Drakeford wanted Adam and Davies to agree to adopt a Privy Council relationship with him in terms of receiving background information and briefing papers about Brexit. This was to help in producing a more consensual and collegiate approach to what threatened to become a full-blown crisis, in the event of a no-deal crash out of the EU on 29 March – in the national (meaning, of course, Welsh) interest. In the discussion that followed Drakeford also said that, assuming the No Confidence vote would fail later that evening (as it did), he felt events were making another referendum more likely. Afterwards we discussed the Privy Council proposal. I voiced scepticism. Where was the crisis that suggested it? Not only that, it would tend to diminish accountability, drawing the opposition into the government's web. It was typical of Drakeford's preference for avoiding confrontation. The idea was left unresolved.

When he returned to our office Adam told Steffan to send a sternly-worded letter demanding an apology. In their response Labour lied, saying their understanding was that the BBC had informed us they would be there. At one level the whole thing was relatively insignificant. At another level, however, such things matter in the relationship between party leaders since they can either enhance, or erode, trust.

This minor episode occurred amidst the unfolding of grief within the party over Steffan Lewis's death. Early on Tuesday, before the start of the meeting of Shadow Cabinet, Adam called in all the staff. There was standing room only, with many people sitting on the window ledges. It was a sombre occasion, but Adam spoke movingly, weeping at times, saying it was a mistake to hold your emotions in. This caused many in the room also to crack up. It was a strangely unifying moment in a party organisation that remains oddly destabilised more than three months after the leadership contest. Dai Lloyd offered counselling, as a GP with some experience. So did Helen Mary Jones, who said she had training, as did Siân Gwenllian, who has direct experience of bereavement. It felt like a fractured family coming together.

I realised, too, that Adam was suffering a good deal of strain, though it was not obvious. That day the Plenary timetable was cleared to make way for more than an hour of statements of appreciation. At the appointed time the whole staff made their way to the public gallery and sat behind the family, amongst whom I noticed Rhuanedd Richards, Plaid's former Chief Executive, doing the emotional heavy lifting. The number and range of speeches, across the floor were impressive. Adam led and judged the mood perfectly:

> Wales is a small nation, but every now and then we breed giants. I got to know Steffan Lewis first over 20 years ago during the Islwyn

by-election. We heard talk of this incredible young boy from the Gwent Valleys who was not only a member of Plaid Cymru, but of the SNP and Mebyon Kernow too, and had managed to get the WRU to note this in the programme for the Wales-England game when Steffan was a mascot for the Wales team. Steffan never did things by halves.

Within a few years, Steffan was addressing the Plaid conference for the first time, at 14 years of age—two years younger than William Hague and, as he was keen to point out, he was far more effective. And, even at that time, he wasn't little Steffan — Steffan was to be great. There was incredible depth to his character from the outset. His mother, Gail, at the ironing board, and him as a nine-year-old asking all sorts of questions, flowing like water from a well. Where, why and when—and most often, the 'why', like some sort of apprentice Vincent Kane.[13] The potential was spotted and the roots were nurtured and took hold. Gail would highlight articles in the *Western Mail* and buy him books on Welsh history. But writing stories or history books wasn't his destiny; he was to make history.

Steffan was every bit the definition of a passionate Welshman. But he was also a man of Gwent, and he saw in the triumphs and tragedies of that great county the key to understanding the problems and possibilities of the nation as a whole. It was Gwent which brought the first blossoming of Welsh nationalism in the form of Cymru Fydd to a shuddering halt in a stormy meeting in Newport in 1896. But it also produced, in Steffan and, before him, Phil Williams, two of the most cerebral and creative minds in a hundred years of the modern national movement. If our task was to forge a new Wales, then the die would be cast in Gwent—the social laboratory that gave the world socialised medicine. His county was not just the gateway to Wales but the key to its future.

Steffan was obsessed by history, as his sister Nia soon discovered — whose summer holidays growing up were a Wales-wide odyssey of castles, battles and the birthplaces of famous Welsh heroes. But whilst

---

13   Vincent Kane was a broadcaster with BBC Wales for more than 30 years from the 1960s, presenting programmes such as *Good Morning Wales, Wales Today* and *Week In Week Out*.

Steffan wanted us to learn history, he didn't want us imprisoned by it. He tried in vain to get a party that, until recently, still had Lewis Valentine's lyrics to Sibelius's *Finlandia* as its official party anthem, to adopt instead Fleetwood Mac's *Don't Stop*, famously used, of course, by Bill Clinton in his 1992 presidential campaign.

For Steffan, it was the mirror of our past that often offered the vision of our future. A speech he made to our conference after being selected as a candidate for the 2016 election sums this up best, and I'd like to read the closing section now. Here is Steffan in his own words:

> *You know I'm a historian myself by training, and I take a great deal of pleasure looking and learning about our past but, in a few months, I am due to become a father for the first time. That's made me think an awful lot more about our future, rather than our past. What inheritance will there be for the next generation? What accomplishments will that generation look back upon and mark out as decisive points in the course of our country? Friends, all of that is in our hands now.*

He went on to talk about the great inspiration he had drawn from the referendum in Scotland, but the point for Steffan is the choices we made here in Wales. Here's Steffan again:

> *As much as we take inspiration from others, we will thrive as a movement and as a nation only when we find our own path, when we inspire one another, when we come together to resolve to build a new society and a new state. We are going to walk that path together, north and south, local and newcomer, together as one Wales towards the free Wales.*

Steffan, sadly, will not see the Wales of which he dreamed. But for his son, Celyn, and his generation, he has laid the foundation, and it's we who must build the road. He understood, like that other Welsh giant, Brân, that the essence of leadership is to take people with you, to build bridges. In the words of one of his favourite poets, Harri Webb, if we Welsh could only be inseparable, we would be insuperable.

Steffan ended that speech by saying that he wasn't going to be the typical politician and reel off a long list of promises to the electorate.

Instead, he was going to make just one promise: he was going to make us proud. Well, you made us all proud, Steffan — proud of you, proud to have known you, to have called you a friend and colleague. You made us proud to be Welsh by your example, that will endure. You may not get there with us, Steffan, but we will get there because of you. Steffan had all the qualities to become, one day, the father of the nation. That, sadly, cannot be, but he was the nation's perfect son.[14]

Week 14: 21 January 2019
The dud report

The week actually began the Saturday before the Monday. I received a call from Ben O'Keeffe late on Friday night asking if I would speak at a Wales for Europe meeting in Cardiff the next day, briefing activists about the prospects for a second referendum. It seems there'd been a late request for a Plaid speaker, and I was the last port of call.

So I went, and talked about how we should not be afraid of referendums. History has taught us that politically they're an accelerating force. At the same time, based on our experiences in 1997 and 2011, the key to any second referendum would be mobilising the youth vote. And that was also encouraging because all the anecdotal evidence is that young people feel aggrieved by Brexit, sense they're in danger of losing an important asset, indeed a European extension to their Welsh identity, and would be highly motivated to vote this time.

Otherwise, the event was notable because Leighton Andrews was billed as speaking for Labour, which he denied, saying he was speaking purely for himself. Plainly the Carl Sargeant affair still rankles.[15]

---

[14] Shortly after his death a volume of tributes with contributions from fellow politicians, friends and family was published: Rh. Richards (Ed.), *Gwladgarwr Gwent/Son of Gwent – Cofio Steffan Lewis* (Y Lolfa, 2019).

[15] In the various controversies that ensued about the exact nature of the circumstances of his death (see Footnote 9, p.110), Carl Sargeant's friend and fellow Cabinet member Leighton Andrews said that in earlier years Sargeant had been the target of bullying and disinformation in the Assembly. This, he said, had placed 'a strain on his and others' mental health' (BBC News, 9 November 2017).

I went straight from that meeting, at the Tramshed in Grangetown, to Chapter Arts in Canton where a 'working lunch' had been organised for me with Steffan Bryn and Carl Harris. It quickly became clear they were worried about my plans for *New Nation* and Nova Cambria, as an arms-length think tank to run it. Carl was concerned about the money; Steffan about Nova Cambria being arms-length – a Company Limited by Guarantee. It was a good example of Adam's lieutenants being concerned to protect his back. I got the impression they thought I was freelancing. Lurking behind these suspicions was a sense of ownership by Steffan who has been involved in planning Nova Cambria for some time, though nothing has actually got off the ground. His vision is that it should act as an 'in house' Plaid research and publishing portal.

I fundamentally disagreed, and argued it will only function effectively if it is autonomous and has a chance to be outward facing and engage constructively with the political world outside Plaid. We debate all this for an hour-and-a-half, but I remain quietly confident that I have Adam on my side.

This proves to be the case on Monday morning in the Senedd, when we go through all the arguments again, in another nearly two hour-long, tense and fraught meeting. Finally, Adam comes down decisively on my side of the argument: 'This is my view, I know there are difficulties but it's up to you to sort them out.' He says he appreciates the challenge from the others, says it forces him to confront other views and make the argument, but I can see at the end of it he's a bit ragged. Yet what is clear is that he desperately needs what I refer to as facts on the ground. He wants to go to the Spring conference and point to the presence of *New Nation*, plus Nova Cambria, and declare: 'Look, these are concrete achievements, gains we wouldn't have made unless I'd become leader.'

All this has been made considerably more difficult by the appearance of a first draft of the Angus Robertson Report on Plaid's organisation and strategy. Adam circulated it to myself, Carl and Steffan at the end of last week. My first reaction was to ring Adam and ask if Angus had mistakenly sent him the wrong version. The 'report' is terrible. It's just eight pages long, three of which are by way of an extended introduction, being an unnecessary description of the lengths Angus has gone to consult the membership. The rest is just an unconnected mishmash of bullet points, none of which has any supporting argument, evidence or narrative thread. It's worse than terrible, it could be damaging. It threatens to undermine the whole project. Carl puts this well in an e-mail he circulates to Adam, myself and Steffan:

Initial (very brief) thoughts on draft Angus Robertson report:

1. The report is just 8 pages long, with 1 cover page and 2 simply showing how the consultation process was advertised. The remaining 5 pages read more like a summary rather than a comprehensive report.
2. There is a lot of potential for the report, in its current form, to harm Adam's leadership. It has been expensive and is not the game-changing document we had wished to receive or had been expecting.
3. There are a number of key mission-critical issues which we wish to be included in detail in the report in order to progress positively but these are not noted.
4. The mentioned sensitivities regarding Tŷ Gwynfor should not be included if this is, as Angus describes, an 'unrestricted' review.
5. The points noted in the 'Review Feedback' – which consists of just one page – are perhaps the most important aspects of the entire review but are just a series of bullet points. Most if not all of these suggestions, such as changing the party name, need to be far more detailed to justify the points made.

Recommendations:

1. We have to have a far more comprehensive report.
2. Adam to contact Angus initially to discuss a way forward. Suggested approach below.
3. Carl to action whatever is decided – including meeting up with Angus if necessary.

How to pitch discussion with Angus:

1. We are still finding a bit of push back within the party. Not everyone has accepted the leadership result. We need this paper to highlight that Adam's commissioning of the review will lead to a step-change in the way in which Plaid Cymru works/campaigns in future.

2. The report therefore needs to be more substantial in terms of its length and content.
3. There are a number of key items which we need in the document to provide political cover for the type of changes we wish to make. Examples include:

> A: National Campaigns Unit with delegated authority for decision making, including separation from the administrative wing of the party.
> B: Party processes – streamlined and prompt decision-making internally.
> C: 'One Plaid' – improving the way in which the party works across all levels of government and pooling resources if required etc.

4. Angus needs to be comfortable and sign-up to what is in the final document. Ask him how he would wish to proceed. Does he want us to send over sections for inclusion; does he want us to take his document and re-draft; does he want us to meet with him in the next week to work on the document together?
5. Given the delay to meeting at Gregynog, we now have a bit more time to get changes done.

The delay to the Gregynog meeting is due to Steffan Lewis's funeral being on the forthcoming Friday. This has resulted in a postponement of a long-planned Gregynog meeting to discuss the Angus Robertson report.[16]

We agree that Carl and I should put our heads together and, in effect, re-write the Robertson report, giving it some heft and depth, a cogent argument, and the actual recommendations we want. It's a classic, if extreme example of the way consultants work – interview the client, find out what they want, and then tell them – only in this case we're cutting out the mediating role of the consultant. We agree

---

[16] 'Gregynog' refers to the University of Wales conference centre (now a hotel) near Tregynog in the Montgomeryshire hills to the north of Newtown. In 1920 it was bought by the Davies sisters, Gwendoline and Margaret, granddaughters of the 19th Century coal magnate David Davies. They established it as a centre for the arts and bequeathed it to the University of Wales in 1960.

that Carl should deal with the organisational side of things, leaving me to beef up the 'Review Feedback'.

Earlier Adam addressed the 10am Monday staff meeting. He wants to transform the way FMQs are researched and prepared, involving the staff as a whole and not just his immediate entourage. He's circulated a paper, but I can see that the assembled group only get what he's driving at once he starts to give them a lecture. It feels a bit like a university seminar. Adam speaks for a good 20 minutes, but he has their attention. He says there are three purposes to FMQs:

> 'The first is negative, the scrutiny function, to make the First Minister and his government look weak and floundering, running out of steam and drifting. The second is to showcase our own ideas. The third is to present myself as a potential alternative First Minister. All the time their side and the Press are sizing me up. Am I authoritative, trustworthy? Do I have empathy?'

Then he tells us how we judge a FMQ session to have been successful, providing two criteria. First is the feeling in the room. 'You can tell when you've landed a punch, there's a silence on the other side.' Secondly, there's the take up by the press and media: 'When that happens you know you've scored.'

At the meeting with myself, Carl and Steffan, Adam says he wants to institute a regular, routine set of meetings at the beginning of every week. He's just back from a weekend away in Eryri (Snowdonia) with Swami, Ilar, and Andy Street, the West Midlands Conservative Mayor, who has obviously been talking to him. It's another indication of the breadth of Adam's contacts. Street was the managing director of John Lewis from 2007 to 2016, when he ran for Mayor. He's obviously a super-organised guy, and Adam wants to replicate the way he does things.

He says he wants to institute a two-hour series of four half-hour meetings every Monday from 8am. The first should be with the Chiefs of Staff, from the Senedd, Westminster and Tŷ Gwynfor. That should be followed by the Leaders' team. A meeting with the Campaigns Unit should follow that. Finally, there should be a meeting with the Comms staff. All these would bring him up to date, and set the agenda for the coming week.

'Obama had a similar routine,' Adam says. Carl, Steffan and I are a bit sceptical at this ambition, but it's not an immediate prospect, so we don't argue. Adam says, by way of finalising his decision, 'I've learnt from Ilar that human beings love a structure, a routine.'

The following day's Shadow Cabinet leaves Adam deflated. Later he tells me he sensed pushback and resistance – people weren't with him: 'All the oxygen went out of the room. It's quite different with our Grŵp Brexit meetings – they're energising.' It's an indication of how far we have to go.

But later Adam is buoyed up by a Channel 4 News programme, broadcast live from the Senedd, because that day the Welsh Government have brought forward a series of statements about coping with a no deal 'crash out' scenario. Paul Davies for the Tories is interviewed, looking nervous; Mark Drakeford comes across as dull and routine, speaking in monotone. In contrast, Adam is passionate, finds an adrenaline flow and taps into the youthful preacher that he used to be.

Week 15: 4 February 2019
Time is slipping away

This has been another Brexit week. Following FMQs on Tuesday – in which we went after a pointless quest concerning the Permanent Secretary who Mark Drakeford has allegedly asked to resign – Adam set off for Brussels via London. In tow was Math Wiliam, a Senedd researcher who worked with Steffan Lewis. This was a good idea since he is an expert on European politics and also needs a break following Steffan's death. Joining them was Dafydd Wigley, so I imagine they'll have a memorable time.

The point of the exercise was meetings in the European Parliament, facilitated by Jill Evans – though it wasn't clear to me what was to be accomplished, other than contacts and information (never, of course, to be under-estimated).

In any event, while he was there, Adam dreamt up a new Brexit scheme, in which Theresa May might receive cross party support for the Withdrawal Agreement, contingent on her agreeing a referendum at the end of the Transition Period. This seems to be an inventive idea, and as the week goes by gathers legs in Westminster. So much so that on Wednesday, at 6pm, Ben O'Keeffe negotiates a telephone conference call for Adam with Gavin Barwell, May's Chief of Staff in Downing Street.

On the Grŵp Brexit WhatsApp, Ben records the conversation, 'in which they shared some intel on their latest thinking', as follows:

At the moment they are framing their thinking on the new Brexit 'package' they have come up with, around four pillars:

1. Reforms to the Northern Irish Backstop (Parliamentary vote/exit date).
2. EU workers' rights and environmental standards in UK Legislation.
3. Role for Parliament, the Devolved Administrations and UK Government in shaping the future relationship as per the Political Declaration, e.g. in relation to the Shared Prosperity Fund.
4. Extra money for 'left behind areas' above and beyond the Shared Prosperity Fund – to address the causes of Brexit.

It seems that they have also come to realise that the 'stable majority' they need to get the deal through, is not the same majority as the grouping which voted for the Brady amendment[17] – 2, 3 and 4 (particularly 2 and 4) seem to me to be attempts to entice Labour into supporting the deal.

Adam floated the idea of a fifth pillar – a vote at the end of the Transition Period for the UK to re-enter the EU (but on the same terms). I understand that although there are some legal issues with this, conversations in the EU seem to indicate if the political will was there, that this might be possible (as is the case with most things).

This was not shot down out of hand by Barwell, who has agreed to put the idea to the PM and continue talking to us. He also asked how many votes we think this would be worth, but we remained quiet on the issue. The content of this discussion is, of course, important. It does, however, also have the helpful by-product of keeping us on the radar of No 10/Government.

On reflection the nature of this discussion seems to me extraordinary. In the first place No 10/Barwell think it worthwhile to have direct

---

[17] Sir Graham Brady MP was chairman of the 1922 Committee in the House of Commons. On 29 January 2019, the Commons voted 317 to 301 to approve his amendment to the Brexit Next Steps motion, which called for 'the Northern Ireland backstop to be replaced with alternative arrangements to avoid a hard border, supports leaving the European Union with a deal and would therefore support the Withdrawal Agreement subject to this change'.

communication with Adam. As pertinently, in the conversation he comes up with the creative idea of placing a referendum at the end of the Transition Period, which as he says could attract support from both Remainers and Leavers in Parliament. Over the course of the next few days this appears to be the case.

It also contrasts vividly with the parochial event that happened in the Senedd at the beginning of the week. On Tuesday Mark Drakeford's office sent us a message that they would like to undertake an off-the-record briefing about Brexit with Adam and Paul Davies on the terms that had been agreed the previous week (in which we would try out the process for a limited period to see how it went). It transpired, however, that while Drakeford would be bringing his Special Adviser to the meeting, he was not willing to countenance Adam doing the same. On this basis, we refused to take part – though Paul Davies did.

So, in this momentous Brexit week, Adam had a one-to-one conversation with Barwell at No 10, but was excluded from talks in the Senedd itself. Trivial in the order of things, but all the same a bizarre commentary on the nature of Welsh politics.

The week began with more momentous matters, certainly so far as my own position is concerned. At the Monday morning staff meeting, Mabli Jones stunned us by announcing she is leaving – off to work with the Welsh Refugee Council. In the early evening Adam, Steffan and I head for a bar in the Bay. As we walk across, Adam says this should free up resources for me to continue in my Advisor role. There's a gleam in his eye as he talks. Finally, he can see his way clear to putting together a team that can deliver his mandate as leader. He's expansive and enthusiastic, until suddenly he pauses and stares directly over his pint at me: 'Well, have you decided?'

I hesitate, but then tell him I'm happy to commit until the October conference. I say I'm hoping that a year will be enough for me to help him get underway. I can then return to my own preoccupations. 'That's perfect,' he responds, without skipping a beat. 'We need to get on with things, time is slipping away.'

Week 16: 11 February 2019
Plaid Cymru Newydd

The focus this week is on Saturday's meeting in Aberystwyth, where we're unveiling the re-worked Robertson report and getting it through the Executive. Ahead of this I speak to Adam stressing that we need to plan in detail to make sure the thing works out well. So, on the Monday morning we have a meeting with Helen Mary Jones and persuade her to take charge of the day, chair the event, organise the timetable and so on. As it turns out she does a superb job.

The day goes well, though it all seems a bit unreal to me. At the start, in the large Medrus Room on the University campus, Helen hands out the report. The copies are numbered and we're instructed they must all be handed back at the end. It gives the impression of potential controversy and damaging disclosures, but actually the report is pretty mundane, largely about campaign processes and priorities, with hardly any surprises.

Certainly not to me, since I've read it all already, and in fact written a good deal of it. I sit at one of three tables, idly leafing through it during the half-hour we're given to read it before the proceedings start. Next to me is the Treasurer, Marc Phillips, who I've already briefed on the Nova Cambria think tank and *New Nation* aspects. We need his agreement to ensure the finance side of things can be covered – the setting up costs for the website and limited company registration for Nova Cambria. Understandably Marc is somewhat miffed, especially when I show him proof copies of *New Nation*. 'It's the first I've heard of this and you've reached the stage where it's going to print,' he says. 'I feel I'm being bounced. So will the Finance Committee. This is not the way to do things.'

He makes it clear he thinks Nova Cambria and the journal a good idea, but he's plainly cross. I explain that the costs of the first edition are covered, but he still feels bounced, as he puts it again, and I can hardly disagree.

So far as Angus Robertson's report is concerned the most controversial proposal is the idea for a name change. In Welsh it doesn't look particularly radical - Plaid Cymru Newydd. In English, of course, it's quite different – New Wales Party. Most people in the room are totally against. Yet they have no suggestions on how to combat the problem that the name change is supposed to address – the fact that Plaid is seen by very many people as a party for Welsh speakers.

Nobody disagrees with Plaid's need to craft an image and message that will find a common appeal across both Welsh-speaking and English-speaking Wales. But there are no new ideas to counter Robertson's main suggestion on how to achieve this. Plaid Chair, Alun Ffred Jones, underlines the point when he remarks, at the close of the session, that the gathering of about 20 people represents the top leadership of the party, but no-one is making use of the simultaneous translation, apart from Angus Robertson and myself.

At the end of the morning – in which Angus Robertson has proved he's a far better speaker than he is a writer of reports – Adam and I go for a coffee in the campus Arts Centre. There I show him the *New Nation* proofs, including a glowing profile of him by S4C broadcaster Angharad Mair, and he's enthusiastic. He's also still to come down from a high he experienced the previous evening when he appeared on BBC's *Any Questions*, from the Nant Gwrtheyrn National Language Centre at Llithfaen on Pen Llŷn. The first question was about Shamima Begum, a 19-year-old Muslim woman who was groomed to join Isis in Syria when she was 15 and now wants to return home to the UK. All the panellists agreed that she should be taken back, but the audience was totally unresponsive. Listening I felt things weren't going well, though it was the same for all the panellists, but Adam shone later in the programme. As the debate turned to climate change and Brexit, he received applause to every point he made, admittedly from a friendly audience. Now he tells me that, at first, he had had the same feeling as me, but then things got better.

Our discussion is cut short as he heads off to the Executive. Later that evening, Steffan Bryn sends me a text: 'Just a message to let you know that all went well at NEC, including agreement to release funds as seed capital for Nova Cambria.' A good day.

Week 17: 18 February 2019
Nova Cambria

The week begins with a meeting of Grŵp Brexit amidst breaking news of a crop of resignations by eight or nine Labour MPs at Westminster. We immediately launch into an intense discussion of its significance and what it might mean in Welsh terms. Adam makes it clear from the outset that, while we welcome any schism in the Labour Party, the group leaving are on the Right. He refers to Mike Gapes, MP for Ilford South since 1992: 'His politics are in a completely different place to ours. Over Iraq he was a war monger-in-chief, an ultra-Blairite.'

We quickly scan the Welsh horizon and conclude that it is doubtful whether any Welsh MPs might follow them, the only possible exceptions being Anna McMorrin (Cardiff North) who has been campaigning for a People's Vote, and Tonia Antoniazzi (Gower).

The First 100 Days of Plaid's New Leader

Both got in at the 2017 election, and both resigned from their front bench roles last June in protest against Corbyn's Brexit policy.

Adam suggests that we wouldn't want to consider any formal alliance, but a looser arrangement, a 'One Wales' group of Welsh MPs in the House of Commons, might be a possibility. He refers to a precedent in the Canadian Parliament in Ottawa when members of the Parti Québécois formed a Bloc Québécois with defecting members of the Québec Liberals. 'We need to be creative and agile in exploiting any opportunity,' he says. 'If we enlarge our movement in this kind of way it'll be a net gain for Wales.'

Joni Eds predicts there will be further seepage of Labour MPs who are rejecting Corbyn's internal revolution: 'They'll be joined by a few Tory defectors, an understanding with the Lib Dems will follow, and then there'll be the making of a fully-fledged political party, the New Democrats or some such formulation.'

A question then follows whether they can nudge ahead of the SNP's 35 MPs in order to become the third party in the House of Commons. We discuss the prospects of aligning with the SNP to form a Celtic Bloc of 39 MPs to provide an edge over any new grouping. Our MPs counsel against as we'll just be absorbed, lose our distinctive identity and also the advantages we currently have in being called to speak. Dafydd Wigley says: 'I've been here for 40 years. When the SNP have been the same size as us, they're all sweetness and light. When they're bigger they're not interested.'

After this the week quickly disappears. I help prepare FMQs around Mark Drakeford's inconsistency on Brexit, but have to leave early on Tuesday while Adam is asking them in the Chamber. I'm heading west to St. Davids in pursuit of the Festival of Ideas while Adam is off to the States, with Carl Harris, Steffan Bryn and Jill Evans for a week, first in Boston and then Washington DC. The main point of the trip seems to be meeting with Democrat strategists to gain some electioneering tips. Carl volunteered to be part of Obama's campaign a decade ago and made a lot of contacts which he is exploiting.

Meanwhile, I spend two days in Edinburgh, preparing the ground for a visit we're planning for Adam in the early summer. I have meetings with a number of academic friends I've known over the years, to renew contacts and get some first-hand understanding of the state of play north of the border. Professors James Mitchell, Lindsay Paterson and David McCrone are all Edinburgh academic observers of the scene whom I've known for many years. They are all welcoming, and it's heartening to realise that relationships of this kind, established over many years, count for something.

I also meet some new people. On the first day I visit the Scottish Parliament and see Fergus Mutch, the SNP's Director of Communications, and my opposite number, Ewan Crawford, Nicola Sturgeon's Chief Political Adviser (she has nine or ten others as well). I find Crawford interesting, but he's guarded, seeking my views but generally cagey about his own. Before I leave, he startles me by saying that the Scottish and Welsh Governments are negotiating a simultaneous debate next week, opposing a No Deal Brexit and seeking an extension to Article 50. He hopes we will be on board. I don't have the presence of mind to counter this on the spot, but later text him to say I think it essential, from Plaid's point of view, that the motion contains a commitment to a People's Vote.

Week 18: 25 February 2019
Polling our way

This is a week of opinion polls. They've been static, flatlining for more than a year, but now one – a YouGov poll for ITV Wales published on Monday – shows a shift in the tectonic plates and is moderately good for us. Another, by ICM – commissioned by BBC Wales – at the end of the week is much better.

The YouGov poll shows Labour's support falling (compared with last December) and ours edging up, though we're behind the Tories. The constituency result for the National Assembly is as follows

Labour: 32% (-8)
Conservatives: 26% (+1)
Plaid Cymru: 23% (+3)
Liberal Democrats: 8% (+1)
UKIP: 7% (+2)
Others: 5% (+2)

It's similar on the Regional List vote for the Assembly which produces an element of proportionality:

Labour: 29% (-7)
Conservatives: 24% (no change)
Plaid Cymru: 23% (+3)

Liberal Democrats: 6% (+2)
UKIP: 6% (+2)
Greens: 4% (no change)
Abolish the Assembly: 4% (-1)
Others: 4% (+2)

The statistics are projected to produce the following overall result for the Assembly

- Labour: 23 seats (20 constituency, 3 regional)
- Conservatives: 17 seats (10 constituency, 7 regional)
- Plaid Cymru: 16 seats (9 constituency, 7 regional)
- Liberal Democrats: 2 seats (1 constituency, 1 regional)
- UKIP: 2 seats (2 regional)

That gives us another four seats, approaching our target of 18 for the 2021 election, though crucially, of course, one behind the Conservatives. We need to be doing better and be ahead of the Tories to get over the line and have a shout of becoming a minority government. As ever, Labour's saving grace is the lack of a strongly focused opposition, which is split between the Tories and us.

What appears to be happening is that Labour is losing ground, probably due to its disarray at Westminster and Jeremy Corbyn's shortcomings over Brexit and antisemitism. Notably, of course, Mark Drakeford is a supporter of Corbyn. As yet, however, the support Labour is losing is being promiscuously distributed across the parties. We're benefiting, but only marginally better than the others.

In the entrails of the poll are questions about the popularity of the party leaders which provides a clue to why Labour's support is plummeting. Psephologist Roger Awen-Scully, of the Wales Governance Centre, in a piece for the *New Statesman*, comments on the lack of support for both Corbyn and Mark Drakeford, though the latter's position is especially stark in the context of the next Assembly election. He notes that in the past Welsh Labour have benefited from the popularity of Rhodri Morgan and Carwyn Jones but, and as we've predicted, Drakeford is not in their league:

> 'Drakeford faces two problems. The first is that most people in Wales simply have little or no idea who he is. When asked to rate him out of 10, fully 56% of all respondents chose the "Don't Know"

option. This is hardly a problem unique to him. All parties represented in the Welsh Assembly have chosen new leaders in the last 15 months, and none of them are recognised by most Welsh people. But Drakeford has already been First Minister for two months during a highly tumultuous political period. Moreover, Plaid Cymru's Adam Price would likely get a very substantial boost in public visibility during any general election campaign (as did Price's predecessor, Leanne Wood, in 2015).

'The second problem is that even many of those who have a view about Drakeford are not very favourable. This was seen during the Welsh Labour leadership contest last year: public ratings of him tended to lag behind those of the other contenders. Such continues to be the case in the latest poll. Drakeford averages no more than 4.0 out of ten; among those who recognise him Price fares significantly better at 4.6.

'For most of the last two decades, Labour's continuing dominance of politics in Wales has been underpinned by two factors: popular leadership and inept opposition. The first of those is now under significant threat. Meanwhile, under Price Plaid Cymru seem determined to offer a stronger alternative. The path to a serious threat to Labour hegemony in Wales may just be opening up.'

All of this is heartening, but it is eclipsed by the BBC Wales (ICM) poll, published on St. David's Day. These tables include the raw data, that is to say before they were 'adjusted' by the pollsters. Quite why they were adjusted is not clear except the pollsters plainly felt their respondents had exaggerated Plaid Cymru's position. In effect, they re-distributed Don't Knows and some of our vote to the benefit of Labour (up 3) and marginally the Tories (up 1).

Table 2: BBC Wales (ICM) poll (1 March 2019)

Constituency	YouGov	ICM	ICM Adjusted
Lab	32	31	34
Con	26	22	23
PC	23	30	27
LD	8	8	7
UKIP	7	5	5

The First 100 Days of Plaid's New Leader

Region	YouGov	ICM	ICM Adjusted
Lab	29	29	32
Con	24	21	22
PC	23	28	25
LD	6	6	6
UKIP	6	7	6

In any event, in his analysis, Plaid's in-house psephologist Dafydd Trystan judges that:

> 'Based on a detailed seat by seat analysis, these results suggest Plaid have strong prospects in Llanelli, Blaenau Gwent, Caerffili, Neath, and Cardiff West, together with realistic prospects in Aberconwy, Clwyd South, and Carmarthen West and South Pembrokeshire.'

Roger Awen-Scully calculated the seat distribution, based on the poll, as follows:

- Labour: 25 seats (22 constituency, 3 regional)
- Plaid Cymru 19 seats (11 constituency, 8 regional)
- Conservatives: 14 seats (6 constituency, 8 regional)
- Liberal Democrats: 1 seat (1 constituency)
- UKIP: 1 seat (1 regional)

Therefore, we not only exceed our lower end target of 18 seats, but crucially come out ahead of the Tories. This makes a minority government in the wake of 2021 a realistic prospect, and not just something that's a matter of faith amongst Adam's praetorian guard. It's hard to conclude that our efforts within Plaid Cymru over the past six months since Adam won the leadership have done much to contribute to this favourable prospect. It must overwhelmingly be down to Labour's difficulties and poor showing. Nevertheless, it does demonstrate that some Labour people are, at the very least, not averse to supporting us. It's a much-needed fillip to Adam's position and will serve him well as we approach the party's Spring conference in Bangor towards the end of March.

Week 19: 4 March 2019
The Group implodes

If last week felt like travelling along an exhilarating high wire, this one is the complete opposite. It begins late on Sunday evening with a worried e-mail from Adam. I realise I haven't seen him for the best part of a fortnight, during which he's been in Boston and Washington DC in the States. Now he's back and earlier appeared on BBC Wales' *Sunday Politics*, interviewed in the wake of the opinion polls. He thinks he underperformed. His e-mail reveals a raft of worries:

Progress on policy
1. I felt I came up short on *Sunday Politics* earlier. The truth is we haven't developed a single new policy of any significance since my leadership campaign. The emphasis on slow, steady, consensual policy building is understandable. Nova Cambria will help. But the reality is that at the moment we have nothing new or interesting to say on our solutions to Wales's problems. This is damaging to my brand and the one we are trying to build for the party. I need some pretty immediate solutions to this.
2. I need three new big policy ideas for my conference speech. How and where can I get them?
3. I need to hold one-on-ones with the policy leads.
4. My fear is that if we leave it to the spokespersons (as in 2016) we will end up without the necessary ideas. How can I take control of the process?
5. The more I think about it, the 9p income tax cut/LVT idea is a game changer. Are we doing serious work on that?

Newport West
1. How can we ramp up canvassing pretty immediately. I want this to be the best by-election campaign we have fought for 20 years. Are we up for that?
2. Who is in charge of the campaign day to day? There should be a lead staffer and a lead elected member.
3. Can we set targets for all elected members in terms of canvassing sessions and get them organised this week?
4. Can we use it as an opportunity to do genuine A/B testing or randomised control trials?

Spring Conference
1. What are we trying to get out of it? What is the plan to achieve that?
2. Themes for Speech?

USA Follow Up
1. Can I have confirmation that all US meetings have been followed up, with a plan for continued engagement.
2. Can I see the proposed report for the NEC.

This is a large agenda which we partially address as the week unfolds, but Adam only has limited time – Monday and Tuesday, much of which is taken up by Senedd business. We develop a good line on Accident and Emergency waiting lists for FMQs. However, by late on Tuesday he's travelling to Brussels for the annual meeting of the European Free Alliance – an underlying reason is the work he's putting in to bolster his relationship with Jill Evans. Even so, it means he's off again, and he's already been away for nearly two weeks. He won't be home until Sunday, since he's diverting to Edinburgh on the way home, for the Wales /Scotland game there on Saturday. I worry about the stress of all this travelling, not only on Adam himself, but his young family.

Monday and Tuesday disappear in a blur of activity. It begins on Monday with the usual staff meeting, with Steffan Bryn in the chair for the first time. Immediately afterwards Ewan Crawford, Nicola Sturgeon's Special Adviser calls. He tells me that the joint Parliamentary debate between Edinburgh and Cardiff is going ahead. I say we have heard this, via the Whips Office, but that we haven't been consulted. Ewan says he's heard we're determined to put down an amendment on a People's Vote, and urges me 'as a favour' to use my best endeavours to see if it can be withdrawn. I'm doubtful about this, but say I'll consult.

A short while later I call back to say that despite his entreaties, we're going ahead with our People's Vote amendment. He's appalled. Says it will seriously disrupt relationships in the European Parliament where not only Labour, but some SNP members from North-East Scotland are opposed to a People's Vote. 'It will destroy the united front we're trying to achieve,' he says. I advise that the only chance he has of getting Adam to relent is if Nicola Sturgeon makes a direct personal appeal to him.

The Politics of Co-Opposition

At 9am the next morning it's Mike Russell, not Sturgeon, who phones Adam. He argues that the motion, as it stands, represents the best that could be agreed by all parties – the SNP, Scots Lab, Scots Lib Dems, Scots Greens, and Welsh Labour. The SNP could not ensure buy-in from all within their own party and Scottish Labour to including a People's Vote commitment. It would weaken the motion if what is passed is different in two locations

In response Adam points out that in Russell's list of parties consulted, Plaid is notable by its absence: are we being asked to support a motion without having sight of the text that's already been shared with all the other parties? Plaid has recently succeeded in bouncing Drakeford to support a People's Vote, but he has since been rowing back. Passing this motion without an effort to amend it would achieve Drakeford's aim of excising a People's Vote from his lexicon. In addition, Plaid has an upcoming by-election in Newport West, so cosying up to Labour at the current time is not in our strategic interests. Moreover, and in any event, the Welsh Government will probably be able to vote our amendment down, so the SNP's aim of ensuring identical motions passed will still probably be achieved.

There's a meeting of Grŵp Brexit immediately following this call, and there is unanimity in supporting Adam's position. This is followed by similar agreement at the Shadow Cabinet. Indeed, for the most part the Shadow Cabinet is remarkably harmonious. This is partly because we're all buoyed by the opinion polls, to which Adam draws attention. Then there's the appearance of *New Nation* which has been laid out on the table. It provokes a generally constructive debate about its role, the place of Nova Cambria and its relationship with the party. Following this there's a very good presentation on policy development by our new research officer Fflur Elin.

However, under any other business, comes a bombshell when South-West Wales List AM Bethan Sayed announces that if Neil McEvoy is let back in the party, following his re-application to rejoin, she will leave. There is a stunned silence. Bethan elaborates a little before dissolving into tears. There is a rush of emotion, as other members around the table come to her support – Leanne Wood and Helen Mary Jones in particular.

Adam looks on appalled. He speaks lamely that we shouldn't be discussing this, as due process is underway. His own position is quite clear. As party leader he cannot, and will not, comment. However, it is agreed that Dai Lloyd and Helen Mary Jones will draw up a dossier to present to the party's Membership, Discipline and Standards Committee that will be dealing with the McEvoy application. This will need to demonstrate, with facts and paper trails, that his behaviour has not altered in the past year.

The meeting breaks up in despair and acrimony. Most repair to Leanne's office to console each other. Adam, myself, Steffan Bryn, and Siân Gwenllian repair to his. They're next door to each other so people speak in hushed tones.

Adam is distraught. 'This thing is taking over,' he says. 'People have more invested in this than getting into government in 2021.' Siân says she is sure she can persuade Bethan not to resign. I say something about the claimed misogyny endemic in the party mirroring Labour's problems over antisemitism. Adam concludes that, whichever way the panel's verdict goes, we cannot win. Whether McEvoy is kept out or allowed back in we lose. 'We're damned if we don't and damned if we do,' he says.

Week 20: 11 March 2019
Upping our game

Adam arrives in the office, mid-morning on Monday looking reasonably chipper. He has a full day ahead but calls me over for a brief chat in the meeting room. As I enter, I close the door and we settle down. 'I've something to tell you,' he says. I lean forward, worried that this might mean some unwelcome revelation, but no, it's just a story about his time at the game in Edinburgh.

It seems that late on Saturday night he found himself in the Sheraton Hotel where the Welsh team were staying. Most of them had gone to bed, but Ken Owens, the Welsh hooker was at the bar. He's from Carmarthenshire and Adam knows him a bit. They got into a conversation. Adam tells me Ken Owens is interested in politics. He's Labour but a supporter of independence. Likes him and Joni Eds. 'I think he's typical of those who could swing to us.'

'Be great to get an endorsement from him,' I say. Adam laughs. Then says he asked what Warren Gatland said when he came into the changing room after the game –after all it had been a bit scrappy, and the Welsh nearly blew it.

'Three words,' Owens told him. 'You fucking won.' I laugh, but Adam gets serious. 'No, really, we've got to get some of that. We've got to get a bit of self-belief into the Group. How do we do that? Gatland says the Welsh team have forgotten how to lose. That's what we need to do, forget how to lose. We need a coach, like Gatland. I can lead, but I can't be the coach as well. Could we get Gatland to come and talk to us, do you think?'

I suggest that Rhun ap Iorwerth might fit the bill. Adam looks thoughtful, then our conversation turns to *New Nation* and Nova Cambria which we launched over the weekend, in the sense that the Nova Cambria website went live, and *New Nation* landed on members' doorsteps.

Moreover, Martin Shipton has done us proud in the *Western Mail* today. I had lunch with him last week and gave him a copy, asking him to hold the story until after the weekend. The headline is 'Plaid aims to win war of ideas with think tank' and in it he quotes me in the following terms:

> 'Since Adam Price was elected as party leader, there has been a growing sense that Plaid could be in power after the next election. There's something in the air and recent opinion polls have confirmed that support is rising. But if the party is to have a real chance of success, it needs to be prepared – and that means whatever it does has to be based on solid intellectual foundations.
>
> 'Neither Nova Cambria nor *New Nation* will be controlled by Plaid, and those who contribute will have the freedom to think creatively. With Labour having been in charge of the Assembly since the outset, it's important for Welsh democracy that change comes. In the two years until the next election, we shall do what we can to ensure that happens.'

Martin has also written the day's editorial, helpfully welcoming our initiative:

> 'Plaid Cymru's announcement that it is launching an arms-length think tank and a new journal is evidence that the party leadership is taking seriously the aim of winning power at the next Senedd election in 2021.'

However, there's been some pushback because *New Nation* is completely in English, with no Welsh language element. Adam is resentful at the reaction. Says he was much influenced by *Radical*

Wales during the 1980s that was also published wholly in English. 'Do we want to prevent that happening to today's new generation that is coming through?' I say that Cynog Dafis' advice is to beef up *Y Ddraig Goch*, by appointing an editor who can commission some longer, more thoughtful articles. Adam agrees and asks me to find an editor.

In Edinburgh Adam had also run into Alun Davies, the Blaenau Gwent MS who in a previous life was a leading Plaid activist and is still friendly to the cause. He's also seriously disaffected over Corbyn and Brexit. It seems he's given Adam some feedback on First Minister's Questions. He says we need to improve our performance in two respects. We need to do more research and find firmer evidence on where the government is under-performing before launching into an attack. He also says Adam needs to use more humour to get under Drakeford's skin.

Adam takes these suggestions seriously. 'We need to up our game,' he tells me. This is all very well, given our resources. The fact of the matter is that while our researchers are well meaning, they are not very pro-active in coming up with new angles. Most of the ideas come from Adam or myself, and necessarily – given the other pressures on us – this tends to be hand-to-mouth, from week to week. Rattling Drakeford with jokes is even more difficult, but the points are well made.

This week we decide to go on health, which is an area we need to do more to occupy, since in recent months it has been a favoured Conservative topic. Between us we do some research and come up with the following questions which result in one of the more constructive exchanges we've achieved in recent months, not least because we're batting on Drakeford's own turf.

Adam Price: First Minister, last week in your speech to the Scottish Labour Party conference, you stated that social class, rather than geographical accident at birth, is the single most powerful factor in shaping people's lives. But, surely, seen through the prism of Welsh experience, poverty and place are hardly unconnected. Poverty is indeed the single most important determinant of life outcomes, but poverty is unevenly distributed, and is particularly concentrated in Wales – and that's, of course, after two decades of devolved Labour Government.

You referred to falling life expectancy across the UK, but it is true, is it not, that life expectancy is falling in Wales faster than anywhere else – indeed faster than anywhere in western Europe. To depart from the language of the seminar here, let's spell out what that actually means: the chances of a child born today in Wales living to the age of 90 are significantly lower than they are in England. Will you accept that this now represents a full-scale public health crisis here in Wales?

Mark Drakeford: I think the Member needs to be careful in the way that he deploys figures, because the evidence of falling life expectancy is very recent, and I don't think that you would sensibly project trends into a 90-year future on the basis of what we know so far. But I want to agree with the basic premise of what Adam Price has said. Of course, poverty has a shaping impact on people's lives, and that is why we are determined as a government to do everything we can to address the circumstances of people who live in poverty, and to use the levers that are in the hands of the Welsh Government to make a difference wherever we can. And that's something that we have been doing since the start of the devolution era and which we are determined to go on doing, even in the very constraining circumstances that austerity puts on our ability to fund all the public services to the extent that we know those services ideally would require.

Adam Price: Let's delve a little deeper into particular aspects of what I certainly regard as a growing public health crisis in Wales. Take the incidence of diabetes: the numbers diagnosed in Wales with diabetes is increasing and is now higher than anywhere else in the UK. The highest number of all in Wales and among the worst in the UK – 8% of the population – is in Gwent. Only last week the Assembly's Health Committee said that Wales is facing a national crisis in terms of our children's health. The latest figures from Public Health Wales show an increase in the numbers of obese four-to-five-years-olds over the last two years, with 27% overall now overweight or obese, compared with just 23% in England. The lack of physical activity among children is a primary factor, but surely the key drivers of this worrying trend are the limited role of physical activity in the curriculum and the lack of wider public interventions against obesity. And, surely, in this context, the biggest inactivity of all has been your own as a government.

Mark Drakeford: That was a question that was doing quite well until the end. So, where I agree with Adam Price on this, Llywydd, is that when you look at rising incidence of diabetes, when you look at rising incidence of obesity, the answer isn't, 'What is the health service going to do about it?' The answer is in that wider public health agenda that he outlined, and we look at the shaping causes that lie behind those figures. And they are to be found in poverty that drives people to have to shop in particular sorts of ways. So, diet and food poverty are part of all of this. The figures that were published of children arriving at the school door already overweight cannot have been caused by lack of exercise at school, because these children weren't in school at that point. But it is to do with ways in which people live their lives and it is up to Government to create the conditions in which people are able to take the actions that allow them to promote their own health into the future. So, it is that combination of actions that people themselves can take, but Governments have to act in order to give them the opportunities to act in that way. That is a public health agenda, and, to that extent, I agree with the points the Member was making.

Adam Price: Obviously, the determinants of this public health crisis are complex, interrelated, multiple. They're the result of a toxic cocktail of low incomes, poor housing, poor diet, low physical activity and high pollution. Some of these matters are reserved to Westminster, but many are within your sphere of control. Let's take cancer, for example. In the last six years for which figures are available, the long-term decline in cancer death rates has slowed markedly in Wales. Over the same period, the rate of decline in Scotland, which has a similar deprivation profile, has increased. Public Health Wales has said that the causes of these and other changes to death rates are not fully understood and are being explored further. Now, can I suggest that doesn't exactly convey a sense of urgency? Can I put it to you that the need to understand what is happening here and find answers is a matter of utmost urgency? People's lives literally are at stake. Your spokesman's response to the Health Committee's report was that the new school curriculum, due to come in effect in 2022, will include a focus on health and well-being. But that's three years away. Can we afford to wait three years when the crisis is happening to our children right now?

Mark Drakeford: Well, Llywydd, Adam Price is right when he points to some of the long-term trends that we are dealing with here. Every single generation since 1945 has been heavier than the generation that preceded it. And that has been true in times of economic success as well as times of economic decline. These are really long-term trends in which actions by Government cannot be expected to make a short-term difference. But we are not waiting for particular events in order to make a difference. We're already doing things. The Active Travel (Wales) Act 2013 passed by this Assembly makes a difference every day to the chances that children can walk or cycle to school. The actions that we are taking in the food field to try and make sure that those families that need the most help to access the type of diet that they need, to provide families with the skills to prepare the food that is good for the long-term health of their children – those are programmes that are happening in Wales today. If there are more things that we can do, as we will through the new curriculum, of course we will do them. Because we want to focus, as I said, Llywydd, on those levers that are most directly in the hands of the Welsh Government and then maximise the impact that they can have in the lives of families and children in Wales.

We don't score any instant hits out of this exchange – one of Adam's criteria of success is the extent to which we generate a news story, on the BBC website or in the *Western Mail*. However, the overall weakness of Drakeford's answers – generally agreeing with the points made in our questions and referring to long-term trends which are difficult to engage with in any way that indicates a specific policy success – reveals an administration that is struggling to come up with a policy agenda that can really address the fundamentals of the problems we've raised.

That evening I attend a Group dinner in the Senedd. Apparently, these are supposed to happen on the first Tuesday of each month – as an informal, get together – but this seems to be the first one held since I've been here, symptomatic perhaps of the lack of appetite for bonding. In any event it is a depleted Group that turns up – just six of the original twelve that were elected in 2016 (minus Steffan Lewis, of course, and also Simon Thomas). It's a reminder that the Group has declined to ten because of Dafydd Elis-Thomas's defection to serve in the Labour Cabinet, and Neil McEvoy's expulsion from the Group just over a year ago. Of the remaining ten, six attend the dinner: Adam, Delyth Jewell (who has replaced Steffan Lewis), Siân Gwenllian, Helen Mary Jones, Llyr Huws Gruffydd, and Rhun ap Iorwerth who arrives late. Dai Lloyd, Chair of the Group is away for some good reason, but also absent are Bethan Sayed and Leanne Wood. Apart from them there's me and Steffan Bryn, regarded apparently as 'senior staff who should attend'.

The event is held in a featureless oblong room with a long table that we occupy at one end. To begin with the lighting is extremely harsh, but Adam finds a way of dimming it, which helps. The conversation is cordial and cheerful enough, until Adam begins an exchange around how well things are going. Someone comments that it was in a room like this one, not far away, that the leadership question came to a head last April. Siân says it was then she first realised that the Group could not carry on without a contest. And it was following that dinner that Leanne invited a leadership challenge, saying, in effect, 'bring it on'. This prompts a wide-ranging discussion about the way things are going. It's mainly about how Leanne must be feeling, with a good deal of sympathy for the position in which she finds herself as a leader rejected by the party. It is a reminder of how much there is to do, to get the Group working together as a real team shaping up for 2021.

Week 21: 18 March 2019
The speech

For me this week began last week, so to speak. I'm producing a first draft of Adam's conference speech, which he is delivering in Bangor this coming Friday. It feels like a culmination of the first period of Adam's leadership, and indeed it is the end of the first part of his three-phase strategy to get into government in 2021.

The conference is plainly important for Adam's campaign. It is vital that it be seen as a success. He has to have visible acceptance by the party. He has to come over as a unifying figure. He has to cut through the Brexit noise and get some clear messages across – about our seriousness in campaigning to be the next government, our belief that we will be, and also that we have a stand-out programme for policy delivery when in government. In short, he has to make an outstanding speech – and I have to write it, or at least the first draft.

Adam, Carl, Steffan and myself met briefly last Wednesday to go over the conference narrative and the lines we wanted to pull out. I made the following notes about the speech:

- Explain what we've done so far in our progress to victory – changing the party, creation of Nova Cambria and *New Nation*, up in the polls, the string of local by-election victories, the momentum we're creating.
- Wales and Europe - our position in the Brexit debate.
- The New Wales we want to build – in contrast with Drakeford's 'begging bowl Wales' (Adam says it's a 'begging bowl with bells on') and his continued belief that everything will be OK just so long as Corbyn is elected.
- Concrete policy ideas – for the economy, education, and health – a 21st Century WDA; removing bureaucracy from teachers to let them get on with teaching; I have to come up with some ideas on health – so I come up with legislating to bring down waiting lists, following the example of the SNP government.
- We have to have something on the north-west – in the wake of the demise of Wylfa B in Anglesey. Adam suggests I get in touch with Carl Clowes[18] and mentions the importance of the western corridor and his Arfor idea.
- I suggest we end up with something emotional on Plaid's European vocation, in light of the London People's Vote march during our conference weekend.

It's a framework at least. Later I ask Adam about his trip to Brussels for the European Free Alliance annual conference at the end of last week. He says his speech received a good reception. 'I did the Greece and Rome thing,' he says. 'Got them crying in the aisles.' Later I hear this confirmed by Jill Evans. I ask him to send it to me. He does, and building on it, my final version of this section of his speech for conference comes out like this:

---

18 The late Dr Carl Clowes, a medical practitioner, was the founder of the Nant Gwrtheyrn National Language Centre near Llanaelhaearn; inaugural chair of the Antur Aelhaearn Community Co-operative; President of Dolen Cymru, the Wales-Lesotho relationship; and an ardent campaigner against nuclear power on Ynys Môn.

The First 100 Days of Plaid's New Leader

As I said at the outset, these are perilous times for our country. The British State looks close to cracking up. And yet at the same time its so-called political élite wants to drag us out of the European Union.

Tomorrow hundreds of thousands of concerned citizens from throughout these islands will march through London in opposition to this wilful destruction. Our thoughts and our hearts will be with them. We say to them, and to our friends across Europe:

> *You can try and take Wales out of the heart of Europe, but you cannot take Europe out of our hearts!*

And let's be clear about one thing. Brexit does not represent taking back control for our people. It involves moving power from one end of the Eurostar to the other, at neither of which do we currently have a seat at the top table. And no, Alun Cairns[19] does not count.

And if you don't have a seat at the table, you'll find that you're on the menu.

Leaving the European Union is no answer to our democratic deficit as a nation. We want to join the European Union as an independent member, trebling our MEPs, giving us a Commissioner, the Presidency of the Council on a rotating basis, and £billions of Cohesion funding until we are brought back up to decent levels of prosperity. When did London ever offer us that?

In the words of Winnie Ewing, "Stop the World we want to get on."

The young, in Wales as in Catalonia, will no longer accept our democracy denied, our future deferred.

And by young, I mean those not just young in age, but young in spirit too.

Like the 90-year-olds I met outside a polling station in Barcelona in the 2017 Independence referendum. They would not go home until

---

[19] At the time Alun Cairns, Conservative MP for the Vale of Glamorgan, was Secretary of State for Wales with a seat in the UK Cabinet.

they had voted. They had been waiting for that moment all of their lives. This is what they said and what we say here now too:

> *Our goal is a modest one.*
> *But we cannot renounce it.*
> *Though you place us in chains, real or metaphorical.*
> *We want to be. Ourselves. Together.*
> *We want to be free. And, sooner not later, we will.*

It's interesting to reflect how that early line about being at the heart of Europe evolved. I recalled how my daughter Morwenna used to wear a T-shirt with the slogan: 'You can take the girl out of Wales/ But you can't take Wales out of the girl'. I turned that into:

> You can take Wales out of the European Union
> But you can't take Europe out of Wales.

Which Adam adapted to:

> You can take Wales out of the heart of Europe
> But you can't take Europe out of our hearts.

This kind of iteration took place over the whole week leading up to the speech. I delivered the first draft to Adam last Sunday, early afternoon, having worked through most of the weekend. I took a break to watch the Wales game against Ireland, and was glad that Wales won, not least because I'd deployed Warren Gatland in our cause:

> The new Wales we're fighting for is one that is self-confident, optimistic, ambitious, dynamic. To get there we need a bit of Warren Gatland's spirit.

> As well as having a rugby team that's forgotten how to lose, we need to be a nation that forgets how to lose. It's about building belief and confidence: This is what Gatland says:

>> *"If you want something badly enough and really believe it can happen, it often does."*

By the time we'd got to Thursday morning, Adam had added in so much new stuff the speech was running to 7,000 words, which was 2,000 words too long. I spent much of the morning cutting it back to 5,000. Then I jumped in the car and headed north to Bangor.

Meanwhile, the *Western Mail*'s Martin Shipton comes up with a piece on the Friday morning of the conference. Entitled 'Price scrums down to carry leadership vision forward', it's supportive of our ambition to become a party of government:

> At a time when Brexit is squeezing the life out of political discourse, it's refreshing to see a political party concentrate on developing its own policy programme.
>
> For a while, then, we can set to one side the unprecedented chaos at Westminster and assess how realistic Plaid Cymru's aspiration to take over the Welsh Government in 2021 may be.
>
> Plaid's leader, Adam Price, is certainly trying to stir up a sense of momentum. Buoyed by recent polling figures suggesting his party may be within striking distance of Labour in a notional Assembly election, he has tapped into the zeitgeist created by Wales's Grand Slam victory to propose a transition from support for the national rugby team into support for the Welsh party that markets itself on the basis of putting Wales first.
>
> This is a bold ambition and one that has not proved spectacularly successful in the past. Plaid loyalists have frequently reflected ruefully on the Welsh public's ability to restrict nationalistic inclinations to sporting contests. But we are living through strange political times, and the conventional wisdom that Plaid does best when there's a Labour government at Westminster doesn't necessarily hold.
>
> Ironically, it's Brexit that may have turned such wisdom on its head. Looking at Plaid's prospects as dispassionately as possible, the party has a number of advantages as well as a number of "challenges" – the habitual presumption by some that the party is for Welsh speakers only, the antagonism towards Welsh independence and the difficulty in getting its message across.

However much Plaid might like to develop its policy agenda in a space discrete to Wales, Brexit is inescapably the issue of the moment. Since Mr Price was elected leader six months ago the party has been unequivocal in its support for a further referendum. By settling on a clear Brexit policy, Plaid is now able to distinguish itself from the Conservatives and Labour, both of which parties have equivocated to the point of incoherence.

Having a clear policy on Brexit marks Plaid out as a party that is not afraid to come off the fence and adopt a position it argues would clearly be to Wales's advantage.

Such a stance plays into Plaid's second advantage: having elected Adam Price as its leader. Through its 90-plus years of existence, Plaid has veered between being a campaigning pressure group and being a party that wants to wield power. Before devolution, that was understandable. As a party that only fields candidates in Wales, Plaid was never going to be involved in government in Westminster. The most it could hope for was the ability to extract concessions from the larger parties when neither had a working majority. Sometimes that led to a degree of self-indulgence, a trait that persists in the party to this day.

But in the post devolution era, where Plaid has a chance of entering government, it's important to have a leader who takes the broadest view of policy and takes improving the Welsh economy and public services as seriously as possible. As an economist with ideas of his own, Mr Price is well placed to keep his party focused on this bigger picture.

At the end of a hundred days of Adam's leadership this is as good and fair – and also optimistic – a summary of where we have arrived that we could reasonably have hoped for at the outset.

Blown off Course

Here my weekly diary, of the first hundred days, ends. After this point I felt, perhaps subconsciously, that the prospects for our project of getting Adam Price elected as leader of a Minority Government in 2021, were fading fast. This was directly attributable to Brexit. Not only was it draining our energy and momentum, it was completely transforming the Conservative Party. In England the Conservatives had become an English nationalist party, and that same process was eviscerating any autonomous Welsh identity out of the Conservatives in Wales. Instead, they were becoming a mere echo of the values and priorities of the Conservatives at Westminster. They were now an alien force with whom collaboration was impossible. There could be no possibility of Plaid leading a minority Government in the Senedd. To do so we would have to rely on Conservative support. Now, due to fall-out from Brexit that would be neither forthcoming nor acceptable.

Nonetheless, the momentum built up during the first six months of Adam Price's leadership kept the party going into the European Parliament elections in May when Plaid polled ahead of Labour for the first time in a Wales-wide election. Compared with the European elections in 2014 it was as though a kaleidoscope had been shaken with a completely different pattern emerging. The most successful parties were those that most strongly identified with either the Leave or Remain position on the European Union, as shown in the table below.

Table 3: European Parliament Elections in Wales: % votes for the parties [20]

Party	2019	2014	2009
Brexit Party	32.5	0	0
Plaid Cymru	19.6	15.3	18.5
Welsh Labour	15.3	28.1	20.3
Welsh Liberal Democrats	13.6	3.9	10.7
Welsh Conservatives	6.5	17.4	21.2
Wales Green Party	6.3	4.5	5.6
UKIP	3.3	27.6	12.8

The newly formed Brexit Party headed the poll, at the expense of both UKIP and the Welsh Conservatives. On the other side, Plaid campaigned strongly for Remain and a second referendum, a position that shored up its support. At the same time Plaid's second place was largely due to the collapse in support for Labour which had been ambivalent on the European Union. In the wake of the election

---

20 Senedd Research, *How did Wales vote? European election results*, 4 June 2019.

Mark Drakeford came out in support of a referendum, but by then it was too late.

Moreover, Plaid maintained its momentum into the summer months. In July a YouGov poll placed Plaid in the lead for the forthcoming 2021 Senedd election for the first time ever. Again, however, it was due to a substantial fall in Labour support rather than any major increase for Plaid. In the 2016 Assembly election Labour won 34.7% of the constituency vote and Plaid 20.5%.

Table 4: Senedd Constituency vote: ITV Cymru and Wales Governance Centre (YouGov, July 2019)[21]

Plaid	Labour	Con	Reform UK	Lib Dem	Green	Other
24%	21%	19%	19%	12%	4%	2%

By now Adam Price himself had veered to the view that the Brexit debate was fatally undermining our prospects for forming a minority government after the 2021 election. The day after the European Parliament election he sent me an email acknowledging that our project was blown off course. We urgently needed an alternative. He wanted ideas on what our options might be. In response I drafted a paper entitled *Strategic Themes 2019-2020*. This began by pointing out how Welsh Labour had consistently out-manoeuvred us by the simple tactic of owning Plaid territory. Calling itself **Welsh** Labour, it had morphed into a soft nationalist party, one with which Welsh identifying people could feel safe in placing their allegiance:

> Welsh Labour has self-consciously underlined this tactic by constantly declaring it is 'standing up for Wales'. It has cleverly distanced itself from London Labour, although only in terms of political rhetoric. Hence it adopted "clear red water" to distance itself from unpopular London Labour interventions, such as the Private Finance Initiative for investing in public services, or the war in Iraq. However, we have seen this approach unravel in recent weeks with the European election campaign and the leadership of Mark Drakeford.

> Against the overwhelming sentiment of its supporters in Wales, London Labour continued to blindly pursue a course of "constructive

---

21 www.itv.com/news/wales/2019-07-29

ambiguity" on a People's Vote through the European election campaign. And far from 'standing up for Wales' by opposing this, Drakeford aligned himself with the London leadership's approach. The result was a collapse in Labour's vote while Plaid's firm and unambiguous stance in favour of a People's Vote reaped the dividend of increased support. We now need to follow up this breakthrough inside Welsh Labour's outer defences with a deliberate strategy of placing our tanks firmly on the lawn of its inner sanctum. We need to colonise policy areas that have traditionally been most associated with Welsh Labour. We need to demonstrate not only that they have been indolent and ineffective in their approach in these areas, but that we have the energy, urgency and innovation to tackle them more successfully.

I suggested three areas as examples of where we should develop our policy and profile: child poverty, climate change, and the Valleys Metro.

A third of Welsh children – some 206,000 – were living in poverty, with most of them concentrated in Labour voting areas, in the Valleys and the poorer parts of Wrexham, Cardiff, Newport and Swansea. The numbers were emblematic of Labour's record of promising much but delivering little. In the early years of devolution, Communities First, an extensive largely European-funded programme, comprised a multitude of schemes of varying quality, spread too thinly across Wales. Partly because of that it was largely ineffective. We needed a more focused policy which should be free school meals for all primary school children in Wales. This had the additional advantage of chiming well with Mark Drakeford's signature approach of progressive universalism. Despite this, on the three occasions leading to the 2021 election when Plaid proposed motions on the floor of the Senedd calling for free school meals, Labour voted them down.

Labour had followed our lead in the Senedd by declaring a 'Climate Emergency', but what would that mean in terms of delivery? On past form, and left to itself, the Government was unlikely to come up with an agenda beyond warm declaratory support. There was an opportunity for Plaid to produce practical policies. These, I suggested, should focus on small-scale community-owned energy initiatives, promoted by a Renewable Energy Agency.

The South Wales Metro had the potential for being transformative for the economy of the Valleys. If the project as originally conceived was to be delivered, there would be an extensive network of light rail with complementary bus services and through-ticketing.[22] New housing would be aligned with the network and new stations would be associated with economic and community development hubs. A project at scale on these lines would cost at least £3 billion, way beyond what Labour had in mind. There was also a strong case for establishing a Valleys Development Agency to ensure the project was delivered. Here again, was a contrast with Labour's approach. It was failing to deliver the necessary investment and would certainly oppose an agency through fear of losing control.

The paper marked the beginning of a process that led to Plaid's 2021 election Manifesto. It was a return to the approach the party had traditionally relied upon: first, developing distinctive policies for building Wales as a nation; and then seeing how far we could bring Welsh Labour along with us in supporting them.

Part III describes how we utilised this familiar role into forging the Co-operation Agreement.

---

22 The original proposal for an electrified, light rail Metro to integrate Cardiff and its Valleys hinterland was made by M. Barry, *A Metro for Wales's Capital City Region: Connecting Cardiff, Newport and the Valleys* (IWA, 2011).

Part III

The Agreement

4

Negotiating the Agreement

In late May 2021, shortly before the opening of the first exploratory stage of the negotiations that resulted in the Co-operation Agreement, Adam Price sent me an email: 'We have an opportunity to snatch an historic victory from the yawning jaws of defeat.' At the election earlier that month Labour had equalled its best ever result, also achieved in 2003 and 2011, when it increased its constituency vote by 5% to 39.9% to gain a seat and win 30 MSs, exactly half of the 60 Senedd seats. The Conservatives also had a good result, increasing their constituency vote by 5% to 26%, gaining five seats and raising their seat count from 11 to 16. As a result, Plaid was forced into third place with a static vote share of 20% though increasing its seats from 12 to 13.

Judged by these statistics, the election was certainly a defeat for Plaid. However, the party had broadly sustained its position in what was a difficult and unprecedented contest dominated almost entirely by Covid in which Mark Drakeford had commendably played to his strengths. Effortlessly, it seemed, he floated to victory on an incoming tide of recognition and approval. Yet before the onset of the Covid lockdown he had been virtually unknown to the Welsh electorate. Indeed, until then many voters were barely aware of the existence of the Senedd, let alone a Welsh Government that made vital decisions about their everyday lives. For instance, many had believed it was the Westminster Government that was responsible for the Welsh health service.

The pandemic changed all that. For more than a year leading to the election Mark Drakeford held forth in daily televised press conferences on the life and death decisions he'd made due to the pandemic. In the Senedd, the opposition parties were left with walk-on parts. Little wonder that during the election the three words most associated with the Labour Party in voters' minds were 'Welsh', 'Mark' and 'Drakeford', as illustrated in the pollster's word cloud displayed on page 15.

Plaid's performance, measured by the party's own expectations, was disappointing. Overall, it gained a seat and came within a handful of votes of adding another on the the North Wales Regional List. In addition, Plaid won substantial majorities in all five constituencies in its heartland – Ynys Môn, Arfon, Dwyfor Meirionnydd, Ceredigion, and Carmarthen East and Dinefwr. This underlined the importance and opportunity of its Arfor proposals. At the same time, however, Plaid lost the Rhondda, while the overall outcome of a 13-strong Senedd Group was at the lower end of its expectations. Crucially, Plaid remained in third place behind the Conservatives, and so was nowhere near being able to form or be part of the government for the sixth Senedd. Five more years of opposition politics beckoned.

Nevertheless, soon after the election Mark Drakeford and Adam Price agreed to open exploratory negotiations on reaching a shared programme. Drakeford made it clear that he was interested in tackling substantive issues. The way he put it was that he wanted more than the 'low hanging fruit'. The question was why? With 30 seats Labour could continue governing on its own. What were the attractions of a deal with Plaid? It became clear there were three.

In the first place Labour had long anticipated that there would be a need for an agreement of some kind and, despite the unexpected success of the result, dealing with the fallout from the pandemic still argued in favour of co-operation on what it described as a shared agenda. It was noteworthy, too, that Labour's 2021 manifesto was short of policies and there was a need for new ideas for the forthcoming Senedd term. Moreover, polling among Labour supporters revealed strong support for collaboration with Plaid.

Secondly, the Welsh Government needed consistent and reliable support on the floor of the Senedd if it was to tackle some of its major policy challenges. Difficult problems included climate change, the second homes crisis, and developing a long-term plan for social care. Concerted opposition would undermine the prospects of real achievement, but co-operation between Plaid and Labour would provide an 'unstoppable force' – a phrase the Labour side used in the negotiations.

However, the most immediate reason for a deal was the concerted attack on Welsh devolution by the Westminster Tory Government. In early June 2021, Drakeford attended an inter-governmental Covid response meeting at Number 10 where he stressed the importance of a four-nation approach. He argued that progress would only be possible if the Johnson administration operated in a spirit of mutual respect, and accorded parity of esteem between the Westminster Government and its devolved counterparts. Yet within days the Westminster Government briefed *The Sunday Times* that in future the Foreign Office and other departments were to refer to the UK as 'one country'. They were to also avoid using the 'four nations' description.[1] Mark Drakeford was sure this was a direct response to the points he had made during the Inter-Government meeting. 'We have serious problems,' the Labour negotiators told Plaid. 'They are coming for our country not our parties'.

The Negotiators

One of the more remarkable aspects of the negotiations, which took place over an extended period of nearly six months, was that they remained confidential. For much of this time, outside the small number of people immediately involved, no-one else in their respective parties, nor indeed within the wider civil service or Welsh Cabinet knew that they were even happening.

This proved controversial for some in both parties when the Agreement was first revealed to them, but it was vital if the talks were to have a chance of success. At the start there was no clear agenda and there were potential risks to both sides. If word had leaked out, there were plenty of factions that would have found reasons to sabotage the discussions. Compromises were inevitable and, for this reason, Plaid insisted from the outset that nothing could be agreed until everything was agreed. It was always going to be easier to sell the deal once it could be seen in the round, rather than allow the inevitable trade-offs to be argued in isolation.

On each side were three negotiators: two political advisors and the respective chief whips, part of their leaders' most immediate support teams.

For Labour, Mark Drakeford fielded two of his closest political advisors, Jane Runeckles and David Davies. First recruited in 2003, Runeckles worked as a political adviser within the government until 2009 when she left to become Campaigns and Policy Officer with the Wales TUC. She returned to the government in 2016 and became

---

[1] *The Sunday Times*, 6 June 2021.

Drakeford's Principal Special Adviser when he was elected First Minister two years later. This extended experience provided her with an expert knowledge of the innermost workings of the government, which proved vital in shaping the operational architecture of the Co-operation Agreement, especially in the later phases of the negotiations.

David Davies was a more recent recruit into the role though he had known Drakeford for many years as chair of his Cardiff West constituency Labour Party. A retired senior NHS Wales manager, Davies also had a track record of involvement with cross party organisations, including Cymru Yfory.[2]

Plaid's political advisors in the negotiations were myself, as Adam Price's Special Adviser, and key staffer Steffan Bryn. Although still in his 20s, Bryn had already gained considerable political experience having led campaigns in the student movement, worked for the Welsh Language Commissioner, and as a researcher with Adam Price following his election to the Senedd in 2016. Shortly after Price became leader, Bryn was appointed to the role of Chief of Staff to the Senedd Group.

The remaining members of each team were Vale of Glamorgan MS Jane Hutt and Arfon MS Siân Gwenllian. Hutt was Labour's chief whip and a close Drakeford ally who had experience as one of Labour's lead negotiators in the talks that led to the One Wales coalition in 2007. Gwenllian was Plaid's chief whip and a leading supporter of Adam Price in his campaign for the party leadership in 2018.

The negotiations took place in three phases. The first, from June to late August involved just the Special Advisers. Over a series of meetings, mainly over Zoom, the broad scope of the policy commitments was agreed, areas of disagreement identified, the narrative established, and the initial versions of the Agreement drafted. During September and into October the composition of the negotiating teams changed. The politicians, Jane Hutt and Siân Gwenllian now took the lead, joined by Jane Runeckles and Steffan Bryn, plus a few senior civil servants and communications advisers

---

2   Cymru Yfory/Tomorrow's Wales, chaired by the Archbishop of Wales Dr Barry Morgan, was set up in 2004 to campaign for implementation of the recommendations of the Richard Commission: legislative powers, increased membership and proportional representation for the Senedd, partially delivered in the 2011 referendum.

from both sides. Whereas the earlier period had focused on policy, these weeks were largely devoted to hammering out the mechanisms for implementing the Agreement.

Finally, in late October and into November, Mark Drakeford and Adam Price had a series of long one-to-one meetings, usually on Sunday afternoons in Cathays Park, to finalise the most difficult areas and to hammer out the detailed wording. Both had to take hard decisions, but by then the shape of the Agreement, with its extensive list of policies desirable to both sides had come into full view. The overall offer proved an alluring incentive to prevent either side walking away due to concessions they felt constrained to make.

Negotiating a Programme for Government

Before the election Labour undertook a comparative analysis of the two party's manifestos and placed Plaid's generally more ambitious policy proposals into three categories of difficulty:

- Affordability: in many cases there simply wasn't the money to implement them.
- Competence: in some cases, implementation required powers that were not devolved to the Senedd.
- New structures: many proposals entailed the creation of new executive agencies, which created a problem for Labour – that is to say, they would require a reversal of the 'Bonfire of the Quangos' that had taken place in the early 2000s.

Nonetheless, it was agreed that as a starting point, both sides would produce a paper listing ten priorities on which agreement might be reached. Labour's list was minimalist, making clear an intention to limit any agreement's breadth and extent. Not only that, most of the items on the list were sure to attract Plaid support, and indeed many had been previously announced, or were so relatively uncontroversial that they hardly needed an agreement to make progress:

1. Senedd reform
2. Constitution Commission
3. National Care Service / Welsh speakers in social care
4. Second homes
5. Reform of the school day / terms

6. Council tax reform
7. New medical school in the north
8. Basic income pilot
9. Peace Academy
10. Growth of indigenous Welsh firms

In contrast Plaid Cymru tabled a list of ten themes rather than topics, covering:

1. All-Wales spatial planning and development, with special attention for the Arfor and Valleys regions
2. Welsh-medium early years education
3. A new Welsh democracy and constitution based on Wales's right to self-determination
4. The Climate Emergency
5. A Welsh Green Deal
6. A National Health and Social Care Service
7. Reducing child poverty
8. Farming and sustainable food production
9. Young People
10. Action on the housing crisis

Labour stated that there was nothing in Plaid's paper that they were ideologically against. However, there were constraints in terms of the budget and Welsh Government powers. Plaid's position was there was no point to an agreement unless it produced gains of national significance. After some weeks of discussion, it was agreed to move forward on the basis of four pillars, following a pattern that had been set out in the One Wales agreement in 2007:

Pillar 1 – Context and narrative of why Plaid and Labour were coming together to present a joint programme for the forthcoming three years
Pillar 2 – Constitutional and Senedd Reform
Pillar 3 – Policy Programme
Pillar 4 – Machinery for Implementation

The negotiations that ensued concentrated on the last two, with Plaid giving most attention to policy and Labour to the operational aspects. In many respects the latter were the most novel part of the agreement, certainly in Welsh and wider British experience. From the outset there was tacit agreement that a formal coalition, with Plaid Ministers in the government, was not on the table. In the first place Labour's commanding position, with 30 Senedd members to Plaid's 13, made it politically difficult for Labour to justify. Moreover, from Plaid's perspective, there was a strong wish to retain its distinctive role as an Opposition party which Ministerial posts would inevitably compromise.

However, towards the end of August this tacit understanding was de-stabilised when the coalition deal negotiated between the Greens and the SNP in Scotland resulted in the Greens having two Cabinet Ministers. The contrast with the position in Wales was stark. The Greens had seven out of 129 members in the Scottish Parliament, while Plaid had 13 out of 60 members in the Senedd.

Moreover, in the previous administration the Welsh Government had been happy to accept two non-Labour members as Ministers, the Liberal Democrat leader Kirsty Williams and former Plaid MS Dafydd Elis-Thomas. The answer to this point was that, in effect, the two Opposition members had entered the government as individuals rather than party representatives, and had voted with Labour almost without exception. It was also clear, however, that if Plaid persisted in seeking representation in the Cabinet there would be no deal.

During the early months of the negotiations Adam Price took no direct role. Nevertheless, throughout he kept a close eye on progress and made critical internal interventions at key moments. This was one, in which he argued:

> 'In any negotiations getting a "No" is one of the best things that can happen, especially if it's the first time the other side give you a definite answer. It's a gift. We should step back and leave emotion behind. It's an opportunity to explore their thinking: Why are they're saying no? What lies behind it?
>
> Why are they saying "No" to our demand for Ministers in the Government? Is it just the thought of having Plaid inside their tent? We know Labour, or parts of it anyway, hate Plaid Cymru. Is it a fear of having me involved, with me putting my ego first? But I'm not at all interested in becoming a Minister. This demand of ours is not driven by ego. For us the programme is far more important. At

the same time, our argument for Ministerial involvement has two powerful reasons:

- In order for us to be able to sell the Agreement to the party.
- Plus, we need to have our people in there to ensure delivery, through our knowledge, commitment and representation.

How much leverage do we have? We need to inspire them with the positive reasons for doing a deal. It's not just a matter of providing them with confidence and supply but, more fundamentally, it's providing Drakeford with a legacy. Nonetheless, at this stage we shouldn't compromise on our position or give in. Just say we're interested in hearing the arguments for their "No". We could then say to them: "Over to you... what are you prepared to give us and will you put it on paper? What are you willing to accept?" After all, they've mentioned a bespoke, creative alternative to Ministers. What would that look like?'

What then transpired was that while Plaid conceded on Ministerial positions – instead agreeing to the involvement in government of two Plaid Designated Senedd Members and two Plaid Special Advisers – it made substantial progress on the depth and breadth of agreed policy positions. In effect, what was negotiated was a Programme for Government framed by Plaid Cymru. Not all the party's objectives were achieved – especially in the field of economic development and an all-Wales approach to spatial planning, with the creation of economic regions and development agencies for the western seaboard and the southern valleys. Nevertheless, significant advances were made in constitutional, social, and environmental policy.

Co-opposition

Over the course of six months the Agreement went through many iterations but finally ended up with 46 specific commitments under four main themes, which are detailed in the Appendix. As discussed in the opening chapter, the greater proportion of these commitments emanated from Plaid Cymru's manifesto. However, what caused most controversy in the weeks following the Agreement was not the policies it contained, but rather the mechanisms put in place to implement it. By the end of the negotiations both parties were clear that while they wanted an ambitious policy programme, they did not, for different reasons, want a formal coalition. Having fought a successful election, Labour would have found agreeing to Plaid Ministers within its government difficult to sell to its membership. As for Plaid Cymru, it was anxious to sustain its separate identity as an opposition party, not least to ensure that it could continue receiving funding for its Group in the Senedd.

The compromise, drawing on precedents beyond the UK – and especially the co-operation agreements in 1995 and 2002 between the Swedish Social Democratic Minority Government and the Swedish Left and Green Parties – was a half-way house, what Adam Price termed Co-Opposition. In summary the mechanisms negotiated included:

- A Joint Oversight Board convened jointly by the First Minister and the Leader of Plaid Cymru to provide strategic focus for the implementation of the Agreement.
- A Co-operation Agreement Unit led by a senior civil servant, and staffed by a further half-dozen civil servants to: (i) provide logistical and organisational support for joint decision-making by Plaid Cymru and Welsh Ministers; (ii) support delivery of the Co-operation Agreement policy commitments; and (iii) serve as a gateway to the wider Welsh Government civil service.
- Two designated Lead Members from the Plaid Cymru Group, plus deputies from the Group to oversee progression of the Agreement.
- Joint Policy Committees comprising Welsh Ministers and designated members of the Plaid Cymru Group to meet regularly and reach agreement by consensus on issues covered by the Co-operation Agreement.
- Appointment of two Special Advisers within the Co-operation Agreement Unit nominated by the Leader of Plaid Cymru to provide day-to-day support.
- Additional specialist advisers with appropriate expertise appointed, if required, to work with the Plaid Cymru designated members on specific areas of the Co-operation Agreement by the mutual agreement of the First Minister and the Leader of Plaid Cymru.

By the time the Agreement was brought to an end, after two-and-a-half years, Plaid had five Special Advisers working within the Co-operation Agreement Unit, located in Cathays Park at the heart of the Welsh Government. The Unit began with two officials providing support, but by the end these had expanded to seven, with the administration being conducted through the medium of Welsh.

All of this amounted to 'impressive creativity', according to Laura McAllister, Professor of Public Policy at Cardiff University:

> '... the creation of designated members (who look like quasi-ministers?) is a clever move as it protects party independence and the resources and status that come with it. Plaid has also secured two Special Advisers, which is an important win, but it's going to be a strange and unusual role, working to a Labour-only Cabinet, and on a day-to-day basis with a Labour-appointed Spad team.
>
> Providing "day-to-day support for the range of areas covered in the Co-operation Agreement" is the remit of those advisers, and it's normal for Special Advisers not to work on party political or campaigning matters. There isn't an obvious precedent for this kind of arrangement, but overall this looks imaginative and might be critical for holding the co-operation agreement together. However, I'd wager that to do this for three years is going to require emotional and personal skills as much as committees and political savvy.'[3]

The Welsh Conservatives attacked the collaboration as anti-democratic. Their leader in the Senedd, Andrew R.T. Davies wrote:

> 'To say this deal places the Senedd and the structure of governance in Wales in unchartered territory is an understatement. Before us, we see a coalition in all but name. To underline this, Plaid Leader Adam Price will regularly join Mark Drakeford at Cathays Park for joint press conferences. But at the same time, he'll supposedly be scrutinising him at First Minister's Questions every Tuesday afternoon. And the Coalition Agreement is so wide-ranging, there will be few issues Plaid will actually be able to scrutinise. Forty-six areas of governance are now covered by this coalition deal. And Adam Price is riding two horses, simultaneously acting as a coalition partner while being an opposition party leader too.'[4]

---

3   L. McAllister, 'Labour have signed a deal but what does it mean for the future of politics in Wales?' (*Western Mail*, 4 December 2021).
4   A.R.T. Davies, 'Labour-Plaid deal poses serious questions for the Welsh Parliament' (www.iwa.wales, 6 December 2021).

Similar worries were echoed by several Labour backbenchers. Caerphilly MS Hefin David said:

> 'The key issue is that designated members are accountable – that's the most important thing. I think you can't have government ministers answering questions in the chamber and not Plaid Cymru members if they are involved in taking government decisions. I want to scrutinise them. I want to ask them the questions and the mechanisms need to be in place for that.'[5]

Alun Davies, the MS for Blaenau Gwent added that while the Cooperation Agreement might not be declared a coalition, it certainly looked like one:

> 'Plaid is clearly part of the executive. In having access to the civil service and a clear supervision role overseeing the budget they cannot maintain their position as simply another opposition party.'[6]

These views prompted Elin Jones, the Senedd Presiding Officer, to take legal advice on whether Plaid Cymru's new status meant they could continue as a Group in the Senedd or should be regarded as being part of the Welsh Government. Her view was the former, confirmed by the legal advice.[7] However, in a written statement she acknowledged that while Plaid Cymru remained an opposition party, it was also co-operating with the Welsh Government on an agreed policy programme. She added that, 'as an evolving democracy we should be prepared to govern in different ways which work in the interests of the people of Wales and I welcome any move by political parties that seeks to bring together different views for the common

---

[5] BBC Wales, 2 December 2021.
[6] *Ibid.*
[7] From Lord Pannick KC and Marlena Valles of Blackstone Chambers, London: 'The Government of Wales Act 2006 [GoWA] sets out the position with clarity. Section 25(8) of the Act states: 'For the purposes of this Act a political group is a political group with an executive role if the First Minister or one or more of the Welsh Ministers appointed under section 48 belong to it.' As Elin Jones commented, 'As far as GoWA is concerned, therefore, the references to 'executive role' only apply to a party group that has entered government in the sense of having at least one member appointed as a Welsh Minister or as the First Minister.'

good.' Nonetheless she resolved that the scrutiny functions of the Senedd should be altered in a range of ways. Most importantly, she said, 'The Leader of Plaid Cymru will continue to be able to ask three questions without notice to the First Minister each week, although I would not expect those questions to be used to promote any policy areas covered by the Agreement.'[8]

Delivery

The Co-operation Agreement's commitments were not set in stone. All of them required further policy development. Even the most eye-catching and immediately deliverable commitment, free school meals for all primary school pupils, needed further research, on how locally sourced food provision could be guaranteed. The same was the case with the commitment to increase public sector procurement within Wales: 'We will carry out a detailed analysis of the public sector supply chains and promote the purchasing of made-in-Wales products and services.'

Much would also depend on Ministers providing an effective lead to their civil servants. There are all manner of ways in which civil servants can delay, divert, otherwise obstruct, or even sabotage policies they dislike or think impractical. A classic example was the fate of the Welsh Baccalaureate, negotiated in 2000 as part of a coalition deal between the Liberal Democrats and Labour.[9]

---

8   Elin Jones MS, Llywydd / Presiding Officer, 'The Co-operation Agreement – Senedd Business', Written Statement, 15 December 2021.

9   Developed over nearly a decade by the Institute of Welsh Affairs, the WelshBac as it became known, was thoroughly disliked by civil servants in the Welsh Government's Education Division. It sought to broaden the range of subjects studied by sixth formers, involving a mix of arts and sciences, requiring the study of maths and a foreign language, and adding topics such as 'theory of knowledge' and 'community engagement'. Some civil servants thought the WelshBac too challenging, educationally, and too radical, politically, in providing Wales with a separate qualification from England. It was based on the International Baccalaureate (IB) and that in itself was regarded as problematic. One of the leading civil servants in the Education Division had a child studying the IB at Atlantic College on the Glamorgan coast near Llantwit Major. On the basis of that experience, he believed that most Welsh pupils would simply be unable to cope with the WelshBac. But that was a misreading of the qualification. For built into it were vocational streams that would make it accessible to a much broader range of the cohort than just the academically

Negotiating the Agreement

Against such potential difficulties in implementation, the 46 commitments in the Co-operation Agreement could divided into three categories:

1. Commitments that were understood and agreed between the parties in some detail and could start being implemented from Year 1.
2. Commitments where there was broad agreement between the parties, but which required significant policy development.
3. Commitments where significant policy development was required but where there was a lack of clarity on the direction of travel.

The third category was mostly focused on 'nation-building' policies that were derived from Plaid Cymru's manifesto. Despite this they were under-developed in the sense of being in a position to be simply handed over to the civil service for delivery. Consequently, there was a danger that they could become bogged down in arguments over their practicality, their cost, or otherwise deflected or delayed.

One example was the commitment to establish *Unnos*, a National Construction Company to improve the supply of social housing. However, there was no detail on how this should be implemented. The Agreement stated, 'We will take advice together on its remit, parameters and location.' The definition of *Unnos* in the Agreement as a 'National Construction Company' was much narrower than the role described in Plaid's manifesto. There it was envisaged that it should be established as a public authority, with a strategic role in land assembly and co-ordination of housing associations and local authorities in providing more social housing. If these broader functions were not put in place there was little likelihood that the Welsh Government would meet the large and growing demand for social housing across Wales that both Labour and Plaid agreed existed.

---

inclined. Before the WelshBac could be delivered on a wide scale it was agreed that it should be piloted in a small number of schools. However, for those taking part it would be more than a rehearsal, so there had to be a back-up qualification. What could that be? Uniquely, the International Baccalaureate Organisation in Geneva offered the Welsh Government the IB, but the civil servants turned that down. Instead, they opted for the only alternative, A Levels, the very qualification the WelshBac was seeking to replace. Mixing the two qualifications was unworkable, as the civil servants knew, so the WelshBac was destined to fail before it started.

Moreover, Labour remained wary about creating new agencies at arms-length from the Welsh Government. They feared the potential for conflict with government policy if they went off in their own direction and believed they undermined democratic control. Yet, as discussed in Chapter 2, the opposite is the case. Arms-length agencies remain accountable to government through their annual remit memoranda and, in practice, are more transparent than the civil service because of their regular appearances in front of Senedd committees.

Even so, such considerations lay behind Labour's refusal to accede to new economic agencies for Arfor and the Valleys yet, without radical intervention, the under-development of these two regions would persist. In relation to the agency for the southern valleys, the case was powerfully made by Alun Davies, Labour's MS for Blaenau Gwent:

> 'It is time to accept the conclusion that without a Valleys development agency rooted in the Valleys and with the single objective of delivering a clear vision with the capacity and resources to do so, then we will continue to have a sterile debate where targets are set, but where delivery is forgotten.'[10]

Despite Labour's refusal, the Co-operation Agreement did, however, keep the notion of those development agencies alive with a commitment to commission the Organisation for Economic Co-operation and Development (OECD) to undertake an examination of the case. It is noteworthy that the OECD, commissioned by Welsh Government to examine its economic policy in 2020, recommended a revival of a development agency for Wales as a whole. It noted that the deployment of such agencies was on an upward trend among OECD countries, pointing to examples of their advantages in Canada, Finland, Ireland, Scotland, and France.[11]

The urgent need for new institutions to bolster the economies of the poorer parts of Wales had been inadvertently revealed by the wealthiest part of the country. In March 2022, Cardiff County

---

10 *Western Mail*, 14 October 2020.
11 OECD, *The Future of Regional Development and Public Investment in Wales*, 2020, p.191. In the event Kevin Morgan, Professor of Governance and Development at Cardiff University, was commissioned to examine options for taking forward the western seaboard and southern valleys development proposals.

Council extolled a list of its success stories on social media. Among them was 'almost four out of every five jobs in Wales being created in Cardiff between 2015 and 2020.'[12] So with just 13% of Wales's population, the capital was generating around 80% of the nation's new jobs. Cardiff Council's leader Huw Thomas rationalised the imbalance by arguing that if they had not come to the Welsh capital they would have gone to cities elsewhere in the UK:

> 'The types of jobs we're creating in Cardiff now aren't stolen from elsewhere in Wales, they're jobs we have competed for with other British cities. They're jobs in fintech, creative industries, and cyber which otherwise would be based in Bristol or Birmingham or Edinburgh. Twenty years ago, far more people would leave university and look eastwards down the M4 for their career. Over half of the population of Wales live within less than an hour of Cardiff city centre. Creating jobs here is creating work accessible to the majority of people in Wales. This isn't taking jobs away from other parts of Wales. There's certainly a tension, a drive from the Welsh Government to encourage businesses to invest in other parts of Wales—but when a company is either going to come to Cardiff or go to Birmingham, we should be in the game and bring those companies to Cardiff.'[13]

Yet the reason the jobs are so overwhelmingly attracted to Cardiff is because the city has the connectivity and facilities that most other Welsh communities lack. That is why, for example, creating a Valleys, rather than a Cardiff, Metro, with major investment in cross-valley connections in addition to the lines to and from Cardiff, is so mission-critical for rebalancing the Welsh economy. Otherwise, Wales will merely continue to replicate the economic imbalance that afflicts the UK, with London and the south-east gaining the lion's share of investment and wealth. It's not just England that needs 'levelling-up', it's Wales too.

A united Wales

There is a saying in politics that you campaign in poetry, but govern in prose. It is all too tempting to become mired in the detail and

---

12   Cardiff County Council, *Twitter*, 2 March 2022.
13   *Nation Cymru*, 'Cardiff "not taking jobs away from other parts of Wales": Council leader's revealing election interview', 20 April, 2022.

difficulties of something like the Co-operation Agreement, especially its delivery. Yet in doing so one can lose sight of the policy gains and the inventive mechanisms for cross-party working.

Plaid believed that the commitment to guarantee a free school meal for all primary pupils in Wales would be transformational for thousands of families. Extensive research shows that children (particularly those from disadvantaged backgrounds) benefit from free school meals, not only from a nutritional point of view but also from an educational one, improving engagement and concentration in the learning environment. For example, a survey of all primary headteachers in Gwynedd on the provision of free school meals revealed:

- 75% believed pupils were eating more healthily;
- 49% stated an improvement in concentration levels;
- 40% stated an increase in pupil's commitment;
- 36% recorded improvement in pupil behaviour;
- 40% noted improved achievement in the afternoons.[14]

The commitments to expand free childcare to all two-year-olds, with a special focus on strengthening Welsh-medium provision, will also be transformational. As will Welsh history becoming a mandatory part of the school curriculum, overcoming previous Labour opposition.

Radical action to address the proliferation of second homes was another key result of the Agreement, including a cap on the number of second and holiday homes within local authority regions; measures to bring more homes into common ownership; a statutory licensing scheme for holiday lets; and greater powers for local authorities to charge council tax premiums on second homes.

Also included are policies to reach net zero by 2035 (replacing the previous 2050 target), plant more trees and protect biodiversity, adopt a targeted approach to addressing agricultural pollution, and support the family farm.

In political terms, Plaid and Labour came together to form a united front against the Westminster Conservative Government's attempts to roll back the powers of the Senedd. Instead, there was a determination to confirm its place as the home of Welsh democracy.

---

14 Gwynedd Education and Economy Scrutiny Committee, *Free School Meals* report, 21 March 2024.

Negotiating the Agreement

In early May 2022 Mark Drakeford and Adam Price agreed that the Senedd elected in 2026 would have 96 members (an increase of 36), with six members elected by the d'Hondt proportional formula for each of 16 new constituencies.[15] Within weeks, this substantial advance in the architecture of Welsh devolution was endorsed by Plaid's National Executive and a special conference called by Welsh Labour.

The two parties also agreed that the Senedd needs greater powers, in particular over the police and justice system, leading to the creation of a distinctive Welsh jurisdiction. The Constitutional Commission, established under the terms of the Agreement, was designed to promote a consensus on the need for greater powers for the Senedd and to move Welsh autonomy forward.

Moreover, the Agreement marked a moment when Plaid Cymru transformed itself from an opposition party into one that was working at the heart of government to deliver a programme that included much that was in its manifesto. It created a bespoke model of inter-party relationships that stood somewhere on a spectrum between full coalition and one-off budget arrangements. There was no precedent for it in the British Isles, though it had happened elsewhere – notably in Scandinavian countries such as Sweden, Denmark, and Norway; and in Commonwealth countries such as New Zealand, Canada and Malaysia.

At the heart of the Agreement lay the idea of a Welsh Demos, a Welsh political nationhood, which transcends party and embodies enduring values. Wales will not move decisively towards independence without Plaid Cymru being in Government. Even then, of course, a majority of the people of Wales would need to be persuaded to unite around Welsh autonomy, and necessarily that would also mean a majority of Labour supporters. The Co-operation Agreement established a path towards that united Wales.

---

15 The new constituencies would be based on the 32 new Westminster seats proposed by the Boundary Commission for Wales, once it had concluded its 2023 Parliamentary Review. These constituencies would be paired on a contiguous basis in order to create the 16 Senedd constituencies. The new Senedd members would be elected using closed proportional lists with integrated statutory gender quotas and mandatory zipping – that is, listing candidates alternately according to their gender. See the following chapter for how these commitments came to be implemented in practice.

5

Senedd Reform

Increasing the number of elected members in Wales's devolved institution was a matter of controversy even before the National Assembly was first elected in 1999. A panel of constitutional experts convened by the Institute of Welsh Affairs pointed out that 60 members were simply not enough to do the job.[1] Their commentary on the government's White Paper *A Voice for Wales*, the framework for the legislation that established the Assembly, noted that there would need to be at least 16 committees, which led them to conclude:

> 'There is a strong case for increasing the size of the Assembly to eighty or even more members, just from the point of view of the effective working of the Committee structure.'[2]

Their report left the matter there, but I vividly recall a further argument made by one of the panel's members, Keith Patchett, Emeritus Professor of Law at Cardiff University. He had been a consultant in legislative drafting for countries across the globe, from Albania, Armenia, Bermuda and Bulgaria, to Kenya, Kiribati, Slovenia, Portugal, and Malaysia. An annexe to his house in Cyncoed in Cardiff, was lined with volumes of legal texts. This library was host to a stream of young clerks and lawyers from emerging countries to learn the art of constitution writing. In his biography, Rhodri Morgan

---

[1] Chaired by Ivor Lightman, a former Deputy Secretary at the Welsh Office, the panel comprised Professor Keith Patchett, Emeritus Professor of Law at Cardiff University; Robert Hazell, Director of the Constitution Unit at University College, London; Sir John Gray, former British Ambassador to Brussels and Chair of the Welsh Centre for International Affairs; J. Barry Jones, Director of Political Studies at Cardiff University; His Honour Judge Dewi Watkin Powell; Dr Gareth Jones, Chair of the IWA Research Panel; and Dr Denis Balsom, Warden of Gregynog.

[2] Report of the Expert Panel, *Making the Assembly Work* (IWA, November 1997), p.9.

says his first choice to chair what, in the event, turned out to be the Richard Commission was Keith Patchett. However, the then First Minister was persuaded Patchett wouldn't carry the required weight in Whitehall. Like myself, Rhodri was entertained by the Professor at his house and library, recalling: 'When I visited, a team from the Palestinian Authority was learning the pros and cons of different types of constitutional arrangements. It was fascinating to watch.'[3]

Patchett's argument on the size of the Assembly was as follows: 'You can apply the principle of thirds to every organisation you can think of, whether it's a business, a school, a university, or a public authority.' When I queried what he meant, he continued, 'It's like this. In any organisation about a third of its people are capable of taking on a leadership role, and another third are competent enough to undertake tasks that are assigned to them.' When I asked him about the remainder, he laughed. 'Well, the final third just shouldn't be there.'

Apply that principle to the 60 members of the Senedd and Professor Patchett's argument becomes clear. The Senedd has the following key leadership roles: the First Minister plus ten Cabinet Ministers and three Deputy Ministers; the 17 chairs of Committees; the Presiding and Deputy Presiding Officer; and the three Opposition Leaders. That totals 36. Yet according to Professor Patchett's principle of thirds, the Senedd would only have 20 members fully capable of undertaking these tasks.

Patchett's argument may appear tendentious, but it does underline the reality that an institution with just 60 members provides a very small pool within which to find political leadership. Alongside that, the intense committee workload results in the Senedd having few 'backbenchers' in the sense of the relatively independent, free-floating legislators of the kind who form a significant proportion of the MPs at Westminster. Of the 60 members, 16 are office-holders: the First Minister, ten Cabinet Ministers and three Deputy Ministers, together with the Presiding Officer and his or her Deputy. The remaining 46 Members have, between them, to cover a broad range of policy areas, often as Committee Chairs or party spokespersons. That is to say, they have to oversee matters that at Westminster occupy the attention of some 400 backbench MPs, albeit that these also have to engage with defence and foreign affairs.

---

3   Rh. Morgan, *Rhodri: A Political Life in Wales and Westminster*, op. cit., p.245.

Why 60 Members?

It is salutary to examine how the decision to provide the National Assembly with 60 members came about. The story begins in 1996, just eight months before Labour won the Westminster election in May the following year. At that point Labour was committed to devolution for Scotland and Wales, and was intending to include the commitment in its forthcoming election manifesto to provide the political legitimacy that these major constitutional measures required.

However, still uncertain of his victory, and exhibiting extreme caution over tax and spending commitments, Tony Blair visited Scotland in July 1996 determined to remove from the election agenda Labour's promise of tax varying powers for its proposed Scottish Parliament. The mechanism was to be a referendum in which the people of Scotland would be asked two questions, one on whether they supported a Parliament and, crucially, a second on whether they agreed that it should have the power to vary income tax by 3p in the pound up or down. By placing the tax decision directly in the hands of the Scottish people, it was calculated that the referendum would remove it from the immediate general election debate. The commitment to a Scottish referendum was therefore driven entirely by the exigencies of Scottish politics and the impact it was feared they might have on Labour's electoral prospects in the United Kingdom as a whole. However, the most immediate effect was on Wales. For it was soon appreciated that it would be impossible to have a referendum in Scotland without also having one in Wales.

Tony Blair's referendum ploy came out of the blue. The Shadow Secretary of State for Scotland, George Robertson, was informed beforehand, but the Shadow Secretary of State for Wales, Ron Davies, was left in the dark. In fact on the eve of the announcement, he was taking part in a BBC Wales television programme on the forthcoming election and, under persistent questioning, insisted Labour had no plans for a referendum to endorse devolution. Yet within days Ron Davies was locked in negotiations with Blair on the help he would need if he were to lead the Labour Party in Wales through the forthcoming general election and into a referendum. There was one pivotal requirement. Blair would have to lean on the party in Wales to reverse its conference decision, in 1995, in favour of first-past-the-post for a Welsh Assembly, and opt instead for some variation of proportional representation. Davies argued that without a commitment to PR it would be very difficult for Labour to win a referendum in Wales. Certainly, without PR it would be impossible to persuade Plaid Cymru and the Welsh Liberal Democrats to campaign for a Yes vote.

There was a further argument that doubtless concerned Blair. Labour was already committed to the Additional Member system of PR for elections to a Scottish Parliament, the result of protracted negotiations that had taken place during the previous decade within the Scottish Constitutional Convention. It would surely look anomalous for the party to fight for a Yes vote in parallel referendums in Scotland and Wales for institutions which would have a different electoral mandate. In any event, Ron Davies won his concession and went on to lead the Yes campaign to the wafer-thin majority in the referendum that was held a little over a year later, in September 1997. There is little doubt, given the closeness of the result, that without the PR commitment the referendum would have been lost.

At the same time Labour's commitment to proportional representation was minimal. Its plans for the Assembly, based on its 1995 conference decision, were to have two members for each of the 40 Westminster constituencies, elected by first past the post. This would have resulted in an Assembly of 80 members. The 1995 Welsh Labour conference rejected an alternative it was offered, a German-style additional member system, incorporating a further 20 'top-up seats' allocated on a proportionate basis, thus providing 100 members.[4]

However, once it was forced to introduce an element of proportionality, by creating a hybrid additional member system, Welsh Labour decided that 40 should be elected by first-past-the post to represent the constituencies, but with only 20 additional members to inject an element of proportionality. It argued that keeping members to a minimum was to reduce costs, but the underlying purpose was to ensure the party continued to benefit from the first-past-the-post system in a plurality of seats. How minimalist and grudging was this commitment to proportionality can be seen when Wales is compared with Scotland and Northern Ireland, as shown in the following table.

---

4   See Welsh Labour Party, *Shaping the Vision: a report on the Powers and Structure of the Welsh Assembly*, 1995.

Table 5: Size and electoral systems of devolved institutions in UK 1999[5]

UK devolved institutions	Constituency Members	Regional Members	Total Members	Ratio FPTP: List	Ratio Member: Population
Wales	40	20	60	67%: 33%	1: 48,600
Scotland	73	56	129	57%: 43%	1: 39,200
Northern Ireland	Elected by STV		108	n/a	1: 15,700

The table shows that while having the smallest membership of the devolved institutions, the Senedd has the largest proportion of members to population. In particular, in comparison with Scotland the relatively small size results in disproportionately fewer List members. Wales has only 33% of its membership adjusted by PR compared with 43% in Scotland (Northern Ireland, of course, has the wholly proportional Single Transferable Vote system). There can be little doubt that the decision to give the National Assembly just 60 members was based on a narrow political calculation of allowing the maximum proportionality consistent with providing a Labour majority. And indeed, in an unguarded moment, Rhodri Morgan confessed that the system had been devised to ensure that Labour would achieve a majority of seats in at least three elections out of four.[6]

The Richard Commission

Of all the many inquiries, conventions and commissions that have been established to examine the powers, procedures and structures of the Senedd there is little doubt that the Richard Commission, which reported in March 2004, has proved the most cogent and far reaching.[7] Established as a result of the coalition between Labour

---

5   The table is taken from the report of the Richard Commission, 2004, p.229.
6   See J. Osmond (Ed.), *Welsh Politics Come of Age – Responses to the Richard Commission* (IWA, 2005), p.7.
7   One constitutional expert described it as 'the most serious analysis produced in the UK since the Royal Commission on the Constitution chaired by Lord Kilbrandon reported in 1973 – even more thoughtful and detailed than the documents produced by the Scottish Constitutional Convention' (see A. Trench,

Senedd Reform

and the Liberal Democrats, four of its members were nominated by the political parties and another five were appointed as a result of an advertisement and interviewing process, following the Nolan Principles.[8] None of the political nominees were chosen from the front ranks of their parties and neither did the public appointments produce any high-profile personalities. On the other hand, they could be seen as broadly representing the middle ground of opinion in Wales.

Lord Ivor Richard of Ammanford was an ideal chair. He had been the Labour MP for Barons Court in London for ten years from 1964. Following that he was the UK Permanent Representative at the United Nations, chairing the Rhodesia Conference in 1976. Between 1981 and 1984 he was a European Commissioner. He was a member of the UK Shadow Cabinet from 1992-97 and a member of the Cabinet 1997-98, as Leader of the House of Lords. Overall, he brought a unique combination of Labour links, independence and experience, together with influence in Whitehall. As Rhodri Morgan put it, he was, '...halfway between being 100% Labour Government loyalist, never departing from the party line, and an independent who is outside the party. He is the right kind of person in terms of having clout in Whitehall and Westminster.'[9]

At the beginning Lord Richard said he had been sceptical that any change was needed so soon after the Assembly had been established. However, when the report was published 18 months later, he said the weight of the evidence had influenced him to change his mind. He described the Assembly's powers, procedures and relationship with Westminster as 'grotesque' and 'a lawyers' nightmare.'[10] The evidence showed that its operations were poorly understood, even by some Members let alone the wider public, and that it was failing to deliver in promoting through Westminster the primary legislation it wanted. Lord Richard quoted the view of one speaker at a public meeting held by the Commission in Newport, which he said had stuck

---

'The Assembly's Future as a Legislative Body' in J. Osmond (Ed.), *Welsh Politics Come of Age, op. cit.*, p.35.

8   These were the principles established by the Committee on Standards in Public Life, first chaired by Lord Nolan, and appointed by Prime Minister John Major in 1994, following the 'cash for questions' scandal in Parliament.
9   National Assembly for Wales, *Record*, 18 April 2002.
10 Speech at the IWA's 'Responding to Richard' conference, Cardiff, 23 April 2004.

in his mind: "We were short-changed on the devolution argument compared with Scotland."[11]

Moreover, there was an inherent instability in a system whose smooth operation depended on governments of the same complexion being in place in both Westminster and Cardiff Bay. What would happen if, sometime in the future, there was a Labour administration in Cardiff, and an unsympathetic Conservative administration in Westminster? Lord Richard concluded that, 'This prospect of different colour administrations was one we could not ignore.'[12] So the weight of the evidence pointed to more powers. It was not that the system was currently breaking down, operating as it was with co-operative Labour administrations in Cardiff and London. As Lord Richard put it:

> 'The surprising thing – and I want to emphasise this – is that we didn't reach this conclusion because the present system isn't working. Almost the opposite in fact. It is precisely the success of the Assembly and the Welsh Assembly Government in establishing itself as the government of Wales in the key public policy areas that creates the pressure for change. We examined in detail the dynamics of the present situation and found that the Assembly is increasingly setting the legislative agenda for Wales in devolved areas and negotiating with Whitehall and Westminster for the legislation it needs. Since this is already happening and likely to happen increasingly in future, it seemed to us that the most efficient and straightforward process would be for the Assembly itself to pass this legislation in Cardiff.'[13]

The force of the Richard Commission's recommendations followed from the logic it applied to the evidence it accumulated. Indeed, it was extraordinary that representatives nominated by each of the four parties could agree, not only on the Assembly becoming a legislative parliament, but that its members should be increased from 60 to 80 and elected by the Single Transferable Vote proportional system. As Lord Richard himself declared, 'I didn't expect that the political representatives would be able to come to an agreed understanding.

---

11 Ibid.
12 Speech by Lord Richard at the press launch of his report, Cardiff, 31 March 2004.
13 Ibid.

The reason they did was because they looked at the evidence.'[14] As one of those representatives, Professor Laura McAllister, who would continue to be a major influence on the debate, put it:

> '...the Commission set itself two important principles: first, that size follows function, and second, that an increase in numbers would be justified only by a greater workload for AMs. These were hardly earth-shattering conclusions, and simply underlined the practical, logical impetus that drove the Commission's deliberations... If the Commission was convinced that the Assembly should accrue additional powers, then the number of AMs should increase. This then meant revisiting the electoral system to ensure proper operational capacity and human resources for effective scrutiny.'[15]

The Commission applied the same logical process when it came to consider which proportional system it should recommend. As Laura McAllister, also explained:

> 'The flaws in alternative systems, together with unconvincing suggestions for amendments to the Additional Member System, left the Commission staring STV in the face. It is fair to say that few Commissioners rejoiced at this. There was certainly no evangelical conversion to STV. Nevertheless, it was clear that in order to follow the guiding principle of an evidentially based analysis, motivated by providing the Assembly with the tools for good governance, STV met more of the Commission's criteria than any alternative. That is not to say that STV was Hobson's choice. Some Commissioners were positive and supportive of it as a system that met most of the Commission's requirements, whilst others were more pragmatically in favour. Nevertheless, the recommendation gained unanimous support.'[16]

The key argument *for* STV was that it was proportional, whilst allowing clear constituency member links. For the Commission, the

---

[14] Speech at the IWA's 'Responding to Richard' conference, Cardiff 23 April, 2004.
[15] L. McAllister, 'The Best Electoral System', in J. Osmond (Ed.), *Welsh Politics Come of Age, op. cit.*, p.53.
[16] *Ibid.*, p.58.

merits of STV over the other proportional systems it considered were three-fold:

1. All Members would have equal status and share the same relationship with the electors.
2. Most votes count, meaning 'safe' seats are unlikely, thus offering an incentive for all parties to campaign actively in every constituency.
3. There would remain opportunities for improving the representation of various interests, most especially the ethnic minority communities, from which no current Member was currently drawn.[17]

However, in politics as in life more generally, reason and logic can only take you so far. It is a necessary condition for persuasion, but invariably there has to be an additional political impulse or emotional charge if change is to happen. This was certainly the case with the arguments put forward by the Richard Commission. Indeed, it was two decades before circumstances aligned to allow its recommendations to be implemented, more or less, in the round. Throughout it was Labour, neuralgically opposed to proportional representation, that stood in the way. Broadly speaking, Labour accepted the case for primary legislative powers for the Assembly, subject to a referendum, but it remained emphatically opposed to more members and any change to the electoral system. Its response was unequivocal:

> 'We reject the Richard Commission proposal for the use of the proportional representation system of Single Transferable Vote with a boundary reorganisation, and constituencies of four to six members.'[18]

The rationalisation was the unpopularity of increasing the number of politicians. According to Rhodri Morgan it 'would screw up any chances of getting the other conclusions on law-making powers through — the people of Wales were simply not ready to accept any argument for more AMs, however logical the reasoning over

---

17   Richard Commission, p.237.
18   Wales Labour Party, *Better Governance for Wales* [response to the Richard Commission], August 2004, para.7.

increased work on the legislative front needing more legislators to carry it out.'[19]

Underlying such arguments was a visceral opposition from Welsh Labour MPs at Westminster, fearful that any increase in the size of the Senedd would lead to a reduction in their own numbers. There was also opposition from the wider party to any hint of proportional representation that, they believed, would undermine Labour's hegemony. It was only under the pressure of negotiating with Plaid Cymru that Welsh Labour compromised. First, it was the One Wales coalition between Labour and Plaid in 2007 that paved the way to the referendum on legislative powers. Then it took another 14 years before the Co-operation Agreement finally reached a deal on the remainder of the Richard Commission package.

Size matters

The 2011 referendum which gave approval to the National Assembly becoming a parliament provided an important boost to the case for enlargement. The Richard Commission had argued that the Assembly already did not have enough members to populate its committees or undertake its scrutiny functions effectively. A move to full legislative powers, as it recommended, would make the scrutiny gap even more intolerable.

The case was amplified in 2012 by the recommendations of the Commission chaired by former House of Commons and National Assembly Clerk Sir Paul Silk, on devolving taxation powers. In its second report on legislative powers in 2014, deliberately straying beyond its brief, the Silk Commission said there should be 'at least' 80 members.

However, apart from the case made by both the Richard and Silk Commissions, there was a further democratic argument why the size of the Senedd with its currently small membership matters.[20] This was due to the relationship between numbers and effective scrutiny which determines the balance of power between a legislature and the executive component of government.

---

19   Rh. Morgan, *Rhodri: A Political Life in Wales and Westminster*, op. cit., p.245.
20   J. Osmond, *Size Matters: Making the National Assembly more effective*, 2014, jointly published by the UK Changing Union Partnership, comprising the Institute of Welsh Affairs, the Wales Governance Centre, and Cymru Yfory/ Tomorrow's Wales, together with the Electoral Reform Society Cymru.

Proportional representation has a tendency to lead to power sharing in government, whether this takes the form of a coalition or more informal arrangements such as confidence and supply, or more elaborate policy accords such as the Co-operation Agreement. As a result of proportional representation, the Senedd operates a more consensual style of governance compared with the majoritarian culture in Westminster. The Senedd lies somewhere in between majoritarian and consensual governance, whose characteristics are set out in the table below:

Table 6: Contrast between majoritarian and consensual political systems[21]

	Majoritarian governance	**Consensual governance**
Executive	Single party Cabinet system	Multi-party Coalition, Compact or Agreement arrangements
Balance of powers	Executive dominance	Executive-Legislative balance
Electoral system	Majoritarian	PR Multi-party systems

Wales's semi-proportional system (where a third of Assembly is elected on the proportional regional list) allows for a greater level of party competition than is the case with the Welsh MPs elected by Westminster's majoritarian first-past-the-post system. However, in terms of governance, the Senedd has moved towards centralisation of government power in the Executive.

The original 1998 Government of Wales Act established the National Assembly as a local government style corporate body, with the Assembly as a whole taking an active part in formulating policy under a consensus model. The 2006 Act changed this to a Westminster model of centralised Executive dominance. Legislative power is now exercised by the Cabinet, with the rest of the Senedd Members responsible for scrutinising it.

During the One Wales coalition between 2007-11, 41 members were either from Labour or Plaid Cymru, leaving only 19

---

21 This classification is derived from the political scientist Arend Lijphart and his work on consociational democracy, in which cross-party relationships can ameliorate endemic societal divisions. His book *Patterns of Democracy* (1999) also argued that consensual democracies fare better than majoritarian ones for democratic authenticity and government performance, including stimulating economic growth and controlling inflation.

AMs from a non-governing party. This did not provide for a strong opposition or effective scrutiny. Since then, Labour has governed alone allowing for a more effective opposition in terms of numbers, but the tendency in the system is for cross-party arrangements, as was the case with the Co-operation Agreement. Inevitably this results in a weaker opposition as a result of the relatively small number of members remaining outside the parties participating in government. The overall result is to strengthen the executive and weaken the legislature. There follows a move from 'Executive-legislative balance' towards 'Executive dominance', in which the opposition has a more limited capacity to amend laws and hold the Government to account. This is the fundamental democratic case for increasing the members of the Senedd. It is needed to address the imbalance between the strength of the executive and the weakness of the legislature.

The decision becomes ours

The tipping point in the tortuous 25-year process towards Senedd reform came with the Silk Commission's recommendation that the 'size of the National Assembly be increased so that it can perform its scrutiny role better.'[22] This recommendation prompted some controversy since it could be argued that the Commission had exceeded its terms of reference, which stated that:

> 'The Commission will not consider the structure of the National Assembly for Wales, including issues relating to the election of Assembly members.'[23]

The insertion of this caveat was testimony to the political sensitivity of these questions, especially for the Conservative-led government in London which drew up the remit. Nonetheless, the Commission felt compelled that it should take a view. It reviewed the evidence and found the case overwhelming. As it explained:

> 'The size and the capacity of the National Assembly is a contentious issue on which there is no overall consensus in Wales. Robust views

---

22 Commission on Devolution in Wales, *Empowerment and Responsibility: Legislative Powers to Strengthen Wales*, March 2014, p.157.
23 Ibid., p.4

are expressed against any suggestion that members need to be increased, and political parties are naturally cautious about making any recommendations that might appear to support the case for more politicians. It is all the more incumbent upon us to come to a view on this question.'[24]

The Commission addressed the question of its remit – whether or not it was able to consider the 'structure' of the Assembly – head-on:

'On the narrow linguistic point, we are quite clear that size and structure are different concepts. Objects of different size can have the same structure. No-one suggested that the "structure" of the House of Commons was altered by the reduction of the number of seats provided for under the Parliamentary Voting Systems and Constituencies Act 2011. What would alter the structure would be, say, a proposal that Ministers should not be Assembly Members. More generally, what is clearly within our terms of reference is anything that we believe will enable the National Assembly to better serve the interests of Wales. It is our clear judgement that, without its enlargement, the National Assembly cannot serve the people of Wales as it ought.'[25]

The Commission's report was influential. Within a year the Westminster Government published a White Paper proposing to devolve all powers relating to elections to the Assembly, subject to a two-thirds majority in the chamber. This duly became law with the passing of the Wales Act 2017. Immediately, the Llywydd (Presiding Officer) Elin Jones appointed an Expert Panel to come up with recommendations on the number of Senedd members and how they should be elected. Chaired by Professor Laura McAllister, who had also been a member of the Richard Commission, the Panel took only eight months to produce recommendations that included expanding the Senedd to 'at least 80 and preferably closer to 90 members', elected by STV.[26]

---

[24] Ibid., p.155.
[25] Ibid., p.156.
[26] Report of the Expert Panel on Assembly Electoral Reform, *A Parliament that Works for Wales*, November 2017.

Senedd Reform

There was then a hiatus in substantive progress until, in July 2019, the Senedd debated a Plaid Cymru motion calling for the Expert Panel's recommendations to be taken forward. Following the debate, the Senedd voted by a majority that an increase in members was needed and that there should be further cross-party work. Subsequently a committee was established, chaired by Dawn Bowden the Labour MS for Merthyr. However, the Conservatives refused to participate. Initially, a Brexit Party MS, David Rowlands, did take part but withdrew before the committee's report was published, in September 2020. Nevertheless, the committee, now comprising two Labour members and two Plaid members, recommended that legislation should be introduced shortly after the forthcoming 2021 Senedd election to increase the size to between 80 and 90 members, elected by STV in multi-member constituencies. In summary it found that:

- The new electoral system should be simple for voters to complete their ballot papers and there should be a clear constituency link between constituents and their representatives.
- Votes should be translated into seats fairly, and the electoral system should produce broadly proportional outcomes.
- All Members should be elected by the same route to resolve the recurrent debate over whether regional Members are accountable to voters or parties.
- Multi-member constituencies would offer more choice to voters and enable parties to put forward multiple candidates, allowing them to diversify their selection processes and encourage the election of a more diverse Senedd.[27]

This was the first concrete signal that Labour and Plaid, who together commanded a two-thirds majority in the Senedd, were able to agree on a reform agenda, although the precise form it should take and the priority it would be given were still matters to be resolved. This was made evident by the content of the Plaid and Labour manifestos at the 2021 election. Plaid Cymru's was unequivocal:

---

27   Committee on Senedd Electoral Reform, *Senedd reform: The next steps*, September 2020. The Labour members of the committee were Dawn Bowden (Merthyr), and Huw Irranca-Davies (Bridgend); the Plaid members were Delyth Jewell (South-East Wales) and Dai Lloyd (South-West Wales).

> 'We will implement the recommendations of the Expert Panel on Assembly Electoral Reform, in particular on Single Transferable Voting, gender quotas and expanding the Senedd.'[28]

Whereas, Labour's manifesto lacked specificity:

> 'We will build on the work of the Senedd Committee on electoral reform, chaired by Welsh Labour's Dawn Bowden, and develop proposals to improve the representation of the people of Wales in their Parliament.'[29]

In the weeks leading up to the 2021 election, I prepared an internal paper analysing the two manifestos to assess the prospects for finding common ground. Under a heading 'Size of the Senedd and Electoral Reform' I commented:

> 'In theory Labour should be on board for this, especially since Dawn Bowden (name-checked in their manifesto) chaired the Senedd Committee on electoral reform that approved the key recommendations that the size of the Senedd be increased to between 80 and 90 and that elections should be by STV. However, on its own and without pressure Labour will be unlikely to pursue this agenda, especially STV, since it would perceive it being against its electoral interests. However, for Plaid Cymru this is a crucial step, calculated to prise open the door for further constitutional advance for Wales. In terms of its importance in this regard it is analogous to the achievement of law-making powers by the 2007 One Wales coalition. Given that during the coming Senedd term Wales's Westminster constituencies will be reduced from 40 to 32, we should press for these also to be new multi-member constituencies for the Senedd at the 2026 election. Each should return three Senedd members, elected by STV, making a total of 96.'[30]

As a prediction of what eventually happened this was not far out. The difference was that the 32 new constituencies will be merged to

---

28   Plaid Cymru, *Let Us Face the Future Together*, May 2021, p.117.
29   Welsh Labour, *Moving Wales Forward*, May 2021, p.64
30   J. Osmond, *Coalition Days in May 2021: Green – Red Lines* (unpublished).

create 16, and each will return six members, arriving at the same total of 96.

Negotiating Senedd reform

Early on in the Co-operation Agreement negotiations it became clear that while there was a consensus within Labour on the need for more members, beyond that there was no agreement on other aspects of Senedd reform, including PR and the representation of women. An internal party working group was being established to address these questions and would table a position paper at a forthcoming conference before the end of the year. Final proposals would then be put to Welsh Labour's Spring Conference in March 2022. Accordingly, the Labour side proposed that it would be helpful if the Agreement set out overarching principles rather than defining a position. It was explained that while Mark Drakeford and the leadership in the Senedd were in favour of reform as set out by Dawn Bowden's committee, powerful sections of the party, including the MPs and some trade unions, had yet to be convinced. The Labour negotiators argued that it would be counter-productive if Labour was seen to being pressurised by a competing party.

Plaid Cymru accepted this position, so long as the 'overarching principles' included:

- Increasing the size of the Senedd should be accompanied by broadening the proportionality in the election of Members.
- All Members should be of equal status, thus removing the contrasting mandates of FPTP and List Members.
- There should be a mechanism to ensure gender parity of Members.

Over the ensuing weeks, these principles were subjected to a great deal of detailed discussion, with the final wording in the Agreement condensed into just one sentence: 'Support plans to reform the Senedd, based on 80 to 100 Members; a voting system which is as proportional – or more – than the current one; and have gender quotas in law.' This position was finalised towards the end of the negotiations, in November. By then sufficient trust had developed to enable the Plaid Cymru side to have confidence that its fundamental objective of substantially increasing the size of the Senedd would be met.

However, in order to close the deal Adam Price was forced to make three concessions – to accept Westminster boundaries; to abandon STV in favour of the d'Hondt formula of proportional representation; and to agree to closed party lists. The last was to cause much controversy. It meant that although the broad outline of Senedd reform would be achieved, the detailed provisions of its enactment would remain unfinished business. The terms were set out in a joint statement, published by Mark Drakeford and Adam Price in May 2022:

- The Senedd should have 96 Members.
- It should be elected using closed proportional lists with integrated statutory gender quotas and mandatory zipping.
- Seats should be allocated to parties using the d'Hondt counting formula.
- The 2026 Senedd election should use the final 32 UK Parliament constituencies proposed by the Boundary Commission for Wales once it has concluded its 2023 Parliamentary Review.
- These constituencies should be paired to create 16 Senedd constituencies. Each constituency should elect 6 Members.[31]

Labour preferred closed lists because they give more control to the party machine, crucially by enabling the party to determine the order in which their candidates can be elected. Labour also preferred the d'Hondt counting formula because it tends to allocate more seats to larger parties, compared with alternatives such as the St. Lague method. On the other hand, an important characteristic of STV is that it enables votes to be cast for individual candidates rather than for parties, giving the electorate more control of the way lists are ordered.

The Senedd reform legislation also:

- Reduced the length of time between Senedd general elections from five to four years.
- Increased the number of Deputy Presiding Officers from one to two.

---

[31] Welsh Government press release: 'First Minister Mark Drakeford and Plaid Cymru Leader Adam Price have today set out a way forward for Senedd reform', 10 May 2022.

- Increased the limit on the number of Welsh Government ministers from 13 to 17, in addition to the First Minister and Counsel General.
- Required Senedd Members to be resident in Wales.
- Provided for a review of the operation of the new legislative provisions following the 2026 election.[32]

Closed lists

Closed lists were condemned by most observers who gave evidence to the Senedd Committee that undertook scrutiny of the Senedd Cymru (Members and Elections) Bill. For example, Professor Alan Renwick, Deputy Director of the Constitution Unit at University College London, and a member of the Expert Panel on Senedd Reform, told the Committee that closed lists 'put Wales out of line both with the British democratic tradition and with modern European democratic practice.' He also added:

> 'It just seems to me very, very clear that to remove that ability for voters to vote for individual candidates would create a significant danger of increasing public disaffection with the system. And when we're talking about a reform to increase the number of politicians... the suggestion that you also then change the voting system in order to give voters less power to determine who the individual politicians filling those seats are, seems to me really dangerous.'[33]

The Committee supported this view, finding that closed lists:

> '...would reduce voter choice, prioritise the influence and wishes of political parties over those of voters, erode Members' links and accountability to their constituents, and introduce an effective electoral threshold of around 12% at a constituency level, with

---

32 Further measures: (i) Require the Seventh Senedd to consider job-sharing of offices; and (ii) Renames the Local Democracy and Boundary Commission for Wales as the Democracy and Boundary Commission Cymru with powers to establish new Senedd constituencies and undertake ongoing reviews of their boundaries.
33 Welsh Parliament Reform Bill Committee, *Senedd Cymru (Members and Elections) Bill, Stage 1 Report*, January 2024, p.99.

potential implications for the electoral chances of individuals and smaller parties.'[34]

Nonetheless, Plaid Cymru gritted its teeth and supported the package during the passage of the Bill, acknowledging that it was the price for achieving the necessary two-thirds majority. As Heledd Fychan, MS for South Wales Central, put it:

> 'We in Plaid Cymru have been open from the outset that this Bill doesn't deliver everything that we would wish to see in terms of Senedd reform. Our policy as a party, which is well known to all, is that we support STV rather than the closed list system that will be implemented by this Bill, and we will continue with our calls that we will be using the closed list system but once, using the review mechanism, following 2026, to refine the system further by 2030. However, we also acknowledge that no one party in the Senedd has the two-thirds majority required to secure reform alone, according to the terms set by the Conservatives in Westminster as the architects of the Wales Act 2017, which gives us the powers to amend our electoral systems. Therefore, we have as a party worked pragmatically with the Government to develop a set of proposals that will enable us to reach that threshold.'[35]

In a response to a question about closed lists, at the Institute for Government in London in January 2024, Mark Drakeford also suggested that they would be for one election only:

> 'This is a closely balanced argument between closed and open lists but in the first election I think that balance just tips in favour of closed lists because from my party's point of view at least, this is the only way that we can be sure that we will deliver on our promises to our black members, to our disabled members, that they will be in prominent positions on those lists and will end up in the Senedd. For me the closed list is a one-off opportunity to guarantee that we end up, at least in my party's case, with a cadre of members of the Senedd who properly reflect the diversity of contemporary Wales. And without the closed list you can't guarantee that. Once that's done,

---

34   Ibid., p.119
35   Senedd Record, 5 March 2024.

we're committed to a review of the system. After the first election the balance of the arguments may move back in favour of open lists. But for the time being, for that first election, I think the closed list system offer us that extra advantage in establishing the new enlarged Senedd in that genuinely diverse way.'[36]

Gender parity

The Co-operation Agreement's commitment to create equality in the Senedd by legislating for 'gender quotas in law' proved highly problematic. So much so that this aspect of Senedd reform was the subject of a separate Senedd Cymru (Electoral Candidates Lists) Bill in March 2024, six months after the main Senedd Cymru (Members and Elections) Bill had been introduced. The reason was a large question mark over whether the Senedd had the power to pass it. Separating the two meant that if the Senedd's competence was successfully challenged, the bulk of the Senedd reform agenda would still go ahead.

The wisdom of this decision became clear when Elin Jones, the Llywydd, declared that the Bill was outside the legislative competence of the Senedd, because it:

1. related to the reserved matters of equal opportunities; and
2. modified the law on reserved matters, namely the Equality Act 2010.[37]

The provisions of the Bill require:

- At least half of the candidates on a party's list in each Senedd constituency to be women. In addition, the Bill requires that a list must be ordered so that a candidate on a list who is not a woman must be followed immediately by a candidate who is a woman – known as the vertical placement criteria.

---

36 M. Drakeford, Interview, Institute for Government, London, 24 January 2024.
37 Presiding Officer's Statement on Legislative Competence, 11 March 2024. This was the first time the Presiding Officer had stated that she considered a Bill being introduced into the Senedd would be wholly outside its legislative competence. The Bill had been due to be published in November 2023 but was delayed until the following March after the Presiding Officer's view of its competence became known.

- The first on at least half of the lists submitted by a party should be a woman – known as the horizontal placement criteria.
- All candidates on a party's list must state either whether they are, or are not, a woman.

The Senedd's Special Purpose Committee that examined the legislation had recommended 'zipping' – that is, listing candidates alternately according to their gender.[38] However, the Government argued this would place a ceiling on the number of women candidates who could stand. Instead, parties would now be able to put more than one woman in succession on a list.

The Government insisted that because its proposals were about the way elections to the Senedd were organised they came within its legislative competence and so were not a reserved matter. In its Explanatory Memorandum, it argued that increased representation of women would lead to a more effective Senedd, improved democracy, and better policy making. Quoting extensive academic research, it argued women in politics had been found to:

- Prioritise different policy and legislative matters.
- Champion particular ways of working.
- Drive a higher calibre of candidates.
- Create role models in positions of political leadership.
- Increase minority representation.
- Decrease corruption and unethical activity.[39]

Nonetheless, the Presiding Officer, was quite clear that the Bill trespassed powers reserved to Westminster. As Elin Jones put it:

'While I accept the Bill has the devolved purpose of making the Senedd a more effective legislature, in my view the Bill also has the reserved purpose of equal opportunities. "Equal opportunities" is a reserved matter in Schedule 7A to the 2006 Act and includes the prevention, elimination or regulation of discrimination between

---

38 Special Purpose Committee on Senedd Reform, 'Reforming our Senedd: A Stronger Voice for the People of Wales', May 2022

39 Welsh Government, *Senedd Cymru (Electoral Candidate Lists Bill) Explanatory Memorandum* (March 2004), p.11.

persons on grounds of sex. From reading the Bill and the Explanatory Memorandum, I concluded that the Bill:

> (a) seeks to address disadvantages and barriers that women face during the candidate selection process;
> (b) will require political parties to treat a man (who would otherwise be more likely to be selected for a place on the list that must be allocated to a woman) less favourably than a woman, because of the man's sex.

Having considered the purpose and effect of the Bill, I concluded that the Bill has more than a "loose or consequential"[40] connection with the prevention, elimination or regulation of discrimination between persons on the grounds of sex. In other words, in my view, the Bill relates to the reserved matter of equal opportunities and would not be within the legislative competence of the Senedd.'[41]

She also found that the Bill would modify the Equality Act 2010, which was another reserved matter:

'Section 104 of the 2010 Act makes special provision for political parties by permitting them (voluntarily) to adopt discriminatory selection arrangements in order to address under-representation in their candidate selection processes. Therefore, section 104 **permits** political parties to address under-representation, but does not **require** them to do so. The Bill, however, requires political parties to address under-representation: it requires at least half of candidates on lists submitted by political parties to be women, and it requires that the first or only candidate on at least half of those lists be a woman. In the context of Senedd elections, in my view, the Bill effectively turns the voluntary power to address under-representation in section 104 into a duty to address under-representation.'[42]

---

40 The 'loose or consequential' test as applied by the Supreme Court in numerous devolution cases.
41 Presiding Officer E. Jones, Letter to D. Rees MS, Chair of the Reform Bill Committee, 11 March 2024.
42 Ibid.

The Bill attracted further controversy because of its provision that candidates would be able to self-identify as the gender of their choice. Women's Rights Network Cymru declared this would be 'met with full scale legal resistance':

> 'This Bill is meant to address female political representation but once again the Government is using it as a lever to push through the first formal steps towards self-ID in Wales... Men are not women, and they can never become one either. There should be no provision for men to self-identify as women on electoral lists.'[43]

For all these reasons, if it was passed unamended, the Bill would very probably be challenged by the UK Government in the Supreme Court. A clear warning of this eventuality was given by David T.C. Davies, Secretary of State for Wales, in a letter to then First Minister Vaughan Gething in late March 2024:

> 'Given that a key aspect of the role of Secretary of State for Wales is ensuring that legislation in both the UK Parliament and Senedd reflects the devolution boundary, I am duty bound to express my grave concern that the Llywydd and the Welsh Government are not in agreement on this Bill. While improving the gender diversity of parliaments across the UK is an ambition we share, I am concerned that Welsh Ministers are yet to make clear how relevant UK legislation, including the Equalities Act 2010 and the Gender Recognition Act 2004, relates to the provisions in the Bill, particularly in regard to the definition of a "woman".'[44]

This view was underlined a few weeks later when the Equality and Human Rights Commission warned the Welsh Government that it does not have the power to allow anyone to self-identify with their chosen gender at Senedd elections. The Commission noted that when it had given evidence to the Special Purpose Committee on Senedd Reform in early 2022, it said that in addressing the under-

---

43 M. Shipton, 'Legal battle looms over Senedd gender balance Bill' (*Nation Cymru*, 11 March 2024).
44 M. Shipton, 'Vaughan Gething faces constitutional battle over Senedd Gender balance Bill' (*Nation Cymru*, 22 March 2024).

representation of women, the relevant protected characteristic in the Equality Act 2010 was sex, not gender:

> 'The protected characteristic of 'sex' refers to a person's legal sex, as stated on their birth certificate or as acquired through obtaining a Gender Recognition Certificate. Further to our evidence, the Scottish Court of Session Inner House gave judgment in a case which determined that "sex", for the purposes of the Act, is not determined by "self-identification". Whilst it is to be noted that Scottish judgments are not binding on courts in England and Wales and that the judgment is currently under appeal to the Supreme Court, we consider it the leading authority on the point.'[45]

The force of these arguments was conceded by the Welsh Government in June 2024 when it said that the 2030 election would be a 'more prudent' timetable for implementation of the reform than 2026.[46] Instead, Jane Hutt, the Trefnydd (Business Manager), said that progress in the 2026 election would have to be made as a result of voluntary action by the parties.[47] As she explained, although the general principles of the Bill, aimed at creating a gender-balanced Welsh Parliament, had been agreed by the Senedd:

> 'Protecting the outcome and integrity of the 2026 Senedd election, including implementation of the Senedd Cymru (Members and Elections) Act, is of utmost importance, and I've concluded that the more responsible approach is for this Bill to be implemented for the scheduled 2030 Senedd election. This will ensure that the legislation can be implemented in an orderly way, and gives time for any potential legal challenges to be resolved well in advance of that election.'[48]

Siân Gwenllian, Hutt's opposite number on the Plaid benches, acknowledged that approval for the Bill 'in principle' was 'an historical

---

45 M. Shipton, 'Equalities watchdog warns that plan to allow any Senedd candidate to self-identify as a woman is unlawful' (*Nation Cymru*, 18 April 2024).
46 C. Haines, 'Major step back as Senedd quotas bill postponed' (*Nation Cymru*, 19 June 2024).
47 *Senedd Record*, 18 June 2024.
48 M. Shipton, 'Gender balanced Senedd agreed in principle – but not until 2030, and only if the Supreme Court agrees' (*Nation Cymru*, 17 July 2024).

and trail-blazing achievement'. However, noting this was a key part of Plaid's Co-operation Agreement with the Welsh Government, she added:

> 'Without quotas, the current reform package is unfinished and incomplete, and I am truly concerned that we will find ourselves with a Senedd that is larger, but one that is even less representative that it has been in previous years.'[49]

A fully-fledged parliament

Regardless of the ultimate fate of the gender quotas Bill, increasing the size of the Senedd will transform it into a fully-fledged parliament. As we have seen, this will be the culmination of a tortuous 25-year process. It also reflects the path Labour have taken to transform itself into a *Welsh* Labour party, one that identifies primarily with Wales ahead of a parallel identification with the rest of Britain. This metamorphosis has only happened as a result of a dialogue with Plaid Cymru. In the process both parties have discovered more about themselves. If Labour has become more politically Welsh, Plaid has had to face the reality that building the nation involves engaging with the greater part of the country and not just those regions where it feels most at home.

In negotiating the Co-operation Agreement both parties responded to what they saw as a hostile right-wing establishment in London, as the preamble to the section of the Agreement containing the details for Senedd reform makes clear:

> 'With devolution under threat from this Conservative UK Government, we must send a clear message to Westminster that the Senedd is here to stay and decisions about Wales are made in Wales.'[50]

Senedd reform is a blow for devolution against the centralising forces at Westminster.

---

49 S. Gwenllian, 'It is only by putting a statutory mechanism in place that we will create a Senedd that is truly representative' (*Nation Cymru*, 24 July 2024).
50 See the Appendix.

6

Personalities and Politics Intervene

The Co-operation Agreement was meant to last for three years, from December 2021 to December 2024. In the event, it was cut short by six months due to its coming under the influence of new Plaid and Labour leaders, who brought with them different priorities. On 17 May 2024, Rhun ap Iorwerth, who had taken over the Plaid leadership the previous June, finally lost patience with his new Labour counterpart Vaughan Gething and summarily withdrew from the Agreement.

In March 2024, Vaughan Gething, MS for Cardiff South and Penarth, was narrowly elected leader of the Welsh Labour Party, with 51.7% of the vote, against Neath MS Jeremy Miles. Mark Drakeford had announced his intention to stand down from the leadership the previous December, stating that he had made it clear when he was elected in December 2018 that he would serve for five years. However, it had been thought that he would continue until the Autumn of 2024, not least to guarantee the completion of the Co-operation Agreement. Explaining his decision to leave earlier than anticipated he said the looming prospect of a UK general election was a major reason: 'I think it is better, in Wales, that people know the person who will look to work alongside Keir Starmer.'[1]

However, the flawed and controversial character of Vaughan Gething's leadership campaign during the ensuing three months proved that politics is driven as much by events as good intentions. The first controversy ignited in early January when Gething and Miles took part in a hustings to obtain the nomination of the Unite trade union's political committee. Speeches were made and questions answered but, before a vote could be taken, the process

---

1   BBC News website, 'Wales First Minister Mark Drakeford resigns', 13 March 2023.

was interrupted by the union's regional secretary, Peter Hughes. He ruled that Miles was ineligible to receive Unite's nomination because, he claimed, Miles had never been a lay union official. As a result, the Unite nomination was handed by default to Gething. This rule, whose interpretation was ambiguous, was dredged up only when it became apparent that Miles was likely to win the political committee's vote.[2] Given the closeness of the eventual vote this dubious manoeuvre may well have been decisive.

Even more serious for Gething's credibility, the following month it was revealed that he had received two donations totalling £200,000 from David Neal, a businessman who had previously been convicted of environmental offences as head of two companies, Atlantic Recycling and Neal Soil Suppliers. It also transpired that Gething had written to Natural Resources Wales in 2016 and 2018 asking the public body to ease restrictions on Atlantic Recycling which is based in his constituency.[3] Then it emerged that in February 2023 the Development Bank for Wales, owned by the Welsh Government and responsible to the Minister for Economic Development, had provided a £400,000 loan to Neal Soil Suppliers for the purchase of a solar farm. At the time Vaughan Gething was the Minister for Economic Development.[4]

During the leadership campaign Gething received £254,600 in donations, compared with £58,800 raised by Jeremy Miles.[5] Questions about the sources, the size and character of Gething's donations continued unabated for months following his becoming First Minister. Throughout, he insisted he hadn't contravened the Labour Party rulebook, though he commissioned former First Minister Carwyn Jones to produce a report on how future leadership campaigns should be funded.

Then in early May came further damaging claims, this time that Gething had misled the UK Covid-19 Inquiry in evidence he had

---

2 M. Shipton, 'Vaughan Gething only joined "stitch-up union" months ago' (*Nation Cymru*, 29 January 2024). It transpired that Gething himself had joined Unite only during the previous year.

3 BBC News website, 'Vaughan Gething helped waste offence company', 12 March 2024.

4 BBC News website, 'Gething refuses independent donations inquiry', 23 April 2024.

5 R. Mosalski, 'Huge sum Vaughan Gething spent in his fight to be Wales's new First Minister revealed' (*WalesOnline*, 16 May 2024).

presented about his activities while Health Minister in August 2020. At the centre of this story was a text Gething had sent on a group chat to nine other Ministers when the Welsh Government's main preoccupation was handling the Covid crisis. It emerged that the subject of their exchanges was the Welsh Government's intention that, because of Covid, GCSE and A-level grades should be awarded on the basis of teacher assessments. Gething wrote, 'I'm deleting the messages in this group. They can be captured in an FOI [Freedom of Information request] and I think we are all in the right place on the choice being made.' However, he had told the Covid Inquiry that no messages sent by him had been deleted.[6]

Responding to questions about the deleted message, Gething insisted that it was a Labour Group political exchange and not directly about Government business, so therefore he had not withheld information from the Covid Inquiry. However, he undermined that position when, a little over a week later, he sacked one of his junior Ministers Hannah Blythyn for being the source of the leak, an accusation she vehemently denied.[7] It was this event that proved the last straw for Rhun ap Iorwerth. Explaining why he had withdrawn Plaid from the Co-operation Agreement he wrote:

> 'I believe that it was an error of judgement for the First Minister to accept a donation from a company that had been found guilty of environmental offences, and remain convinced that the only proper way to address this error would have been for him to repay the donation. Money left over is in Labour party coffers. I'm also worried by the circumstances around the First Minister's decision to sack a Minister. Whether or not Hannah Blythyn leaked iMessages is not the issue. The real question at play is why did Vaughan Gething not provide the information to the UK Covid Inquiry in the first place and why the determination to try and find the whistle-blower rather than

---

6   M. Shipton, 'Vaughan Gething misled UK Covid Inquiry by not admitting he deleted messages' (*Nation Cymru*, 7 May 2024).

7   E. Price, 'Vaughan Gething axes Cabinet Secretary in unprecedented move' (*Nation Cymru*, 16 May 2024). In another unprecedented move, this time for a news outlet, on 17 July *Nation Cymru* revealed that Hannah Blythyn had not been the source of their story about the leak.

owning his own mistake? Finding scapegoats for the purposes of self-preservation is never a good look.'[8]

It was noteworthy that just days later Andrew Whyte, UK Labour's Director of Governance and Legal, decided that rather than keeping the £31,600 residue from Vaughan Gething's campaign donations, the money should instead be redirected to 'progressive causes'.[9] This enabled Rhun ap Iorwerth to claim it was further proof of Gething's error of judgement: 'The right thing to do all along would be to pay back the entire amount'.[10]

Personalities matter in politics. The Co-operation Agreement would not have occurred without Mark Drakeford's strong backing. After all, he had the option of governing without such a deal. Neither would the Agreement have been so extensive and far reaching without the political imagination that Adam Price brought to the table.

Price had been forced to resign in May 2023 because of circumstances in which he had no part. An accumulation of accusations and complaints prompted Price to commission a report into the party's culture and procedures. The report, by former MS Nerys Evans, published in April 2023, found a systemic pattern of misogyny, bullying and sexual harassment within the party, and made 82 recommendations to address it.[11] Evans exonerated Price of any direct involvement, and he accepted her recommendations in full. Indeed, she urged him to stay on as leader to ensure her recommendations would be implemented. However, some members of the Senedd Group decided that a change of leadership was necessary to demonstrate they accepted the need for fundamental change. Despite pleas from members of the National Executive and the party at Westminster, Price decided he no longer had the united support of the Senedd Group.

---

8   Rh. ap Iorwerth, 'Why Plaid Cymru decided to withdraw from the Co-operation Agreement with the Welsh Government' (*Nation Cymru*, 18 May 2024).

9   M. Shipton, 'Top Labour figure close to Starmer decided not to accept what's left of Gething's "dodgy donation"' (*Nation Cymru*, 23 May 2024). The episode also provided confirmation that Welsh Labour's finances are controlled in London.

10   'Labour not keeping Vaughan Gething's leftover cash' (*Nation Cymru*, 21 May 2024).

11   Nerys Evans, *Prosiect Pawb* [Everybody's Project], April 2023.

Personalities and Politics Intervene

By the end of the year Mark Drakeford had also left the stage. This placed the Co-operation Agreement in the hands of new leaders who, necessarily, could not have the same personal investment in it as their predecessors who had negotiated its terms. Any political agreement, regardless of the constitutional framework or guarantees it embodies, ultimately relies on trust between the participants. As we have seen, this was swiftly eroded once Vaughan Gething assumed leadership of Welsh Labour. Moreover, in late May the calling of a UK general election made competitive party politics an overriding priority.

On 5 June a motion of no-confidence was brought against Gething by the Conservatives in the Senedd. Albeit that Labour was able to ignore the vote, because it was held in Opposition time and so not binding on the government, the motion was passed by 29 members to 27. This was because two Labour members, Hannah Blythyn and Lee Waters, failed to vote. The surface explanation was that both were away from the Senedd on sick leave, agreed to and therefore covered by, the Labour chief whip Jane Hutt.[12] Was it a coincidence, however, that Blythyn had been sacked by Gething for allegedly leaking his Covid iMessage, and Waters had a few weeks earlier broken ranks to call on him to return the £200,000 loan? Both could have voted remotely in support of the First Minister.

Six weeks later, in a message to members of his Llanelli constituency party and following Vaughan Gething's resignation, Waters revealed why he had not supported the First Minister:

> 'It is clear that Vaughan very sincerely does not believe that he did anything wrong. And for me that was the fundamental problem. One of the reasons why the last three months has been so painful in the Welsh Labour Party is that the schism that has surfaced has revealed a genuine tension in values. I literally felt sick when I felt compelled to speak out against what I saw as 'norm spoiling' behaviour; and when my cry of pain was ignored I made myself ill with the thought of endorsing this amorality in a confidence vote. I couldn't do it, and didn't do it. I drafted a private note to Vaughan which, in the end I didn't send as he hadn't responded to any of my messages, but it summed up how I felt:

---

12 Normally in such circumstances the opposition parties pair their votes with Labour MSs, but on this occasion neither the Conservatives nor Plaid Cymru agreed to do so.

> *I know you think you are being held to a higher standard than others. I honestly don't – unless you are comparing donations at a UK level that we have rightly condemned. It is a terrible argument to make, and one contradicted by your decision to advise the UK party that they should not keep the underspend. If it was a problem for them to use it, why wasn't it a problem for you? The argument that you won't be involved in any decisions is disingenuous and beside the point. It reinforces the view that we are slippery, venal and insincere. The polls now clearly show that this has cut-through and people feel you should not have taken the donation, and having taken it should give it back. The way you have dealt with the situation has revealed further character traits that clash with the values I expect from a leader.*[13]

As Adam Price put it in the debate, the Government had become shallow and rudderless, 'shorn of any sense of greater purpose other than the political survival of the First Minister himself ':

> 'The question of dirty money, which bedevils most western democracies, has thankfully not been much of an issue for us in Wales. Welsh millionaires have not been interested in politics and Welsh politics has not been interested in millionaires. That happy circumstance the First Minister has brought crashing to an end.'[14]

Despite Gething ignoring the confidence vote, which his supporters among Welsh and other MPs at Westminster described as a 'gimmick', pressure continued to mount from within the Labour Group in the Senedd. Initially, he was helped by the need for Labour to retain an outward appearance of unity during the UK general election campaign that was underway. However, as soon that ended, on 4 July, his position rapidly became untenable. The Conservatives tabled a motion for 17 July that would have compelled him to reveal the evidence he used in his decision to dismiss Hannah Blythyn. On the morning of the day before that motion was to be debated, in a co-ordinated move, four of his Ministers resigned: the Counsel General Mick Antoniw, Economy Minister and his rival for the leadership

---

13 M. Shipton, 'Ex Minister Lee Waters warns Welsh Labour it's in danger of losing power in wake of Gething crisis' (*Nation Cymru*, 22 July 2024).
14 *Senedd Record*, 5 June 2024.

Jeremy Miles, Housing Minister Julie James, and Culture Minister Leslie Griffiths. Significantly, all four cited the First Minister's refusal to respond to the No Confidence motion in their resignation letters. Within hours Gething was gone.

The Co-operation Agreement's Inheritance

Despite the Co-operation Agreement being wound up prematurely, both the new party leaders declared support for the collaboration it represented and the policies it contained. Responding to Plaid's decision Vaughan Gething said:

> 'The Co-operation Agreement was about mature politics, working together on areas where we agree. While it was always a time-limited agreement, we are disappointed Plaid Cymru has decided to walk away from their opportunity to deliver for the people of Wales... By working together we have achieved a great deal, including free school meals for all pupils in primary schools, providing more free childcare, introducing a radical package of measures to create thriving local communities, helping people to live locally and addressing high numbers of second homes in many areas of Wales.'[15]

For his part, Rhun ap Iorwerth observed:

> 'The Agreement was both an innovative and mature way of doing politics, which in the best traditions of Plaid Cymru put the interests of Wales first. It was an antidote to the UK Conservative government's politics of division, and a constructive response to the chaos and uncertainty of Brexit and the Covid pandemic. I'm proud of what we achieved and know that what Plaid Cymru has been able to put into action will stand the test of time. Knowing that children won't be hungry in the school day, that measures to control the housing market will allow more of our young people to live in the communities where they were brought up, and that the climate crisis is being taken seriously by way of establishing a national energy company is what progressive politics should be about.'[16]

---

15 'Plaid pulls out of Co-operation Agreement' (*Nation Cymru*, 17 May 2024).
16 Rhun ap Iorwerth, 'Why Plaid Cymru decided to withdraw from the Co-operation Agreement with the Welsh Government', *op. cit.*

Such accolades suggest that, in future, Plaid and Labour may not be averse to negotiating a fresh iteration of the Co-operation Agreement. As always this will be determined by the personalities and the politics at the time. The latter will take the form of the numbers – that is to say, the outcome of the 2026 Senedd election in terms of the seats won will be the most decisive factor. That election promises to bring together a set of circumstances designed to require further party co-operation. By May 2026 Labour will have been in power in London for approaching two years, enough time for the shine of a newly minted Westminster government to have worn off. Further, the Welsh electoral landscape will be completely different, with 16 new Senedd constituencies each returning six members, under a completely proportional system. In combination, these factors are likely to result in a greater range of representation in the Senedd, in turn increasing the need for further cross-party collaboration.

There is even the possibility that a discredited Conservative Party, losing all its Westminster seats in Wales in July 2024, might be pushed back into third place in the Senedd, with Plaid doing well enough to come second and edging closer to a still dominant Labour that is short of a majority. In those circumstances a straightforward coalition might look a tempting prospect. Nonetheless, in such a situation Plaid would do well to think twice. There is an established record of the smaller parties in coalition governments faring badly in the subsequent election. This was the experience of Plaid itself in the 2011 election following its 'One Wales' coalition with Labour, and of the Liberal Democrats in the 2015 Westminster general election following their coalition with the Conservatives. So, even if a coalition was on offer in the wake of the 2026 Senedd election, with Plaid Ministers in the Welsh Government, a wiser course might be for the party to pursue another Co-operation Agreement.

In any event, much of the agenda for whatever inter-party talks might take place has already been set by the 2021 to 2024 Co-operation Agreement. One indicator was the Welsh Government's decision, announced in May 2024, to delay reform of council tax until 2028. Under the Co-operation Agreement this reform – involving a revaluation of properties and the creation of extra tax bands to make the system fairer – was intended to be undertaken by 2025. The delay schedules the change, which would mean a reduction in bills for poorer households but increased bills for more expensive properties, beyond the 2026 election.

Another, potentially terminal, delay was made to the Co-operation Agreement's commitment to reform the school year. This would have reduced the six-week summer holidays by a week and, instead, added it to the one-week break in October. It was one of the few policies in the Agreement emanating solely from the Labour side, a commitment contained in the party's 2021 Senedd election manifesto. It was also one to which Mark Drakeford was particularly attached. However, in a statement to the Senedd in June 2024 the Education Minister, Lynne Neagle, newly appointed by Vaughan Gething, reported that the 16,000 responses to the Government's consultation on the policy had been evenly divided. Accordingly, she said no final decision would be taken in the current Senedd term:

> 'There is evidence that suggests the summer period contributes to learning loss, and there are obvious concerns around how we support those children for whom school is safer than home. But there is also evidence that shows the benefit of an extended break for the well-being of both children and the workforce, and how that contributes positively to family life.'[17]

Neagle's decision provoked a rare and blistering attack by a former First Minister. Mark Drakeford condemned the abandonment of a Labour manifesto commitment. For him, the policy, though controversial, was an example of a progressive change that had been made possible by the Co-operation Agreement. Now it was a casualty of the Agreement's premature ending. Drakeford claimed the removal of just one week from the summer holiday was far from a radical step and would have been the start of a journey to improve educational outcomes in Wales:

> 'I regret the political damage. I regret the reputational damage that will be done to Wales, just as other parts of the United Kingdom were looking at Wales and pointing to us as an example of what a progressive Government could do.'

Then, pointing to the experience of many children on the Ely estate in his Cardiff West constituency, he added:

---

17   *Senedd Record*, 4 June 2024.

'When those children go away from school in July, in those six weeks, they will not see a book, they will have no opportunity to play in a way that allows them to appreciate what maths can do for them in their lives, and when they come back in September, the school starts all over again. The idea that there is no learning loss in the lives of those children is absolutely absurd. What this policy would have done is it would have begun to close a gap in the lives of those children. Here is a Government that could have done something to help them. But it has decided not to.'[18]

Housing is another area where the ambitions of the Co-operation Agreement fell short. Although measures put in place to tackle the second homes crisis were ground-breaking, there was little progress on wider housing policy. The Welsh Government set a target of delivering 20,000 new low-carbon homes for social rent during the five-year 2021-26 Senedd term, but there is no prospect of that being achieved. In the first two years only 5,775 homes were delivered towards the target.[19]

It hasn't always been this hard to build social housing. In the 30-year period between the mid-1940s and mid-1970s, an average of 8,000 new social homes were built every year in Wales. Compared with this, just 1,203 new homes were built by social landlords in 2022-23. The reason can be traced to the beginning of the sale of council houses in the 1980s and then the withdrawal of many local authorities from house-building altogether. Meanwhile, housing associations couldn't fill the gap. The public sector retreated from the strategic planning, the land assembly and the large-scale development required to provide the volume of social housing that is needed.

Plaid Cymru's proposal for *Unnos* put forward during the Co-operation Agreement negotiations, envisaged a publicly-owned authority, answerable to the Senedd. It would have powers to raise long-term finance, assemble public and private land, co-ordinate housing associations, organise building supply chains, and promote good construction practice. However, what came out of the Agreement did not measure up to this ambition. Financially, the

---

18   Ibid.
19   Senedd Research, *Building Social Housing: can the Welsh Government do more?*, 16 February 2024.

Welsh Government provided *Unnos* with a mere £1 million revenue funding in 2020-23, with another £1 million promised in 2024-25. This was no more than seed-corn funding, making housing policy unfinished business for a successor to the Co-operation Agreement.

An even more intractable policy in the Agreement was its commitment 'to create a National Care Service, free at the point of need'. When this was negotiated in 2021 there was an expectation that the Westminster government was poised, after decades of prevarication, to grasp the nettle of demographic change and invest substantially in a new system of social care for England. Thereby it would have, via the Barnett Consequential, increased the resources available to the Welsh Government for social care. However, as Mark Drakeford explained to the Committee for the Scrutiny of the First Minister in March 2023:

> 'This is one of the areas where the context for the work of the Co-operation Agreement has altered very significantly since the negotiations to come to an Agreement were being carried out. When we were holding those negotiations, the UK Government had committed itself to a social care funding stream, a specific social care funding stream, and it had committed itself to an implementation of its version of the Dilnot report,[20] so it meant that we were able to plan ahead on the basis that there was going to be money available for the development of social care, and we would know the landscape across our border, which has a shaping impact on some of the decisions that we have to make. Neither of those things are true any longer, and inevitably, that has an impact upon the way in which we can take the Co-operation Agreement proposals forward.'[21]

It is a sobering illustration of the extent to which the Welsh Government's discretion remains totally dependent on financial

---

20 The Dilnot Commission, which reported in July 2011, was established to investigate how to deliver a fair, affordable and sustainable funding system for social care in England. It recommended that no-one should have to spend more than 30% of their assets to fund their social care, with a cap of £35,000. It estimated that this would require £1.7 billion in additional annual public expenditure, rising to £3.6 billion by 2025-26. Though the UK Government at the time welcomed the Commission's report no action has been taken on it.
21 *Senedd Record*, Committee for the Scrutiny of the First Minister, 24 March 2023.

choices made at Westminster. Until Wales achieves a fairer financial settlement, based on need rather than the arbitrary population-related Barnett formula, this will continue. As far as social care is concerned, any future inter-party negotiations in the Senedd will have to address two further factors.

The first is a difference between Welsh Labour and Plaid on where responsibility should lie. Labour remains committed to social care being in the hands of local government, while Plaid advocates a seamless Health and Social Care Service, run by the NHS. It believes that only with this mechanism can parity of esteem be assured, and that the principle of 'free at the point of need' be guaranteed.

This leads directly to the second factor which is, of course, funding. Extra money has to be found from somewhere. If the Westminster Government still has not made a commitment by 2026, then there seems little option but to look again at the proposals for a Welsh social care levy. These were first made by Professor Gerald Holtham in a report commissioned by the Welsh Government in 2018.[22] His proposals were incorporated into Plaid Cymru's 2021 Senedd election manifesto.

A further example of where the 2021-24 Co-operation Agreement has set the agenda for inter-party talks that may occur following the 2026 election, is economic development, and specifically the mechanisms that are necessary for an effective policy to be implemented. As was explored in Chapters 2 and 4, this was an area deliberately avoided by Labour during the Agreement negotiations. The idea of reinstating the Welsh Development Agency, abolished by the Welsh Government in 2004 in its so-called 'Bonfire of the Quangos', was an anathema. However, there are signs that Welsh Labour's position is softening. One was Jeremy Miles's willingness to consider the case for a new economic agency, at arms-length from the Welsh Government, during his bid for the leadership of Welsh Labour in early 2024. Plaid Cymru is also advocating a further two related agencies: one for the western seaboard (Arfor) to promote

---

22   G. Holtham, *Paying for Social Care, An independent report commissioned by the Welsh Government*, June 2018. His proposals were incorporated in a paper prepared by the author during 2020 as Plaid's Director of Policy: *A Social Care Fund to Improve and Sustain Social Care for Older People*. This paper proved controversial since there is a strong view within the party that, as with the NHS, social care should be funded from general taxation. However, the policy was eventually accepted by the party's National Council.

housing and economic development alongside language revival; and another for the Valleys, to harness the economic potential of the Metro. Those who argue that this would be an administrative overload, should examine the position in Scotland. There, Scottish Enterprise, the country's long established national development agency, is accompanied by the separate Highlands and Islands Enterprise, and the South of Scotland Enterprise, covering Dumfries and Galloway and the Scottish Borders.

In terms of constitutional development the agenda has been set by the Independent Commission on the Constitutional Future of Wales, established as part of the Co-operation Agreement. As discussed in the following chapter, its final report in January 2024 describes a number of changes that are urgently necessary to protect the present devolution settlement from erosion by the centralising impulses of Westminster governments. These include fairer funding, reform of the House of Lords to give representation to the devolved institutions, and removal of restrictions on the Senedd's powers contained in Westminster legislation. In addition, the Senedd needs more powers, including justice and policing, railways, welfare, the Crown Estate, and broadcasting.

In its response to the Commission's report the Welsh Government agreed with all these recommendations, declaring.

> 'Twenty-five years on, devolution has become an established constitutional reality, underpinned by strong support from people across Wales. Yet as events of recent years have shown, the responsibilities of the Senedd and the broader fabric of devolution – and, indeed, the constitution of the UK – are vulnerable to the actions of a UK Government. Moreover, the future of the UK as whole and its constituent parts remains uncertain. This is the context that makes the final report from the Independent Commission on the Constitutional Future of Wales so relevant, significant and welcome.'[23]

Yet how likely is it that, on its own, a Labour Government in Cardiff Bay will be able to persuade even a Labour Government in Westminster to accede to these demands? It will have more chance if

---

23 *The Welsh Government's Response to the Final Report of the Independent Commission on the Constitutional Future of Wales*, March 2024.

it is able to demonstrate that its remaining in government depends on a cross-party agreement, which in turn requires these concessions. It is an instance of the truth that creating a new Wales is not the work of one party, it is the work of an entire nation, and all of its perspectives.

7

Nation Building

A robust sense of shared national identity is essential for the success of democratic government. It is fundamental to the give-and-take which makes possible the implementation of a coherent programme of national policy. Yet, for very many, perhaps most people in Wales, their national identity is a complex and sometimes ambiguous matter. To varying degrees people identify themselves as Welsh, British, Welsh and British, Welsh and European, or a combination of all three. Others pride themselves on being citizens of Wales while originating from elsewhere. Approximately 20% of people in Wales were born in England, most of whom identify as English or British or both. This diversity of identity is intensified – enriched, it should be said – by the increasing presence of ethnic minority groups within Welsh communities.

In 21st Century Wales it is easier to be relaxed about these varied identities since the presence of the Senedd and the Welsh Government has changed the whole basis of Welsh citizenship. Whatever a person's view of their specific identity, that individual is a voter, is personally affected by the Welsh Government's decisions, and is thus a Welsh citizen in a new and unprecedented way. Attracting all Welsh citizens to participate fully in the life of the nation and to identify with its aspirations and interests is the key to the success of the nation and its government.

However hesitantly, the 1997 referendum set Wales on a course towards greater autonomy. At that time Donald Anderson, then Labour MP for Swansea East and a late convert to devolution, described it as a mystery tour:

> 'I recall the fine story of a bus tour from Cwmrhydyceirw in my constituency. There was a sweep about where the tour would end,

and it is said the driver won. The people of Wales are driving this mystery tour. They will decide the pace and direction.'[1]

More than a quarter of a century later we can see more clearly where the journey is heading. A fledgling Assembly, little more than a version of local government with some parliamentary aspirations tagged on, has developed into today's Senedd with full legislative powers in its fields of competence. Fiscal powers are following and, as a result of the Co-operation Agreement, the Senedd will increase in size to create a fully functioning parliament.

All this has been achieved by Plaid Cymru working with Labour to various degrees and in different contexts. The first occasion was during the One Wales coalition government, which secured the 2011 referendum and legislative powers, then 15 years later it was through the Co-operation Agreement. It suggests that, as the future unfolds, further progress could be made by Plaid and Labour working together. The argument was set out by the late Professor Phil Williams, a leading figure in Plaid Cymru over four decades:

> 'Within the Party of Wales there is a recurring debate as to whether an essential prerequisite for self-government is that Plaid Cymru replaces the Labour Party as the mainstream, dominant party in Wales. Alternatively, is it possible for a single-minded and uncompromising Plaid Cymru to create the conditions whereby other parties deliver self-government, albeit step by step and with some reluctance. Progress over the past 40 years, and especially the establishment of the National Assembly, point to the latter strategy.'[2]

In truth, the party has always followed a dual strategy, challenging the Labour party for power, but all the time seeking to pull it in Plaid's direction. With the Co-operation Agreement this implicit role has now become explicit. Plaid Cymru may lose an electoral battle but, it can be argued, it wins the war of ideas. In 2021 Plaid Cymru failed to secure a breakthrough to power, but its policies found their way to the forefront of the Welsh Government's Programme for Government.

---

1   D. Anderson, *Hansard*, 25 July 1997 - debate on the legislation allowing the 1997 referendum to be held.
2   P. Williams, *The Psychology of Distance* (IWA & Welsh Academic Press, 2003), p.41.

Identity and the language

Throughout the history of Wales, the Welsh language has been a marker of our distinctiveness, and a major source of our separate identity. When Plaid set about popularising the notion of Wales as a political entity, it was perhaps inevitable that Welsh-speakers and Welsh-speaking areas would be the first to convert to political nationalism. After all, they knew they were Welsh. The rest of Wales, in which a large majority of the population speak English only, was not so sure. Put simply, those who don't speak Welsh have a different sense of being Welsh and consequently are more equivocal about political nationalism. In the main, this is what accounted for the success of Plaid in the western half of Wales in the May 2021 election and its relative failure in the east.

Yet rather than a problem for Plaid, this should be seen instead as unfinished business. Wales is a geographic, historic, cultural, psychological, political, and now a constitutional reality. It is diverse and inclusive. It prides itself on the richness of its diversity which, apart from being valuable in itself, is an important resource which can be deployed in the political project of building the nation and attaining independence. Plaid Cymru's *raison d'être* is to lead this national project which is multi-faceted: political, constitutional, economic, social, and cultural.

A key component of the project is the restoration and rejuvenation of the Welsh language which historically has been the badge of our distinct existence as a nation. This will involve reversing the long-term trends associated with our incorporation and marginalisation within the British state, whereby Welsh became a language of a minority. This reversal can only be achieved with the consent of the people. While a majority of the English-speaking Welsh may yet be unready to actively consent to such a linguistic reversal, all the evidence suggests they are not overtly hostile and in most cases are empathetic.

Reversal will require action across a wide range of policy fronts, especially the expansion of Welsh-medium education so that increasing numbers acquire natural fluency in the language. There is also a need to build the confidence and vitality of the communities – whether territorially or network-based – where Welsh is the primary language of choice. The existence and enhancement of such communities is a precondition for the survival and growth of the language across the nation as a whole. It follows that special support is needed for those geographical areas where the language is widely used. This provides the impetus behind Plaid's Arfor policy which is aimed at overturning a long-entrenched pattern of depopulation of the young and in-migration of economically inactive people along the western seaboard of Wales. It recognises that there is clear danger of further decline in the coming decades unless an initiative that combines economic regeneration with language planning is carried through in a determined, and systematic way.

The core implementation of the Arfor strategy requires the creation of three new towns, as extensions of existing settlements on the Menai in Gwynedd, and in the environs of Aberystwyth and Carmarthen. An Arfor development body should have powers in relation to these defined locations in respect of land acquisition and compulsory purchase, together with the funding to provide the necessary infrastructure, housing, and other economic incentives.

Although the Arfor concept is acknowledged in the Co-operation Agreement, together with a gesture towards the defined needs of the southern valleys, there are no commitments beyond pursuing small-scale pilot projects and undertaking further research. Set against the other wide-ranging commitments in the Agreement, the scale and ambition of Arfor were too large for the Labour side in the negotiations to take on board in any systematic way. Nonetheless, the proposals remain as a starting point for consideration in any future agreement.

Wales and England

England is Wales's immediate and, of course, most powerful neighbour. Moreover, the 160-mile border between the two countries is highly permeable. More than half the Welsh population live within 25 miles of it. There has been a long history of often acrimonious relations between the peoples of the two countries. During the Norman era there were times of conquest and revolt, which were followed in later centuries by intermittent periods of repression and exploitation.

Modern Wales emerged in the 19th and early 20th Centuries, led by large-scale in-migration into the industrial south. In 1851, Wales had 1,163,139 inhabitants. By 1913 their number had increased to

2,523,500, a rise of 117% in 63 years.[3] The expansion was largely due to coalmining, especially between the 1870s and the outbreak of the First World War. There was massive migration to the southern Welsh coalfield, to begin with mainly from rural Wales but later also from western England and further afield. In the first decade of the 20th Century Wales gained 120,000 people through immigration from England. More people moved in than out, making Wales unique amongst the nations of Europe in this period. Only America rivalled its rate of population growth as a result of inward migration.

However, the arrival of oil and the collapse of coalmining in the 1920s resulted in massive out-migration. Around 500,000 people left Wales during the inter-war period. The historian Gwyn A. Williams declared this to be our equivalent of the Irish Famine. The exodus of the Welsh was mainly to the English Midlands and South-East, to Dagenham and Slough, the women to service and the men to car factories. In their place came nearly 250,000 people, overwhelmingly English, often retired, making for the holiday coasts and emptied rural villages.

Over three generations, these population movements created massive dislocations, not least in cultural and political affiliations, and a lasting imprint so far as the relationship between Wales and England was concerned. The result, again according to Gwyn A. Williams, was to create a sense of fragmentation and despair:

> 'By the 1980s the Wales which The Successful Century had invented was being dismantled by the force through which the black fuse drove the power, and no one, in his or her heart, no matter which clichés old and new they might parrot in diminishing conviction, knew what was going to happen to us, we who had lived in these two peninsulas, as a people, somehow or other, for a millennium and a half.'[4]

Then miraculously, in a matter of decades some equilibrium was achieved. With the coming of the National Assembly following the referendum in 1997, Wales established itself as a political nation. At the same time, the Welsh economy began to diversify, weaning itself off the dependence on the old extractive industries. Meanwhile,

---

3 J. Davies, *A History of Wales* (Penguin, 2007), p.387.
4 G. A. Williams, *When Was Wales?* (Penguin, 1985), p.260.

shared achievements such as the creation of the NHS, together with many cross-border family interrelations, meant the continuation of a strong social union with England.

This history has bequeathed a complex legacy. There are contrasting views from either side of the border. England seems to view Wales in a quite different way to how it regards Scotland, and certainly Northern Ireland. There is a widespread assumption that Northern Ireland will someday be reunited with the Republic, probably sooner rather than later, and that England has no 'selfish' interest in preventing that happen. Essentially, those were the terms of the 1998 Good Friday Agreement. There is widespread acceptance, too, that the Scots may well vote for independence in another referendum sometime in the coming decades. Many English people would probably think that regrettable. However, in existential terms they would not see it as much of a threat. Certainly, opinion polls illustrated that English Brexiteers were prepared to accept Scottish independence if that was the price of leaving the EU. However disruptive the process, Scotland would merely be following the Irish Republic. The presumption would be that Britain would nonetheless remain, even if significantly diminished. It is not felt – and feelings are crucial in this area – as if England, too, would change substantially as a result. Rather, the English would continue as before, but within a Britain that was smaller.

When examined in this light it can be seen that, although Wales is generally ignored or taken for granted, certainly by policy makers in Westminster, nevertheless it has a highly potent if repressed significance for England. For without Wales there cannot be a 'Britain', and without Britain the English would lose, completely, any sense of an imperial identity, however vestigial that may now be. For England, Wales is indeed the fulcrum as well as the historic starting point of the union. Without Wales the English would have no choice but to address what it means to be English, not least in terms of their place in the world. England's seat on the United Nations Security Council would be in question, if not already in play as a result of Scottish secession. Moreover, England would have to re-examine fundamentally its relations with the rest of the British and Irish archipelago, and the European Union as well. It might even consider in a more cogent way its own internally centralised political and constitutional arrangements (the most centralised in Europe) and the potential for real, English, devolution. Some steps in this direction are being taken, with the emergence of city regions and a good deal of policy analysis by the mainstream media being expressed in terms of England rather than Britain. However, until and unless Wales becomes independent, or at least achieves significantly greater autonomy, it is unlikely there will be any systematic constitutional change within England.

To underscore the force of this argument, we need look no further than to the English resistance to Wales creating its own, distinctive jurisdiction, as has long been the position in both Scotland and Northern Ireland. The argument for a Welsh jurisdiction was powerfully made by the 2017 Commission on Justice in Wales, led by former Chief Justice Lord Thomas of Cwmgiedd, and rehearsed by Plaid Cymru's Independence Commission in 2020. Wales is the only country in the world that has a legislature, but no legal jurisdiction of its own. Yet neither the Westminster Conservative Governments (2010-24) nor Labour's 2022 Commission on the Future of the UK, have been willing to acknowledge or address the fact, let alone the need for change. For to do so would result in there inevitably being created a separate English jurisdiction as well, and thereby a separate English legal personality. From there it would be a short step to confront the political consequences of England no longer being held inside a British framework. The English would have to become politically English.

That is part of the perspective as seen from the English side of the border. Looked at from the Welsh side, the outlook is quite different. The most disturbing prospect is not being left without a union but of remaining inside one that has England as the single partner. This eventuality would be exceedingly problematic for many Welsh people who consider themselves to be unionists, especially many within the Welsh Labour Party. For them the notion of being left inside a union that would comprise only England and Wales is difficult to contemplate. For many, probably most Welsh people, if Northern Ireland were to leave the union in order to re-join the Republic it would not have the same resonance. Indeed, Irish unification would probably be welcomed as restoring the proper order of things. However, if Scotland were to vote for independence that would be a quite different matter.

The stated position of the Welsh Labour leadership is that the union is contractual. Its benefits are seen as providing economic security and an insurance system, in which pensions and other benefits are shared. However, in a much deeper psychological sense, the union is conditional as well. If Wales were to be left in a sole relationship with England, many in Welsh Labour would feel deeply uncomfortable. For feel deeply uncomfortable. For them it is a position that would be unsustainable, anathema even. We need to understand why.

The devolved territories of Wales, Scotland and Northern Ireland comprise some 16% of the population of the UK and by working together they can feasibly hope to have some leverage in a dispute with England. If the UK was reduced, however, to a devolved Wales alongside a Westminster-centric England, with only 5.5% of the total population Welsh influence would shrink to vanishing point. It's not just a question of basic arithmetic, though. Wales is overwhelmingly a social democratic country and leans to the left, while England has historically leaned to the right. So held inside a purely English embrace, more often than not Wales would be subject to right-wing governments at Westminster it didn't elect.

Underlying these political realities are even deeper psychological feelings that have their roots in colonial relationships of the past, and a continued resentment at defeat, humiliation and subordination. These sentiments were encapsulated by the poet Nigel Jenkins in one of his more acerbic verses. He has the Archangel Gabriel asking God to reveal his plans in fashioning Wales. God tells him that the nation will be the finest of his creations, with 'alpine peaks and salmon-packed streams'. Its people will be blessed with laverbread and mineral wealth. They'll be singers and bards and wizards at rugby. Not only that, 'they'll speak the language of heaven itself':

> 'But haven't you, Boss,' the Archangel demurred,
>   'Haven't you somewhat overpaid 'em?'
> 'Not,' replied God with a devilish smirk,
>   'Not if you look at the neighbours I've made 'em.'[5]

Of course, Wales and England have no choice but to remain neighbours, sharing a long and highly porous border, with populations and economies that constantly interact with one another. Politically, the devolution process has created an ongoing question of what constitutional arrangement is best suited to manage the relationship. Devolution involves a sovereign Westminster delegating a measure of its sovereign authority to the Senedd and Welsh Government, but

---

5   Nigel Jenkins, 'The Creation', in his collection *Ambush* (Gomer, 1998), p.16.

devolution is not the same as a transfer of power. Powers that are devolved are, by implication, powers that are retained,[6] and despite the increase in powers that have steadily occurred over the quarter of a century of the National Assembly, now Senedd, devolution remains profoundly unsatisfactory. This was explored in great detail by the Independent Commission on the Constitution.

The Independent Commission on the Constitution

Together with Senedd reform, the Co-operation Agreement's establishment of the Independent Commission on the Constitution was its most significant contribution to a further crafting of the political nation. Chaired by Dr Rowan Williams, former Archbishop of Wales and Canterbury, and Professor Laura McAllister, of the Wales Governance Centre at Cardiff University, its deliberations confirmed that independence is now a mainstream part of the debate. Its final report in January 2024 put forward three options for Wales's constitutional future:

- Enhanced Devolution
- Wales in a federal UK
- Independence

It made no recommendation on which option would be best for Wales. Instead, it set out an elaborate list of criteria against which each option should be evaluated. All of them entailed risks, which it said it was not qualified to assess:

> '...choosing between the criteria and evaluating risk is a choice to be made by citizens and their elected representatives.'[7]

It is a fair question that if an expert group such as the Commission feels unable to reach a judgement, after deliberating for more than

---

6   This point was made very early in the modern era devolution debate by Enoch Powell in a speech at Llwynypia, Rhondda, in May 1974: 'Devolution is not the same as the transfer of power; it is the opposite: power devolved is power retained, and that retention is the very reason which makes devolution acceptable and possible.'

7   The Independent Commission on the Constitutional Future of Wales, *Final Report*, January 2024, p.112.

two years at a cost of some £1.5m, then who could reasonably be expected to do so? However, a close reading of the Commission's report reveals pretty clear pointers to the direction of travel it would adopt if it was pressed. In the first place, there is no doubt that it would rule out the federal option. This is made clear at many points in the text. For example, in its chapter on public attitudes it finds that it was:

> '...the least attractive option for citizens across all the strands of our engagement. For many it was seen as neither one thing nor another, and too complicated and expensive. The structure of the UK was often seen as a barrier, particularly the risk of domination by England due to its population size in relation to the other nations.'[8]

A few pages later it judges:

> '... A federal UK would require a four nations perspective, and all nations to change their relationship with each other. Achieving this requires people across the UK to develop a different conception of what the Union is, and their nation's place within it. At present, public opinion is not heading in that direction...'

And:

> '...research indicates that citizens are not enthusiastic about the changes to English governance that would be required to establish a federal UK. This research found low levels of support for the idea of England being governed by an English Parliament, and even lower levels of support for regional governance arrangements.'[9]

In its summary of its public consultations the Commission judges that: 'Most people in Wales support devolution and would favour greater autonomy, in some form.'[10] It's overall conclusions then say that the choice of options, essentially between enhancing devolution or independence, depends on whether people's priorities are either:

---

8   Ibid., p.80.
9   Ibid., p.84.
10 Ibid., p.112.

a. To achieve greater control by the people of Wales over the widest range of policy areas and the opportunity to shape our future as a nation and change the current economic trajectory – and to accept the risk that this may leave people in Wales financially worse off in at least the short and medium term.

or

b. To pursue a lower-risk strategy, based on whatever reforms of the current settlement can realistically be achieved, and grounded on the idea of solidarity with the rest of the UK's population. This is less disruptive but risks no improvement in Wales's relative economic prospects.[11]

In terms of the Commission's options, the first implies independence, and the second enhanced devolution. The Commission says that, as things stand, most people in Wales would tend towards the lower risk strategy. If that is also the Commission's own, unspoken, view then one is driven to ask to what extent can its proposed reforms to the current settlement, necessary to achieve enhanced devolution be, as it puts it, 'realistically achieved'?

This is an urgent question, since early in its report the Commission finds there is a pressing need to protect the present devolution settlement. The 2017-24 Conservative Westminster governments proved hostile to the devolved administrations. Largely due to Brexit and its consequences, especially the imposition of a UK single market, Westminster constantly intruded on the devolved administrations' powers, undermining previous conventions. Moreover, and more insidiously, the UK Treasury constantly found ways to restrict budgets and financial discretion, treating the devolved governments as, in effect, Whitehall departments.

In short, the Commission comes to the chilling conclusion that, 'without urgent action there will be no viable settlement to protect,'[12] and proposed that the Senedd's powers should be extended over a range of areas, with the following heading the queue:

---

11 Ibid., p.124.
12 Ibid., p.44.

- Justice and policing – and the consequent creation of a distinct Welsh jurisdiction (notably the Conservative member of the Commission, Lauren McEvatt, a former Special Adviser at the Wales Office, resiled from this recommendation 'on the basis of her party's strong commitment to maintaining the single jurisdiction of England and Wales'.[13])
- Transport – particularly the Welsh rail network.
- The Crown Estate – management of which has been legislated for in Scotland, creating 'a new precedent, which should apply to Wales.' [14]
- Broadcasting – 'The Welsh and UK Governments should agree a mechanism for a stronger voice for Wales on broadcasting policy...' [15]

The Commission said that, in addition, there are three further requirements to ensure the present settlement is placed 'on a long-term viable footing':

1. A fundamental review of territorial funding in relation to need across the UK, agreed by the four governments of the UK.
2. The UK government pursues a reform of the Westminster Parliament's second chamber which guarantees a formal voice for the nations and regions of the UK and their devolved institutions.
3. A regular process for reviewing and updating the reservations in Section 7A of the Government of Wales Act to remove reservations which lack a strategic rationale (through primary legislation or Ministerial Order as appropriate), agreed by the Welsh Government and the UK government.[16]

How likely is it that a Westminster Government, of whatever hue, would be at all willing to satisfy these criteria? This is a question that the Commission leaves hanging in the air. We know from experience that less than short change will be produced by the Conservatives. As for Labour, Keir Starmer has made no firm commitments at all on the constitution.

---

13   Ibid., p.67.
14   Ibid., p.67.
15   Ibid., p.71.
16   Ibid., pp.94-5.

The Constitution Commission made clear that the priorities for Wales are, first to protect the current devolution settlement, and second to empower the Welsh Government so it has a better chance to tackle Wales's endemic economic problems. Its proposals for protecting and enhancing devolution would be welcome if they had a realistic chance of being enacted at Westminster. But do they?

As for the economy, it was Plaid's own Independence Commission that demonstrated that Wales has failed to make economic progress, not because the country is too small or too poor, but because it is trapped within an economy overwhelmingly shaped in the interests of the City of London. Wales's average standard of living, or GDP per capita, has hovered very consistently at around 72% of the average UK level since the beginning of electoral devolution in 1999. No expert analysis of any sort believes this is likely to change in any foreseeable future inside the UK. Against this, it is simply a matter of economic fact that states which joined the EU – Ireland, Spain, Portugal and Greece, and more recently countries in central Europe, have seen very considerable economic convergence with EU averages – in a manner which has not happened in the UK.[17]

So, in short, the flawed UK economic model has failed to deliver prosperity for Wales and offers little or no prospect of doing so in the future, while an independent Wales would be free to govern in its own interests. It would no longer be subordinated to the requirements of London and the south east of England or be subject to the fiscal policies determined by the UK Government. There is little doubt, as well, that an independent Wales would seek membership of the EU as soon as was feasible. Certainly, this is already Plaid Cymru policy and may likely become that of Welsh Labour as well.

A close reading of the Constitution Commission's report suggests that, if only it had allowed itself the freedom to express its own view, it would have come to the same conclusion.

Free Association

In its evidence to the Commission on the Constitutional Future of Wales, Plaid Cymru put forward a pathway towards greater

---

17   Plaid Cymru, *Towards an Independent Wales, op. cit.*

autonomy for Wales short of an immediate move to independence.[18] This was a proposal for Free Association, which would guarantee a fully sovereign Senedd whilst retaining, for the time being, a formal constitutional relationship between Wales and the rest of the UK

Free Association is an alternative response to the limitations of devolution on the one hand and the practical difficulties of federalism on the other. It would entail a more fundamental transfer of powers to Wales, limiting those of the Westminster Parliament to England. It would leave the Senedd free to legislate without restriction in relation to Wales except, possibly, on some vestigial subjects. Wales would thereby be more effectively insulated from a tendency for England to exercise reserved powers in a way that disadvantaged Wales (since those reserved powers would be very severely curtailed).

The advantage to England of such a move would be that it would represent a much less disruptive change to the current UK constitution than either a major enhancement of devolution or a move to a federal arrangement. The need to at least give the appearance of accommodating the interests of Wales when making decisions on what are now reserved matters would disappear or at least be greatly reduced. Overlaps between reserved and devolved functions of government would be eliminated. Formal UK sovereignty, however, would not be further diminished.

There are a number of functioning examples of similar arrangements around the world. International law already recognises a category of constitutional arrangement which occupies the space between integration of two territories into a single state (whether with or without partial self-government of the smaller one on a devolutionary basis) and their formal separation into two sovereign states. The term used to denote this intermediate status is that of Free Association, as described in Resolution 1541 adopted by the General Assembly of the United Nations on 15 December 1960.

The development of the concept of Free Association took place in the context of the movement towards decolonisation. The territories to which the UN has needed to apply the concept have been former colonies situated predominantly in the Pacific, Africa and the Caribbean. However, the concept of a status which is neither that of a sovereign independent state nor that of one integrated into a larger

---

18   Plaid Cymru, *The Road to Independence – Evidence to the Independent Commission on the Constitutional Future of Wales* (Y Lolfa, November 2022).

state can also be applied to a number of arrangements which have different historical roots. Some of these, including the Isle of Man, the Channel Islands and the Faroes, are of particular relevance to Wales.

Application of the status of associated state to Wales would inevitably generate a number of practical issues that would have to be resolved. So far, the status has only been applied to island territories remote from the larger state. But it should not be forgotten that not dissimilar questions arise in relation to a number of very small *sovereign* states (for example, Monaco and San Marino) which are contiguous with much larger neighbours and share various services with them. There is no reason to believe that, given the will to move Wales to a status of Free Association, practical solutions could not be found.

Given the close integration of the Welsh and English economies, in particular a shared currency and a single market for trade and labour, it would be essential for the continuation of robust arrangements between England and a Welsh Associated Free State relating to shared services. For example, a shared, common labour market between the two countries would require a continued pensions and social security community linking England and Wales. However, it would be more in line with the concept of Free Association for such arrangements to be governed by inter-governmental relations (subject of course to parliamentary scrutiny in both territories) than by maintaining a nominal Welsh membership of the House of Commons.

Free Association can be seen as akin to the Dominion Status that was the constitutional position of the predecessor to the Republic of Ireland – the Irish Free State – from 1922 to 1949. It was also granted by the 1931 Statute of Westminster to Australia, Canada and New Zealand.[19] In 2016 the late Lord Elystan Morgan moved an

---

19 The 1931 Statute of Westminster was a forerunner of the Sewel Convention that for the early period of devolution, until the Conservative Government elected in 2016, was consistently applied to relations between Westminster and the devolved institutions. Section 4 of the Statute states, 'No Act of Parliament the United Kingdom passes after the commencement of this Act shall extend, or be deemed to extend, to a Dominion as part of the law of that Dominion, unless it is expressly declared in that Act that that Dominion has requested, and consented to, the enactment thereof.' It put into legal language the Balfour Declaration that had been made at the 1926 Imperial Conference. This described Great Britain and the Dominions as 'autonomous communities within the British Empire, equal in status, in no way subordinate one to

amendment proposing Dominion Status to the Wales Bill that was creating a reserved powers arrangement along with devolution of some taxation powers to Wales.[20] Lord Morgan said 'the Welsh people should think big':

> 'For far too long we have begged for the crumbs of devolution and it is highly necessary that we should raise our expectations to be worthy of our status as a mature national entity. The Statute of Westminster 1931 did not create a rigid model of Dominion Status but rather enunciated a principle of immense flexibility and subtleness. It stands to reason that Dominion Status in relation to Wales would be very different from the patterns existing for Australia and New Zealand, but it is a worthy and honourable concept that can enable Wales to play its full part within the life of the UK.'[21]

He also argued that Westminster's plan for a reserved powers constitution was fundamentally flawed:

> 'While a reserve powers system placing Wales on a par with Scotland and Northern Ireland is both just and welcomed, the way in which the Government have proceeded is little short of ludicrous in that they have introduced some 200 reservations with scores of them being utterly trivial and meagre – like licensing dangerous dogs, prostitution, and charitable collections. A reserve powers system in an enlightened society depends entirely upon mutual trust and respect existing between the parent Parliament and the devolved body. It appears, however, that when the question was asked by the Secretary of State for Wales of his Cabinet colleagues, 'What reservations would you desire?' the answer that he seems to have received seems like, "All that we can possibly think of – the meaner and more trivial the better". It is for that reason I have described the

---

another in any aspect of their domestic or external affairs, though united by a common allegiance to the Crown and freely associated as members of the British Commonwealth of Nations'.

20   A leading figure in Plaid Cymru in the 1950s and early 1960s, Elystan Morgan joined Labour in 1965 and became the party's MP for Cardiganshire (now Ceredigion) between 1966 and 1974. He subsequently became a barrister and Circuit Court Judge, gaining a peerage in 1981.

21   M. Shipton, 'Peer set to move amendment which could see Wales given "dominion" status' (*Western Mail*, 7 November 2016).

situation as imperial and colonial and that such tawdry inhibitions would never have been thought of sixty years ago by a Colonial Office dealing with a British Caribbean or African colony. But remember always that Wales was England's first colony and a determination exists in certain circles that it should be its last.'[22]

It was noteworthy, therefore, that in the Senedd debate on the Independent Commission on the Constitution's report, in March 2024, Mark Drakeford also referred to the 'absurdity' of the 2017 Wales Act which meant, he said, that 'we are, in this Chamber, responsible for road, rail, for cycling, but we're explicitly prevented from taking control of Welsh hovercraft.' Then he referred warmly to Elystan Morgan 'who constantly argued that Dominion Status was an option for devolution in Wales that hadn't been properly explored, that ought to be put back on the table.'[23]

The 'Long Revolution'

What has been happening in Wales since 1999 is the result of a long revolution that is slowly gathering pace. The term *Long Revolution* was coined by Raymond Williams in his book of the same name, published in 1961. Williams argued that we were living through a long-term and far-reaching transformation of our society, in which the development of democracy had a leading role. He described it as, 'The rising determination... that people should govern themselves.'[24] Then, in the final chapter he added:

> 'The human energy of the long revolution springs from the conviction that men [sic] can direct their own lives, by breaking through the pressures and restrictions of older forms of society and discovering new common institutions... The nature of the process indicates a perhaps unusual revolutionary activity: open discussion, extending relationships, the practical shaping of institutions.'[25]

---

22   Ibid.
23   Senedd *Record*, 19 March 2004.
24   R. Williams, *The Long Revolution* (Penguin, 1971), p.10.
25   Ibid., pp.375-83

That is a fair summary of Plaid Cymru's essential programme. As Raymond Williams said, the democratic transformation he was advocating is a multi-generational process. Williams's use of the word *process* was echoed by Ron Davies when he famously described devolution in these terms rather than an 'event'.[26] Plaid Cymru's long revolution began almost a hundred years ago, in 1925, when Saunders Lewis set the party on the path to winning national freedom. Since then, it has come a long way in building our nation. Who would have thought in 1925, in 1945, 1966, 1979, or even as late as 1997, that by 2024 we would have a democratically elected legislative Senedd, poised to take another step by extending its membership to become a fully-functioning parliament? It is the long revolution taking place before our eyes, and that is how the significance of the Co-operation Agreement that Plaid negotiated with Labour in the six months following the May 2021 election should be viewed. It has created the outline of a road towards greater autonomy for Wales. However, it will be no ordinary journey. There is no ready-made road. As the Basque saying has it, 'We build the road as we travel'. This is what nation-building means.

One theme of this book has been how Plaid Cymru has shifted its understanding on how nation building and constitutional advance requires the party to collaborate with other progressively minded forces in the Senedd. Of course, the need for cross-party collaboration has been the case since the onset of democratic devolution in 1999. The parliamentary numbers, resulting from the element of proportionality in elections, have made this inevitable. Labour has never had an outright majority. Arrangements have been the norm between it, Plaid and the Liberal Democrats, varying from budget deals to policy compacts and formal coalitions. However, the Co-operation Agreement institutionalised this way of working in a newly imaginative way. It allowed parties to share responsibility for implementing a broad sweep of policy at the same time as continuing to be in a state of opposition with one another. In turn, it has paved the way for more cohesion across the parties in achieving greater autonomy for Wales.

Citizens

In a bar at an academic conference in the mid-1970s I fell into an argument with Exeter University Professor Anthony Birch, a

---

26 R. Davies, 'Devolution a process not an event' (IWA, 1999).

specialist in democracy and federalism, who had been turning his attention to devolution.[27] I objected when he put it to me that the identity of the Welsh people was different to that of the Scots and the English:

> 'You mean you think that we are not so distinctive?' I queried.

> 'Not exactly, you have cultural traits that distinguish you, of course. You have an egalitarian tradition, a concern for education, a love of music ... things of that kind that mark you out as quite different.'

> 'But in other ways not so much?' I bridled, feeling a rising irritation at being placed under a microscope by this urbane Englishman.

> 'Well, there's a degree of ambiguity about Welsh national identity, wouldn't you say?'

> 'As far as I'm concerned, I just feel Welsh.'

> 'But how does one account for the prevalence of such expressions as "very Welsh" and "Welsh Wales", which have no Scottish equivalents? There appears to be a dimension of Welshness, don't you think? Certainly, I think it's an awareness that much of Welsh society has been moving away from the truly Welsh end of that dimension that is responsible for a lot of the passion that has motivated you nationalists in the last few years.'

I disagreed with him at the time, but looking back I think he was right to judge that in those days Welshness could be thought of as a dimension rather than a category, as has always seemed the case in both England and Scotland. Welsh people would commonly say of one another that they possessed degrees of Welshness: 'Oh, s/he is very Welsh.' Moreover, you could also argue that there was a greater duality of identification between Welshness and Britishness than in either Scotland or England.

A high degree of Welshness remains associated with being able to speak the language or registering a strong accent, and generally

---

27 A. Birch, *Political Integration and Disintegration in the British Isles* (George Allen and Unwin, 1977).

being from places associated with these things, western Wales and the southern valleys being typical. In turn these characteristics are closely linked with Plaid Cymru. Moreover many people tend to form the judgement that, if they do not in one way or another possess a strong dimension of Welshness, then they cannot support a political party that typifies that sensibility.

I should have put it to Professor Birch that the Scots do not experience the same gradation or dimension of identity because of their attachment to their civic institutions that they sustained beyond the 1707 parliamentary union. They kept their own European-oriented legal structure, their own church, their own education system, financial institutions, press and media in ways that were simply not available to the Welsh.

As for those institutions that the Welsh regard as British – variously the Westminster Parliament, the monarchy, the armed forces, and the BBC – the English regard them as belonging to one face of a coin, with British on one side and English on the other. It might be said that for most of the time they feel English, but are British when they are abroad, in the wider world. There are differences of emphasis but, in essence, for both the Scots and the English their political institutions provide their identities with the quality of being a straightforward category.

In the Welsh case, until now this has not been so. Until the present generation, Welsh political attachments have generally been felt and described as British. This was something experienced as distinctly separate from being Welsh, which rested on a more diffuse sense of place and culture, with the latter strongly linked to the Welsh language.

However, the creation of the Senedd and Welsh Government, both of which achieved much higher visibility as a result of the Covid pandemic, changed this fundamentally. In the 21st Century Welsh identity is becoming ever more closely associated with a common bond of civic, democratic institutions. These are constantly being extended and elaborated, with Senedd reform, arising from the Co-operation Agreement, being the most recent example. Alongside is the growing status of a distinctively Welsh legal personality, and the separate jurisdiction that will surely follow. These institutions are the foundation of the political nation and provide the democratic support for the Welsh state. Welsh citizenship is a necessary accompaniment. At last, in the 21st Century, the people of Wales are becoming citizens of their own country.

Afterword
The Welsh Experience of Contract Parliamentarianism

A few months after he had stepped down as First Minister, Mark Drakeford gave a lecture in which he identified four systemic difficulties that had confronted those trying to make devolution work in Wales.[1]

- The first was the unstable nature of the devolution settlement itself. Over 25 years the 1998 Government of Wales Act had been constantly revised with subsequent legislation. There had been four periods of constant change: executive devolution between 1999 and 2007; a separation of powers between the Senedd and the Welsh Government from 2007 to 2011; conferred legislative powers between 2011 and 2017; and a new reserved powers legislative model since 2017, bringing Wales in line with Scotland. 'We've never been in a period when the settlement has not been unsettled and challenged,' was the way Drakeford put it.
- Second, was the Westminster establishment's persistent belief in the sovereignty of the London Parliament. In their view power devolved was power retained, a formulation first made by Enoch Powell in 1974.[2] 'But in practice devolution means sovereignty is distributed across the UK,' Drakeford said. 'Recognising this would give us a much more stable way of operating.'
- A third systemic difficulty was that the Senedd had been too small from the outset. In 2004 the Richard Commission had made it clear that 60 members were never going to be enough: 'The gene pool of the Senedd is too small,' Drakeford said. 'It makes the

---

1 M. Drakeford, *Wales: Successes and Challenges* (Honourable Society of Cymmrodorion, 27 June 2004).
2 See Footnote 6, Chapter 7.

Senedd more insular and it's an inhibitor of the boldness that is necessary to make fundamental change.'
- The fourth problem was that Wales had never had fair funding from Westminster. There should be a needs-based formula that operates across the whole of the UK. Instead, the Barnett formula, established as a temporary measure in 1979, had become ingrained. Relying on size of population to determine the distribution of funds is inherently unfair, failing to take account of relative wealth between the nations and regions and other factors. The formula has persisted because changing it would inevitably create losers, and therefore opposition. For example, while Wales would gain, Scotland would lose. Nonetheless unfairness is currently baked into the devolution settlement.

Drakeford might have drawn attention to a further systemic challenge to Welsh devolution, which is one-party government and the undermining of democracy that results. Welsh Labour has won all six elections that have been held since the National Assembly, now Senedd, was established in 1999. It has, though, never won an overall majority, making it necessary to attract the support of other parties to secure its budget and pursue legislation. Since 1999 Labour has entered into no fewer than 14 cross-party deals to secure power, with the Co-operation Agreement being the latest and most innovative. Indeed, it could be argued that the Co-operation Agreement was the next best thing to a change of government. For what it entailed was a governing party lifting the better part of its Programme for Government from an opposing party's manifesto. It was noteworthy that in his lecture Mark Drakeford reflected positively on this turn of events:

> 'What we have learnt is that working with other parties is not some vile necessity, it actually allows you to do the work of government better. In Westminster if the first-past-the-post electoral system results in an inconclusive outcome and people have to work together it's widely regarded as a failure of the system. But in Wales we have demonstrated that it is a success of the system to require progressive parties whose policy agendas overlap to work together for common purposes. I don't think we would have seen it like that in 1999. When Rhodri sent me off to speak with the Liberal Democrats it was because

he thought it was a necessity. We couldn't manage without them. Now we have learnt that you should do it because it yields genuine benefits, for the political culture of the place and for the people more widely, who look to us to make a difference in their lives.'[3]

By the time it reached the 2021 Senedd election Welsh Labour had largely run out of policy ideas. For two decades it's attention had been engaged in the day-to-day managerial business of governing, especially during the Covid pandemic, leaving little time or capacity for policy generation. It had not come up with any distinctive framework of ideas since Drakeford's own formulation of progressive universalism and 'clear red water' in the early 2000s. At the 2021 election the vacuum was filled by Plaid's manifesto whose wide-ranging scope allowed Adam Price to claim that:

> 'In this election Plaid Cymru is presenting the most radically ambitious and transformational programme offered by any party in any Welsh election since 1945.'[4]

Certainly, it provided the basis of what became a straightforward transaction in the Co-operation Agreement, marking it out unambiguously as a clear-cut example of Contract Parliamentarism.

At the same time, the background of constitutional instability that Mark Drakeford drew attention to was an essential context and motivation for the negotiations. What became known as 'muscular unionism' in the period immediately prior to the Co-operation Agreement was a further, vital factor. The abandonment by Boris Johnson's 2019-24 Government of conventions that Westminster would not intrude on the Senedd's legislative competence without consent, was a major stimulus. As Drakeford put it:

> 'The defences that we believed were there to protect devolution turned out not to be defences at all. They were not judiciable by the Supreme Court.'[5]

---

3   M. Drakeford: *Successes and Challenges, op. cit.*
4   'Plaid Cymru, *Let Us Face the Future Together* (2021), p.5.
5   M. Drakeford, *Wales: Successes and Challenges, op. cit.*

Increasing the size of the Senedd was not just a practical response to it being too small to be effective, it was a rejoinder to the threat posed by the Conservatives at Westminster. As the Agreement declared, the reform was a message that 'the Senedd is here to stay and decisions about Wales are made in Wales.'[6]

Experience of negotiating the Co-Operation Agreement demonstrated that three elements are required for success. The first, quite simply is the numbers. The electoral performance of the partners to the negotiation must be such to put an agreement on the agenda at all. In the case of the Co-operation Agreement Welsh Labour had performed exceptionally well in the 2021 election, but was still short of a majority. It needed some Opposition party support to pass its budget, and more sustained support if it was to achieve anything significant with its Programme for Government. As for Plaid Cymru, it had performed disappointingly in the election, coming third behind the Conservatives, and needed a deal with Labour if it was to make any progress at all on its aspirations. In the words of Adam Price, the party sought 'to snatch an historic victory from the yawning jaws of defeat'.[7]

The second element needed for a successful negotiation is a shared aspiration around a policy programme. We've seen with the Co-operation Agreement that, on the Welsh Labour side, its starting agenda was thin. Their list of objectives was modest, and many hardly required an agreement to make progress. On the other hand, Plaid adopted a maximalist position and sought, successfully, to pull Labour in its direction. The party was helped by the Labour First Minister, Mark Drakeford, who was conscious that his time in office was limited. He was keen to create a legacy. A crucial dimension was that both sides shared the substantive goal of Senedd reform, which could only come about with a two-thirds majority that in combination Labour and Plaid could provide.

The third element is a high level of trust between the parties, probably the most elusive and difficult of the three to attain and then sustain. Trust takes a long time to develop and mature. But as was shown when the Co-operation Agreement prematurely ended in May 2024, trust can dissipate very rapidly.

---

6   *The Co-operation Agreement*, see Appendix.
7   See p.171

Afterword

Developing trust requires a combination of shared values, past experience and the reliability of the leading figures on each side. Welsh Labour and Plaid Cymru are both parties of the left and have a shared vision around community solidarity and communitarian ideals. As important, over 25 years working together to grow the power and capacity of the Senedd, they have developed a common belief in a Welsh national interest. This was shown in the tribute Adam Price paid to Carwyn Jones when the latter stood down as First Minister in December 2018.[8] Moreover, as is shown in Chapter 3, Adam Price and Mark Drakeford personally have a great deal in common. Both are convinced socialists, on the left of their parties, and are rooted in radical Carmarthenshire politics. During the three months of the negotiations they developed sufficient trust to enable Price to agree a broad outline for Senedd reform without demanding precise details on numbers and electoral arrangements. These were left to be resolved once Mark Drakeford had had time to steer them through his party's internal procedures. Price understood that he and Drakeford had broadly the same view on what was necessary, but also accepted that elements within Labour, including Welsh MPs at Westminster and some trade unions, had yet to be convinced. He agreed that it would be counter-productive if Drakeford could be presented as being pressurised by Plaid to concede electoral reform.[9]

How quickly trust can break down was shown not long after Adam Price and Mark Drakeford were replaced as leaders of their parties, in 2023 and 2024. Plaid's new leader Rhun ap Iorwerth, who replaced Adam Price in May 2023, worked well enough with Mark Drakeford for nearly a year. But once Vaughan Gething took over in March 2024, his refusal to acknowledge any wrong doing in accepting £200,000 in donations from a businessman in his constituency who had previously been convicted of environmental offences, rapidly led to the breakdown of trust. Plaid Cymru withdrew from the Agreement in May, a decision that was vindicated when Gething refused to resign after a vote of no-confidence was passed by the Senedd a few weeks later. Standing Orders did not require him to respond to a motion that was brought in Opposition time but, nonetheless, by refusing to accept it he undermined the parliamentary character of the Senedd. This was a common theme

---

8 See pps.115-7.
9 See p.203.

in the co-ordinated letters of resignation submitted by four members of his Cabinet in July, letters that prompted Gething's own immediate resignation. As Mick Antoniw, his Counsel General put it:

> 'You have lost a vote of confidence in the Senedd. That is something I regard as being of major constitutional importance. It is clear that you no longer command a majority, that you will be unable to enter into the agreements necessary to pass a budget, and for all intents and purposes the Senedd is rudderless.'[10]

The episode was reminiscent of the demise of Labour's first leader in the Senedd, Alun Michael, in February 2000. He attempted to resign in a brazen attempt to avoid a vote of no confidence. However, the Presiding Officer Dafydd Elis-Thomas refused to accept the resignation letter Michael handed him in open plenary. Within a matter of hours the Labour group refused to back him, and nominated Rhodri Morgan in his place. The immediate reason for the no confidence vote was Michael's inability or unwillingness to fight Wales's corner over the additionality of European Union Objective 1 funding that was subsumed as part of the UK Treasury's block grant. But underlying it was Michael's whole approach to Welsh governance. Prior to becoming leader in the then Assembly he had been Secretary of State for Wales in charge of the Welsh Office that had administered Wales as part of the Whitehall civil service. When he moved across to be leader in the Assembly he attempted to continue as though nothing had really changed, thereby undermining the Assembly's democratic authority. His removal was a critical moment in establishing the legitimacy of the new institution. It also marked the beginning of Labour in Wales evolving into a more autonomous party. As Rhodri Morgan put it, 'We're not Old Labour or New Labour, we're Welsh Labour'. Vaughan Gething's forced resignation marked a similar moment. Quite apart from his questionable behaviour in accepting controversial political donations, he had leant too closely to London and could not be relied upon to epitomise Labour's credentials in 'standing up for Wales'.

---

10   Mick Antoniw MS, letter (via email) to Vaughan Gething, 16 July 2024. The Counsel General is the Welsh Cabinet's chief legal adviser, whose position has to be personally approved by the Monarch along with that of the First Minister.

Afterword

Such considerations weighed heavily in the wake of the July 2024 general election in which there was a sense that the Welsh electoral tectonic plates were beginning to shift. The immediate cause was the impact of Reform UK which split the right of Welsh politics. Its intervention resulted in the Conservatives losing all its 14 seats in Wales. Apart from Brecon and Radnor, which the Lib Dems won back from the Conservatives, all the gains were made by Labour, which emerged with 27 of the 32 Welsh seats, while Plaid held its two seats (Dwyfor Meirionydd and Ceredigion Preseli) and gained two (Ynys Môn and Caerfyrddin). On the face of it Labour performed exceedingly well, but under the surface there were disturbing signs for the party, pointed to by Labour's Llanelli Senedd Member Lee Waters:

> 'After the collapse of the Labour Party in Scotland Jonathan Powell, the PM's Chief of Staff through the whole Blair period in office, said that Scottish Labour had become a hollow tree – all it took was someone to come along and push it for it to fall. Nobody wants to hear this at the moment but this could well apply to Welsh Labour too. There's nothing inevitable about any of this. The difference between us and Scottish Labour in 2011 is that we have a long-record of devolved governments to be proud of, and a proven ability to stand up for Wales. But the voters aren't daft, and the warning signs are clear enough for those who want to look for them in the general election result. Whereas the Westminster voting system this time flattered us, the new more proportional voting system we'll be using in Wales will be far less forgiving if our support levels don't get back beyond the 30% threshold. The last YouGov poll put us at 27% at a Senedd election – just 4 points ahead of Plaid. The d'Hondt voting system [in effect a closed list system, where people vote for a party rather for individual candidates] we've legislated for will actively work against us if our numbers stay at that level and a generation in the wilderness awaits.'[11]

Political forecasting is a hazardous business. Unforeseen events have a way of clouding the clearest projected horizons. Nevertheless, some reasonable predictions can be made when looking ahead to the prospects for cross-party collaboration in the wake of the 2026 Senedd election. The predictions discussed here follow the three

---

11 M. Shipton, 'Ex-Minister Lee Waters warns Welsh Labour it's in danger of losing power in wake of Gething crisis' (*Nation Cymru*, 22 July 2004).

elements that accounted for the successful negotiation of the Co-operation Agreement in 2021 – the electoral numbers, the policies, and the trust associated with the personalities.

On the election outcome, it is reasonable to assume that no party will emerge with a majority of seats. This has not happened so far in any of the six elections to the Senedd under the current partially proportional electoral system. In 2026, an entirely new and completely proportional system for an enlarged Senedd makes a majority for any party even less likely. The YouGov poll referred to by Lee Waters, published just ahead of the July 2024 general election is shown in the following table, along with the results from a Wales Governance Centre Welsh Election Study undertaken a month later. Calculating the number of seats that would be won in the new 96-seat Senedd on the basis of these polls is fraught with uncertainties. However, an estimated result, based on these polls, is illustrated in the table's fifth column. Inclusion of the actual results for the 4 July UK General Election reveals the contrast between voting at different governmental levels in Wales, with Labour's commanding 22% lead over Plaid Cymru at the Westminster election shrinking to a mere 1% for the 2026 Senedd election projected in the Welsh Election Study. The shift is driven primarily driven by a direct transfer of votes from Labour to Plaid. This is the largest predicted contrast in voting intentions for Westminster and Wales since devolution. It is perhaps a reflection of the experience of the Covid pandemic when the Welsh Government and Senedd became much more visible to the Welsh people.

Table 7: Polling (%) for the 2026 Senedd election (July 2024)

	UK General Election 4 July 2024	YouGov/ITV Cymru 27 June – 1 July 2024	Welsh Election Study 29 July 2024	Estimate of members in 96-seat Senedd*
Welsh Labour	37	27	25	29
Plaid Cymru	15	23	24	28
Conservative	18	18	16	16
Reform	17	18	16	16
Lib Dem	7	6	6	3
Green	5	5	6	2
Other	1	3	7	2*

*These estimates are based on an analysis by Dr Jac Larner of the Wales Governance Centre, Cardiff University.

Afterword

More pertinently for the argument being made here, the polls show that both Labour and Plaid Cymru are falling well short of the 49 seats needed for a majority in the reformed 96 member Senedd. This will make cross-party collaboration even more necessary than hitherto. Neither Welsh Labour nor Plaid would contemplate an arrangement with the Conservatives and certainly not Reform which makes collaboration between themselves the only route to secure a majority. The question then is, what kind of arrangement would be considered? In general terms, a formal coalition is more likely the closer the parties are in numbers of seats. Conversely, a reiteration of the 2021 Co-operation Agreement is more likely the further they are apart. A critical factor will be which party comes out ahead of the other. If Labour is ahead then the chances of a coalition or a Co-operation Agreement is more likely. If Plaid is ahead, then Labour might conclude that a period of Opposition is its optimum choice, and offer a Confidence and Supply deal to a minority Plaid Cymru government.

On the matter of policies, as discussed in Chapter 6 the outline of an agenda is already emerging with the unfinished business of the 2021 Co-operation Agreement. Undoubtedly Plaid Cymru would want priority given to policies to develop the Welsh economy which, due to Labour's insistence, were left out of the 2021 Co-operation Agreement. If a coalition was in prospect then it is likely that Plaid would want the economy and transport briefs. These would have to come with a mandate, and budget allocation, to reinstall a Welsh Development Agency, giving precedence to railway infrastructure in the south Wales valleys and associated urban renewal (the Metro), together with development of the western seaboard.

The Co-operation Agreement's Commission on the Constitution has set a comprehensive agenda for extending the powers of the Senedd. Unquestionably the most challenging items are those that require concessions from the UK government, specifically: (i) devolution of justice and policing; (ii) devolution of the Crown Estate; and (iii) a fundamental review of territorial funding and the Barnett formula. There is cross-party agreement on these matters in the Senedd, but Welsh Labour appears to have little leverage with the Labour Government in Westminster to make progress. It is fair to say that the stronger Plaid Cymru is in the Senedd following 2026, the more likely concessions will be made.

Finally, as to trust, it was fortuitous that the Health Minister Eluned Morgan emerged unopposed to take over as First Minister in the wake of Vaughan Gething's resignation. She was put forward as the candidate calculated most likely to unify a fractured Labour group. She also possesses several attributes that would enable her to reach out to Plaid Cymru, such as being a founder member of the Yes for Wales group that campaigned for devolution in the 1997 referendum and an ardent pro-European who was a Welsh member of the European Parliament between 1994 and 2009. Brought up in Cardiff and educated at the capital's first Welsh-medium primary and secondary schools (Ysgol Bryntaf and Ysgol Glantaf), Morgan has also served as the Senedd Member for Mid and West Wales since 2016 so has a keen appreciation of the Welsh-speaking rural heartland.

All this should make her more than compatible with the Plaid leader Ynys Môn MS Rhun ap Iorwerth. Both politicians are instinctively non-tribal, and have a bent for pragmatic solutions rather than ideological preoccupations. Eluned Morgan's political lodestar is undoubtedly Cledwyn Hughes (1916-2001) who was Labour MP for Ynys Môn from 1951 to 1970 and thereafter sat in the House of Lords, where she has also sat, as Baroness Morgan of Ely, since 2011. Emollient and moderate, a unifier, a passionate patriot and early advocate of devolution, Hughes became a Welsh elder statesman in his later years. At the 2004 National Eisteddfod Eluned Morgan founded Cymdeithas Cledwyn (the Cledwyn Society) to promote his thinking within Welsh Labour's ranks.

If Rhun ap Iorwerth had to point to an equivalent mentor it would probably be Gwynfor Evans (1912-2005), Plaid's President from 1945 to 1981 and the party's first MP, winning the Carmarthen by-election in 1966. He and Cledwyn Hughes were of the same generation and, despite their different party affiliation, shared many of the same values, particularly a passionate concern for the Welsh culture and language.[12] Wales could do a lot worse in 2026 than fall back on the inter-twined values of Cledwyn Hughes and Gwynfor Evans to chart a fresh course. And, who knows, Contract Parliamentarianism, may have yet more to offer the country.

---

12   See E. Price, *Lord Cledwyn of Penrhos* (Research Centre Wales, Bangor University, 1990); and Rh. Evans, *Gwynfor Evans, Portrait of a Patriot* (Y Lolfa, 2008).

Appendix

The Co-operation Agreement

Introduction

Almost a quarter of a century ago, people in Wales voted for self-government for Wales, with a promise of a new type of politics.

They placed their trust in a new democracy with an instruction to work differently – inclusively and co-operatively.

Today, as the Welsh Government and Plaid Cymru come together in this Co-operation Agreement, we take another step forward in our collective effort to fulfil that promise of a new politics – radical in content and co-operative in approach.

At the start of the Sixth Senedd, Wales faces great opportunities but also many challenges.

We are continuing to respond to a once-in-a-lifetime global pandemic, which has claimed the lives of millions of people worldwide and affected every aspect of our daily lives.

The climate and nature emergencies together pose a far greater and lasting threat to our country and our way of life than the coronavirus pandemic if we do not take action now to address its worst affects. We have ambitious plans to create a low carbon Wales and move towards net zero – but these plans will need all of us and our public services to make choices and changes.

The UK has now left the European Union but we are still dealing with the aftermath of this decision and we are faced daily with the actions of a Conservative UK Government determined to consolidate power in Westminster and turn back the clock on devolution.

At the start of this Senedd term, it is more important than ever that we have a strong Welsh Parliament able to work together and respond effectively to these challenges and make real and lasting change for people in Wales.

This Co-operation Agreement is a response to these external challenges and that need for a stable Senedd, capable of delivering radical change and reform.

The commitments outlined in this agreement build on a number of shared values – social solidarity, a sustainable planet and a vibrant democracy.

The Welsh Government and Plaid Cymru will work together over the coming three years on the defined policy commitments listed in this document – policies in which we have common interests to implement progressive solutions – from ensuring no child goes hungry to ending homelessness. From working together to explore the long-term future of social care to meeting our shared commitment of a million Welsh speakers by 2050.

Together, we will use this opportunity to address issues which take the greatest political and policy effort to resolve and, together, we will create progressive, made-in-Wales solutions.

Where agreement is possible, people rightly expect political parties to work together. We look forward to making a real and lasting difference for people in Wales.

It is said that those who lead should be a bridge – our hope is that this partnership will help forge the bridge we continue to build together as a nation.

Mark Drakeford MS   **Adam Price MS**
First Minister of Wales   Leader of Plaid Cymru

Policy Programme

Radical action in testing times

The challenges we face in the aftermath of the pandemic call for radical action, which will improve the lives of everyone in Wales.

From school children going hungry to parents juggling the costs of childcare and access to early years education. From rising household bills and a housing crisis affecting every generation to older people worried about whether they can afford care in their later years, this agreement will support people throughout their lives, during the most testing of times.

The Welsh Government and Plaid Cymru will be ambitious in the action we take together to address these issues.

Working together, we will:

- **Free school meals** – Extend free school meals to all primary school pupils, over the lifetime of this agreement, as a further step to reaching our shared ambition that no child should go hungry. We agree that universal free school meals will be a transformational intervention in terms of child hunger and child poverty, which will support educational attainment and child nutrition and local food production and distribution, benefiting local economies.

- **Childcare** – Expand free childcare to all two-year-olds with a particular focus on providing and strengthening Welsh-medium childcare
- **Future of Social Care** – Set up an expert group to support our shared ambition to create a National Care Service, free at the point of need, continuing as a public service. We will agree an implementation plan by the end of 2023. We will continue to better integrate health and care and work towards parity of recognition and reward for health and care workers.
- **Second homes** – Take immediate and radical action to address the proliferation of second homes and unaffordable housing, using the planning, property and taxation systems. Actions being planned include a cap on the number of second and holiday homes; measures to bring more homes into common ownership; a statutory licensing scheme for holiday lets; greater powers for local authorities to charge council tax premiums and increasing taxes on second homes. We will explore local authority mortgages.
- **National construction company** – Establish Unnos, a national construction company, to support councils and social landlords to improve the supply of social and affordable housing.
- **Building safety** – Significantly reform the current system of building safety, which has allowed a culture of cutting corners to the detriment of public safety. We will introduce a second phase of the Welsh Building Safety Fund.
- **Property and Fair Rents** – Publish a White Paper to include proposals for a right to adequate housing, the role a system of fair rents (rent control) could have in making the private rental market affordable for local people on local incomes and new approaches to making homes affordable
- **Homelessness** – End homelessness. If people are made homeless it should be brief, rare and unrepeated. We will reform housing law, enact the Renting Homes Act to give renters greater security and implement the Homeless Action Group recommendations.

Council tax reform – Reform one of the most regressive forms of taxation – which disproportionately impacts poorer areas of Wales – to make it fairer.

Procurement – Explore how to set meaningful targets to increase Welsh public sector procurement from the current 52%. As a first step, we will carry out a detailed analysis of the public sector supply chains and promote the purchasing of made-in-Wales products and services.

Local tourism levies – Introduce local tourism levies using local government finance reform legislation.

A greener Wales to tackle climate change and the nature emergency

The climate and nature emergency are the greatest threats facing our world. If we do not act now, our children and grandchildren will inherit a more polluted, more unstable and more dangerous planet.

By working together to tackle these twin emergencies, we will take bold steps towards a net zero Wales. We will address nature loss, improve biodiversity and plant more trees. As our climate changes, too many people have woken to find their homes flooded and they fear when the next storm will hit. We will learn from past flooding events and invest in flood defences to protect communities.

We will also start the process of reforming farm support to help family farms and agricultural businesses become greener and more sustainable.

Working together, we will:

- **Net zero** – Commission independent advice to examine potential pathways to net zero by 2035 – the current target date is 2050. This will look at the impact on society and sectors of our economy and how any adverse effects may be mitigated, including how the costs and benefits are shared fairly. We support devolution of further powers and resources Wales needs to respond most effectively to reach net zero, specifically the management of the Crown Estate and its assets in Wales.
- **Net zero energy company** – Work towards the creation of Ynni Cymru, a publicly-owned energy company for Wales, over the next two years, to expand community-owned renewable energy generation.
- **Public transport** – Ask Transport for Wales (TfW) to explore the development of transport links between North and South Wales, including how to protect potential travel corridors on the west coast of Wales. We will continue to press ahead with Metro developments to improve connectivity and encourage people to switch to public transport. We will ask TfW to work with local authorities in North West Wales and the Welsh Government to develop plans for an integrated transport system.
- **Biodiversity** – Agree that targets and an environmental governance body have a role to play in helping to protect and restore biodiversity for species and habitats in our terrestrial and marine environments.

- **Tree planting** – Work with the farming community to encourage woodland creation on less productive land and through agroforestry. This will include support for active landowners and farmers through the sustainable farming scheme. We will explore ways of drawing investment for woodland creation that secures local ownership and control.
- **Agricultural pollution** – We will work with the farming community to improve water quality and air quality, deploying the Water Resources Regulations 2021, taking an approach targeted at those activities known to cause pollution.
- **Flood review** – Commission an independent review of the local government section 19 and Natural Resources Wales reports into extreme flooding in winter 2020-21 and act on its recommendations.
- **Flood capital investment and national resilience** – Invest more in flood management and mitigation and plan to respond to the increased risk of flooding. We will ask the National Infrastructure Commission for Wales to assess how the nationwide likelihood of flooding of homes, businesses and infrastructure can be minimised by 2050.
- **Sustainable farming scheme** – Introduce a transition period as we reform the system of farm payments so stability payments will continue to be a feature of the Sustainable Farming Scheme during and beyond this Senedd term. We will agree the longer-term arrangements for Welsh agriculture, recognising the particular needs of family farms and acknowledging ecologically sustainable local food production.
- **Community food strategy** – Develop a community food strategy to encourage the production and supply of locally-sourced food in Wales.

Reforming the foundations of Wales

With devolution under threat from this Conservative UK Government, we must send a clear message to Westminster that the Senedd is here to stay and decisions about Wales are made in Wales.

This means reforming our electoral system to enable Wales's parliamentarians to represent people more effectively and seriously considering all options for the future of our constitution.

We will continue the reform of our education system to support all learners' physical and mental wellbeing and their academic progression, especially disadvantaged children; work to strengthen the media in Wales to address the democratic deficit and protect it from UK Government attacks on its independence, and we will continue to work with and support local government.

Working together we will:

- **Senedd reform** – Support plans to reform the Senedd, based on 80 to 100 Members; a voting system which is as proportional – or more – than the current one and have gender quotas in law. We will support the work of the Senedd Special Purpose Committee and introduce a Senedd reform Bill 12 to 18 months after it reports.
- **Constitutional Commission** – Support the work of the Independent Commission on Wales's Constitutional Future. Both parties are free to make submissions and interact with the commission independently. The commission's interim and final reports will be presented jointly to both parties.
- **Broadcasting** – Explore the creation of a shadow Broadcasting and Communications Authority for Wales, to address our concerns about the current fragility in the media and attacks on its independence. This body would support the use of the Welsh language, particularly in digital and encourage media plurality. We believe broadcasting and communication powers should be devolved to Wales.
- **Media financial support** – Fund existing and new enterprises to improve Welsh-based journalism to tackle the information deficit.
- **Arfor** – Address inequalities between poorer and richer parts of the country by building on the Arfor pilot, which promoted entrepreneurship, business growth, community resilience and the Welsh language. We will create a second phase with local government and ask the OECD to look at and design models for local government to work together in West Wales and the South Wales Valleys to tackle shared challenges and opportunities.
- **National School for Government** – Explore how setting up a National School for Government might contribute to the principle of a One Wales Public Service.
- **Regional partnership arrangements** – Keep regional partnership working under review, together with local government partners, to ensure they are efficient and work for Wales as new Corporate Joint Committee arrangements are introduced. Any changes should be locally led, driven by what works best and based on local priorities and existing relationships.

- **Sustainable public services** – Work with the Wales Governance Centre, the Office for Budget Responsibility and others to understand devolved public finances and the future needs of Welsh public services. We will look for new ways to address any future funding gaps, grow our tax base and consider the funding implications of any recommendations from the Constitutional Commission.
- **Supply teaching and looked after children** – We believe these two vital services should not be run for private profit. We will work with partners to develop options for a more sustainable model of supply teaching with fair work at its heart, which will include local authority-led and school-led alternatives and put in place a framework to remove profit from the care of looked after children.
- **School term dates** – Aim to reform school term dates to bring them more in line with patterns of family life and employment. We will also explore options to reform the rhythm of the school day to create space for more wide-ranging, culturally accessible activities and opportunities.
- **Reforming qualifications** – Focus on experiences and wellbeing as we reform qualifications, in line with Wales' new curriculum. We will significantly expand the range of made-in-Wales vocational qualifications to fit the needs of our learners and our economy.
- **Tertiary Education and Research Bill** – Take forward this Bill to empower education providers to be part of a diverse, agile and collaborative sector that delivers for learners, employers and communities. We will jointly develop a new mission-based national innovation strategy to be implemented across government and by the Commission for Tertiary Education and Research, which has a leading role in promoting innovation in Wales. We will also work together on post-16 curriculum reforms informed by our new national curriculum, an expansion in lifelong learning and workforce professional development.

Creating a united and fairer Wales for all

In recovering from the pandemic, we want to ensure everyone shares in the opportunities of the future, wherever they live, so no one is held back or left behind.

We are opposed to the short-sighted and cruel decision by the Conservative UK Government to cut the £20 Universal Credit uplift, which will drive more households into poverty as we face a cost-of-living crisis. We will do all we can to reduce inequalities and tackle poverty.

We want to make Wales an anti-racist nation and drive out stigma and hatred. We want a Wales where everyone is respected and their diversity celebrated. Wales will continue to provide a warm welcome for all.

Wales has a long and proud history and distinctive culture, built around our language, which thrives today. We will work to strengthen our language and culture, protecting it where needed, promoting it and helping make Welsh an everyday reality for all, as we work towards our shared goal of a million Welsh-speakers.

Working together, we will:

- **Culture strategy** – Develop a new culture strategy, reflecting Wales' diversity, a thriving Welsh language, our arts, culture and heritage sectors and our duties under the Wellbeing of Future Generations Act. We will ensure the financial sustainability of national cultural institutions as we implement the strategy and we will also develop the proposals for a national contemporary art gallery.
- **Curriculum** – Improve the teaching of Welsh history, taking account of the Estyn report. We are committed to Welsh history being mandatory in the new Curriculum for Wales. New curriculum resources will be developed to support Welsh history in all its complexity and diversity. National Network conversations will start in early 2022.
- **Prosiect 2050** – Promote the daily use of the Welsh language in more places. We will lead by example, supporting more sponsored bodies, local authorities and the Welsh civil service to operate through the medium of Welsh.
- **Welsh language education** – Introduce a Welsh Language Education Bill, which together with more immediate non-legislative work, will strengthen Welsh in Education Strategic Plans; set new ambitions and incentives to expand the proportion of the education workforce who can teach and work through the Welsh language; establish and implement a single continuum of Welsh language learning; enable existing schools to move into a higher Welsh language category and incentivise the increase of Welsh-medium provision in all education settings.
- **Welsh Language Standards** – Work with the Welsh Language Commissioner to reduce obstacles in setting Welsh Language Standards; streamline the process for implementing standards, without weakening their impact; implement standards on public

transport; regulators in the health sector; newly established public bodies currently outside the standards regime and water companies; and begin work on implementing standards on housing associations, which will be completed in the Senedd term. We are committed to the full implementation of the Welsh Language (Wales) Measure 2011 and will develop a list to prioritise the further rollout of standards under its schedules beyond the term of this agreement.

- **Welsh language place-names** – Ensure Welsh language place-names in the built and natural environments are safeguarded and promoted.
- **Coleg Cymraeg Cenedlaethol and National Centre for Learning Welsh** – Invest in Coleg Cymraeg Cenedlaethol and the National Centre for Learning Welsh to increase the proportion of Welsh-medium apprenticeships and further education and provide free Welsh language learning for 16 to 25-year-olds.
- **Seren network** – Increase the ability for learners from disadvantaged backgrounds to take part in the Seren Network. We will offer summer schools at each Welsh university for Seren Foundation learners; expand the current partnerships with Aberystwyth and Cardiff universities and set up new pilots in other Welsh institutions.
- **Tackling poverty and inequality** – Support the devolution of the administration of welfare and explore the necessary infrastructure required to prepare for it. Such a transfer of power would need to be accompanied by the transfer of appropriate financial support.
- **Mental health** – Test how community facilities run by trained third sector staff with clear referral pathways into NHS services if needed – the sanctuary model – can help support young people in crisis or with an urgent mental health or emotional wellbeing issue. These would be open evenings and weekends.
- **Disability** – Strengthen the rights of disabled people and tackle the inequalities they continue to face. We are committed to the social model of disability and together we will ensure the success of the Disability Task Force set up to respond to the Locked Out report.
- **Race Equality Action Plan** – Tackle institutionalised and systemic racism and support the publication of the *Race Equality Action Plan*. We will work with communities, stakeholders and partners, including the police and courts, to make the plan as strong as possible. We support efforts to ensure the devolution of policing and justice powers.

- **LGBTQ+** – Make Wales the most LGBTQ+ friendly nation in Europe and support the publication of the LGBTQ+ Action Plan. We will call for the powers to legislate to improve the lives and protect the safety of Trans people in Wales to be devolved.

The Co-operation Agreement: mechanisms

How the Welsh Government and Plaid Cymru will work together during the Co-operation Agreement.

Principles for relations

The Welsh Government and Plaid Cymru's joint objective is to deliver an agreed, shared programme of work through a Co-operation Agreement over a three-year period.

The parties will rely on good will, trust and agreed procedures to facilitate the delivery of the shared programme of work while respecting each party's distinct identity.

Only the business of the Welsh Government and the Plaid Cymru Senedd Group covered by the Co-operation Agreement forms any part of these arrangements.

Close and regular consultation between the First Minister and the Leader of Plaid Cymru, and other designated members from the two partners, will be the foundation of the agreement's success.

This political working arrangement agreed between the First Minister and the Leader of Plaid Cymru will be undertaken according to the following principles:

1. Maintaining positive, trusting relations based on mutual respect.
2. Effective internal and external communication.
3. Sharing information on a 'no surprises' basis and respecting confidentiality.
4. Resolving disputes promptly according to an agreed process.

This Co-operation Agreement is not a coalition and Plaid Cymru will not be represented by Ministerial or Deputy Ministerial appointments in the Welsh Government.

The legal and formal accountability arrangements for the exercise of powers and commitment of resources continues to rest entirely with the Welsh Government. However, at the political level, the Welsh Government agrees to take decisions jointly with Plaid Cymru across the agreed range of co-operation.

The Co-operation Agreement

Machinery

The Welsh Government and Plaid Cymru agree to work together, to make policy decisions, and oversee their delivery, jointly through the Co-operation Agreement. We will always aim to proceed through consensus, and to resolve disagreements promptly. The Co-operation Agreement will be supported by a civil service unit known as the Co-operation Agreement Unit.

This will be led by a senior civil servant whose line management will continue to be through the usual civil service channels. However, the Co-operation Agreement Unit will work even-handedly with the two partners to ensure effective delivery of the agreed work programme.

The functions of the Co-operation Agreement Unit will be to:

1. Support joint decision-making as described in the Co-operation Agreement.
2. Provide logistical and organisational support.
3. Support effective delivery of policy commitments under the Co-operation Agreement.
4. Provide administrative support.
5. Serve as a gateway into the Welsh Government civil service and the provision of advice by officials in relation to the Co-operation Agreement.
6. Promote dispute avoidance through effective communication and governance structures, at official and political levels.
7. Ensure that agreed processes are respected and followed.
8. Oversee communications of joint policy announcements arising out of the Agreement.

On a day-to-day basis, business will be conducted by the respective nominated officials in charge of the policy areas and those with the appropriate expertise to deal with the issues.

The First Minister will appoint two Special Advisers to help provide day-to-day support for the range of areas covered in the Co-operation Agreement, including (i) high-level oversight, delivery and co-ordination of the Agreement; (ii) policy development and engagement; (iii) budget and financing; (iv) communications and presentation of policy outputs; (v) Senedd business; (vi) Group/party liaison and consultation.

Additional specialist advisers with appropriate expertise may be appointed to support the Co-operation Agreement by the mutual agreement of the First Minister and the Leader of Plaid Cymru. The specialist resource and capacity within the Welsh Government to support the shared programme of work will be reviewed on a six-monthly basis.

Welsh Ministers and Plaid Cymru's designated members will, at the political level, jointly agree matters within scope of the Agreement, while recognising that formal and legal responsibility for those decisions still rests with Welsh Ministers.

Committees comprising Welsh Ministers and designated members of the Plaid Cymru Senedd Group will be established to meet regularly and reach agreement by consensus on issues covered by the Co-operation Agreement.

Overall accountability

Overall accountability for the Co-operation Agreement rests with the First Minister and the Leader of Plaid Cymru. Formal structures will be established to facilitate collaboration and to achieve consensus on agreed issues and other areas of mutual interest. The Permanent Secretary will retain responsibility and accountability for Civil Service staffing matters and for discharging his role as Principal Accounting Officer for the proper use of public money across all areas, including those covered by this Agreement.

Governance framework / Oversight arrangements

Plaid Cymru's designated lead member for the Agreement will play a key role in overseeing progression and coordination of the Agreement.

Joint Policy Committees will be established to progress matters within scope of the Agreement. These will be convened jointly by Welsh Government ministers and Plaid Cymru's designated members to consider issues within the Cooperation Agreement. The Joint Policy Committees will develop agendas, agree ways of working, meet regularly and reach agreement by consensus. The frequency of meetings will be determined jointly by the principals according to the rhythm of business over time.

Joint Oversight Board

The Joint Oversight Board will be convened jointly by the First Minister and the Leader of Plaid Cymru and will have a strategic focus. They will be supported by their colleagues and officials as required. The board will meet around monthly but more or less frequently if the parties agree. The Joint Policy Committee(s) will be accountable to the Joint Oversight Board.

The Joint Oversight Board will undertake the following functions, to:

1. Provide strategic direction to the Joint Policy Committees and to remit actions to them.

The Co-operation Agreement

2. Agree timelines and targets for progress on the delivery of commitments contained in the Co-operation Agreement.
3. Resolve disputes/disagreements or blockages which may arise and which cannot be resolved elsewhere.
4. Receive progress reports from Joint Policy Committees and to oversee the delivery of the Agreement as a whole.
5. Receive regular budget updates.
6. Consider Senedd business handling related to the Agreement as required.
7. Provide a forum for sharing wider strategic information which may have implications for the Agreement.

Meetings will be chaired by the First Minister in close consultation with the Leader of Plaid Cymru.

The Joint Oversight Board and any committee(s) established to support it will be supported by the Co-operation Agreement Unit:

1. Determining dates, agenda, location of meetings, with the agreement of the both parties.
2. Commissioning papers for discussion as directed.
3. Recording minutes of meetings and agreed actions.
4. Promoting transparency and accountability to both parties.

The Co-operation Agreement Unit will:

1. Be accountable to the Joint Oversight Board.
2. Serve both parties equally.
3. Co-ordinate and prepare statements on activity arising from the Co-operation Agreement to be presented to the Senedd.

The Civil Service

The Agreement will respect the Civil Service and its obligations, together with the statutory, legal and accountability framework within which the civil service is obliged to operate. Subject to that framework, the Welsh Government civil service will work constructively with Plaid Cymru to enable the successful operation of the Agreement.

Any Special Advisers appointed by the First Minister to help support the Agreement will be required to work within the provisions of the Welsh Government Special Advisers Code of Conduct. As with all Special Advisers, they will have no authority to instruct the civil service. Special Advisers appointed under this agreement will have access to information which is necessary for them to perform their role effectively in relation to the policy areas of the Agreement.

Special Advisers work with Ministers and civil servants as part of considering and deciding on preferred options for delivery and implementation. Special Advisers will contribute to prioritisation of delivery and implementation, which is likely to be an important consideration during the Agreement given other pressures and competing priorities.

Plaid Cymru designated members will not have access to civil servants beyond the machinery agreed by Ministers.

The First Minister and the Permanent Secretary expect the civil service to work constructively with Plaid Cymru designated members in accordance with the terms of this agreement. Plaid Cymru designated members will have the same responsibilities as Welsh Government Ministers to respect the political impartiality of the civil service, the arrangements for management of the civil service by the Permanent Secretary and the provisions of the Civil Service Recruitment Code and the Governance Code for Public Appointments (on GOV.UK). They will not ask civil servants to do anything which might be contrary to the Civil Service Code, or to use public resources for party political purposes. Plaid Cymru designated members, as Ministers do, will treat the civil service with professionalism, courtesy and respect and can expect this to be reciprocated by the civil service.

When working under the provisions of this agreement or when participating in activities under this agreement, the Leader of Plaid Cymru, Plaid Cymru designated lead member, and other Plaid Cymru designated members, will be bound by the Code of Conduct at Annex A, which reflects the analogous sections of the Ministerial Code and the standards and behaviour to which Ministers are expected to adhere.

Plaid Cymru designated members will pay due regard to the advice from the civil service which they receive and, in particular, the advice of the Permanent Secretary as Principal Accounting Officer (or his representatives) on the proper use of public funds. Any conflicts which may arise with the responsibilities of the Principal Accounting Officer would need to be resolved through dialogue and, if necessary, by means of a Ministerial Direction.

Designated members will not divulge the content of advice received from officials, whether written or oral, nor any official documents received or seen by them in the course of their roles. They will also respect the GDPR requirements upon the Welsh Government. In addition, any legal advice of the Counsel General or the Director of Legal Services and their staff should be regarded by Members as carrying legal professional privilege and should not be disclosed or referred to elsewhere whether given orally or in written or electronic format.

Budget

The Co-operation Agreement will be resourced as agreed and oversight of the delivery and budget allocations for it will be jointly monitored through a Finance Committee whose membership shall include the Welsh Minister responsible for Finance and the relevant Plaid Cymru designated member. The frequency of the meetings shall be determined but they will be regularly convened in the period leading up the Senedd's annual Budget procedures, and any discussions on supplementary budgets and on end of year underspends / adjustments.

A three-year budget cycle underpins this Agreement. Any additional resources would be jointly identified and considered on a year-by-year basis by Plaid Cymru and the Welsh Government around the issues in the Co-operation Agreement.

The Welsh Government commits to consultation and collaboration with Plaid Cymru throughout the development and scrutiny of all stages of the annual budget process.

On the basis that the above commitment will result in appropriate funding for the shared policy programme and influence on other budgetary matters, Plaid Cymru agrees to facilitate the passing of Annual and Supplementary Budgets for the duration of this agreement.

The Welsh Government has well established procedures for monitoring and reporting the use of funds allocated through the budget process. These procedures will apply equally to funds allocated under this agreement. The responsibilities of the Permanent Secretary as Principal Accounting Officer will continue to extend to the entirety of Welsh Government expenditure.

Communication

The Welsh Government and Plaid Cymru commit to effective and timely communication with each other, with a joint aim of a "no surprises" relationship in relation to statements and comments on the Co-operation Agreement. Both parties agree to respect the confidentiality of their discussions and to transparency, openness, fairness, and consistency in the conduct of relations.

A full-time experienced member of staff will be appointed to be responsible for the press and communications aspects of the Agreement at official level. They will be based in the Welsh Government communications team, but will work closely with the Co-operation Agreement Unit and the relevant Special Advisers to ensure effective coordination.

The Co-operation Agreement covers the agreed policy areas where the Welsh Government and Plaid Cymru will work together over the next three years. It is important that these are clearly communicated, and that the involvement of Plaid Cymru is recognised as part of normal government communications. This will require effective co-operation and communication between all those involved in the delivery of this Co-operation Agreement. This reflects the 'no surprises' principle, and the need to maintain consistent and agreed messaging between the Welsh Government and Plaid Cymru in the areas relevant to the Cooperation Agreement.

The Civil Service Code makes clear that government resources cannot be used for party political purposes.

Government-produced communications content within the scope of the Cooperation Agreement can reflect Plaid Cymru designated members' contribution in a factual way, although no content should be released which could be construed as providing a platform for promoting Plaid Cymru as a party in the same way as this applies to Welsh Labour. Regular press conferences led by the First Minister and the Leader of Plaid Cymru in Cathays Park or a suitable alternative location to communicate the Co-operation Agreement will be held. An annual report presented by the First Minister and the Leader of Plaid Cymru mapping progress on delivering the agreement's programme will be produced.

Senedd Business

Each party will make its own business management arrangements to ensure the support within the Senedd necessary to deliver the commitments contained within the Co-operation Agreement.

Both parties to this agreement respect the independence of the Senedd committee system and the distinctive roles and functions of the respective parties within the Senedd.

Appropriate procedures and processes are in place inside the Welsh Government, Senedd Labour Party and Plaid Cymru's Senedd Group to ensure that any issues that may arise in relation to Senedd business can be addressed and resolved.

Areas outside the Cooperation Agreement

The Welsh Government and Plaid Cymru committed to working together on an ambitious and far-reaching policy programme.

It is likely there will be occasions over the lifespan of the Agreement where either the government's work or the Plaid Cymru Senedd Group's work may impact on the specific policy areas covered by the Agreement.

To reduce the possibility of friction developing in the relationship between the two partners, it will be important to build trust between the two partners and develop appropriate formal and informal processes to enable information to be shared for this purpose.

The Co-operation Agreement

Distinctive Identities

For matters which lie outside the Co-operation Agreement the Welsh Government and Plaid Cymru recognise the legitimacy of each other's distinctive political identities in the Senedd and elsewhere. For this reason, all issues outside the Agreement will be handled in the normal course of political engagement.

Relationship to other agreements

The Welsh Government agrees not to enter into agreements or relationships with any other party or Member(s) in the Senedd that are inconsistent with this agreement.

Status

This agreement is not justiciable and is a political agreement between the Welsh Labour Government and Plaid Cymru.

Commencement, review and termination of the Co-operation Agreement

The Agreement is for a period of three years from the signing of this document, with annual review and renewal.

Either the First Minister or the Leader of Plaid Cymru may terminate the Agreement earlier by given written notice to this effect.

After three years both parties may decide to renew the terms of the current Agreement, deepen the collaboration further or bring the agreement to an end.

Any decision to widen of the scope of co-operation in this agreement in the interim and any other amendment to it may be made by the joint agreement of the First Minister and the Leader of Plaid Cymru.

Annex A:
Code for Plaid Cymru Designated Members Participating in the Cooperation Agreement

Note: Designated members are those Members of the Plaid Cymru Senedd Group appointed by the Leader of Plaid Cymru and whose names are provided to the First Minister. A list of designated members will be published on the Welsh Government website. Those names may change from time and time and all changes will be reported as soon as practicable to the First Minister. Members of the Plaid Cymru Senedd Group are only bound by this Code during the period of their appointment as designated members.

Introduction

1. This Code is for Plaid Cymru designated members ("Designated Members") when they are participating in activities covered by participation in the Cooperation Agreement and is based upon the relevant sections of the Ministerial Code. The intention is that Designated Members agree to be bound by the same standards and expectations as are placed upon Welsh Government Ministers, insofar as they are relevant and adaptable to the circumstances of the Co-operation Agreement. For the avoidance of doubt, this Code is applicable only when Designated Members are engaged in activities in relation to matters covered by the Co-operation Agreement and nothing in this Code is intended to go beyond the obligations already incumbent upon Welsh Government Ministers.

Conduct

2. Designated Members are expected to maintain high standards of behaviour and to behave in a way that upholds the highest standards of propriety when undertaking activity in matters relating to the Co-operation Agreement, as they are expected to do in their role as MSs. Designated Members should be professional in all their dealings and treat all those with whom they come into contact with consideration and respect. In particular, they are expected to observe the Seven Principles of Public Life.

3. The First Minister and the Leader of Plaid Cymru, in consultation, are the ultimate judge of compliance with this Code.

Designated Members and their Wellbeing

4. Both the First Minister and the Leader of Plaid Cymru recognise that at times the pressure upon Designated Members, as upon Ministers, may be considerable, and they will have regard to the wellbeing of Members engaged in the Co-operation Agreement.

Appointments

5. Designated Members do not have any formal role in public appointments but will be consulted by Welsh Government Ministers for those appointments that relate to the Co-operation Agreement.

The Co-operation Agreement

6. Civil Service appointments are made in accordance with the Civil Service Commission's Recruitment Principles and the Civil Service Code. Public appointments are made in accordance with the requirements of the law and, where appropriate, the Governance Code on Public Appointments under which the Commissioner for Public Appointments carries out his regulatory role. Public appointments follow Welsh Government Public Bodies Unit procedures and reflect and champion the principles of the Welsh Government's Diversity and Inclusion Strategy for Public Appointments. Members, like Welsh Government Ministers, have a duty to ensure that influence over civil service and public appointments is not abused for partisan purposes.

Relations with the Civil Service

7. Designated Members are expected to be professional in their dealings with the civil service and to treat those with whom they come into contact with courtesy and respect. Civil servants who have concerns about the conduct of Designated Members can raise those concerns with the Permanent Secretary, as they can in relation to Ministers. Similarly, Designated Members can expect the civil servants with whom they come into contact to treat them with the courtesy and respect due to their role. If Designated Members have concerns about the conduct of a civil servant, then they should raise those concerns with the Permanent Secretary.

8. Where appropriate under the Co-operation Agreement, it is the responsibility of the civil service to provide Designated Members, alongside Welsh Government Ministers, with impartial, objective and honest advice which includes, to the best of their ability, all relevant information and analysis. Designated Members should pay due consideration to such advice and should not seek to direct civil servants on the advice which they receive, but neither, of course, are they obliged to accept and follow that advice.

9. In order to facilitate the provision of full and frank advice and discussion between Welsh Government Ministers, Designated Members and civil servants, all official papers and documents shared with Designated Members under the Co-operation Agreement, including recommendations and advice, should, unless informed otherwise, be regarded by Designated Members as being supplied in confidence and the contents should not to be shared elsewhere. Similarly, oral advice, policy discussion and debate should be regarded as being conducted in confidence and not for onward transmission. The privacy of opinions expressed and advice given should be maintained. In addition, Designated Members are expected to respect and abide by the GDPR responsibilities of the Welsh Government.

10. Any legal advice of the Counsel General or the Director of Legal Services and their staff should be regarded by Designated Members as carrying legal professional privilege and should not be disclosed or referred to elsewhere, whether orally or in written or electronic format.

11. On leaving their role in the Co-operation Agreement, Designated Members should not retain any official documents in their possession, whether electronic or hard copy.

The Accounting Officer

12. The Permanent Secretary is the Principal Accounting Officer for the Welsh Government with responsibility for the stewardship of all public funds under its control. They have designated other members of Welsh Government staff as additional accounting officers to be responsible for defined areas of the Welsh Government's activities.

13. Accounting Officers and their staff are responsible for ensuring that all advice to Ministers and to Designated Members includes appropriate guidance on the proper use of public funds and draws attention to any possible conflict between the intention of Ministers or Designated Members and the duties of an Accounting Officer. An Accounting Officer cannot simply accept the aims or policies without examination. Designated Members should have due regard to the role of the Accounting Officers in the proper conduct of public business.

Constituency or Party Interests

14. Facilities or support provided by the Welsh Government to Designated Members under the terms of the Co-operation Agreement should not be used for constituency activities or party activities outside the Agreement.

15. Where Designated Members are involved in decisions which might have a particular impact upon their own constituencies or electoral regions, they must take particular care to avoid any possible conflict of interest or apparent conflict.

Designated Members' Private Interests

16. Designated Members must ensure that no conflict arises, or could be perceived to arise, between their activities under the Co-operation Agreement and their private interests. This covers interests which may be financial or otherwise, such as links with organisations which might be funded by the

The Co-operation Agreement

Welsh Government and included in discussions under the Agreement. This also includes the spouse or partner of a Designated Member, as well as close family members.

17. Designated Members should be open in Partnership Discussions to declare any relevant or apparent conflicts. The First Minister and the Leader of Plaid Cymru in consultation are ultimately responsible for deciding how a conflict or apparent conflict which a Designated Member might have is to be treated.

18. Designated Members can seek informal and confidential advice from the Permanent Secretary or Director of Governance and Ethics on identifying conflicts and the measures which might need to be put in place to manage them.

Acceptance of gifts and hospitality

19. Designated Members should not accept any gifts or hospitality which might be perceived as putting them under an obligation in the way in which they discharge their roles under the Co-operation Agreement.

Index

Aberystwyth 51, 89-90, 93, 103, 119, 129, 142, 230, 265
Active Travel (Wales) Act (2013) 158
agricultural pollution 261
Almedalan Week (Sweden) 82n
Albania 188
Amersham International 31
Amman Valley 39, 42-4, 53
Ammanford 43-4, 47, 123, 193
Anderson, Donald 227, 228n
Andrews, Leighton vii, xii-xiv, 135, 135n
Antoniazzi, Tonia 144
Antoniw, Mick 19n, 218, 252
Any Questions (BBC Radio 4) 144
Arcade xii
Arfon (constituency) 100, 123-4, 172, 174
Arfor (western seaboard) 37, 50, 160, 172, 176, 178, 184, 224, 230, 255, 262
Armenia 188
Arnade, Chris 20, 21
Arwel, Fflur vii
Atlantic College 182n
Atlantic Recycling 214
Australia 241-2
Awen-Scully, Roger 147, 149
d'Azeglio, Massimo 55

Baden-Württemberg 48
BAFTA Cymru 46n
Baglioni, Gio Paolo 104
Baker, Steve 120
Balsom, Denis 188n
Bangor 149, 159, 163
Bangor University 86, 256n
Barcelona 104, 161
Barnett formula (consequential) 69, 223-4, 248, 255
Barnier, Michel 103
Barry 71n
Barry (constituency) 71n
Barry, Mark 168n
Barwell, Gavin 140-2
Basic Income 176

Basque Country 104-5, 244
Basque language 244
BBC Wales 4n, 13, 109, 133n, 146, 148, 150, 181n, 190
Begum, Shamima 144
Benllech 50
Berger, Luciana 111
Bermuda 188
Best for Britain 111
Betws 39, 42-4
Bible 44
    King James (1611) 44
    William Morgan (1588) 44
biodiversity 9, 186, 260
Birch, Anthony 244-6
Birmingham 185
Black, Ceri vii
Blackford, Ian 120
Blackstone Chambers 181n
Blaenau Ffestiniog 46
Blaenau Gwent (constituency) 16n, 117, 149, 155, 181, 184
Blair, Tony 33, 51, 59, 65, 71n, 190-1, 253
Blythyn, Hannah 215, 217-18
Bosch 31
'Bonfire of the Quangos' xiv, 33-4, 37, 175, 224
Boston 145, 150
Bourne, Nick 18
Bowden, Dawn 201-3
Bradbury, Jonathan 26
Brady, Sir Graham 141
Brân 134
Brecon and Radnor by-election (2019) 13
Brecon and Radnor (constituency) 253
Brexit x, xii-xiii, xvi-xviii, xix, 3, 5, 11, 13-14, 18, 22, 28, 64, 66, 68, 71n, 75-8, 81, 83-4, 88, 98-103, 107, 110-11, 117, 119-24, 128-31, 135, 140-2, 144-7, 155, 159-61, 163-6, 218-19, 232, 237
    Withdrawal Agreement 88, 101, 103, 111, 120-1, 123, 140, 141n

Index

Brexit, Grŵp (Plaid Cymru) 77-8, 83, 88, 101, 120, 122, 140, 144, 152
Brexit Party xix, 165, 201
Bridgend 130
Bridgend (constituency) 201n
British Airways 31
Brittany 105
Brixton 47
broadcasting 7, 225, 238, 262
Broadcasting Act (1990) xii
Brooks-Jones, Helen 77, 88, 111
Brown, Gordon 66
Brussels 82, 88, 92, 99-100, 103-8, 140, 151, 160, 188
Bryn Glas tunnels 109
Bryn, Steffan vii, 86, 88, 95, 113, 122, 125, 127-32, 136-7, 139, 142, 144-5, 151, 153, 159-60, 174
Bryntaf (see Ysgol Bryntaf)
Buckley, Mary 129
Bulgaria 188
Burgess, Cefyn 100-1
Burry Port 50
Bush, Stephen 5, 6n
Business Finland 35

Cable, Vince 111, 120
Caerau (Cardiff) 57
Caernarfon 109
Caernarfon (constituency) 20
Caerphilly / Caerffili (constituency) 149, 181
Cairns, Alun 84, 161
Callaghan, James 44
Campbell, Alistair 114
Canada 184, 187, 241
Canterbury 56, 235
Cardiff 37, 56-7, 71n, 75, 78, 83, 99-100, 111, 119, 135, 167-8, 185, 188, 194, 225, 256
Cardiff Airport 127, 130
Cardiff Business School vii, 34
Cardiff Central (constituency) 57
Cardiff County Council 184-5
Cardiff Metropolitan University vii
Cardiff North (constituency) 144
Cardiff South (constituency) 213
Cardiff University 8, 32, 48, 57, 180, 188, 235, 265
Cardiff West (constituency) 57, 149, 174, 221
Cardigan 75
Carmarthen 39, 56, 153, 228, 230

Carmarthen by-election (1966) 56, 256
Carmarthen (constituency) 124
Carmarthenshire ix, xvii, 39-40, 42-3, 50, 110, 153, 251
Carmarthen East and Dinefwr (constituency) 51, 83, 172
Carmarthen West and South Pembrokeshire (constituency) 149
Carmel 43
Castle, Barbara 62
Catalan Government (Representation to the EU) 104
Catalan independence referendum (2017) 161
Catalonia / Catalunya 104-5, 161
Cathays Park 9, 93, 175, 179-80, 272
Centre on Constitutional Change (Edinburgh) 40n
Ceredigion 20, 50, 242n
Ceredigion (constituency) 6, 20, 94, 172, 242
Ceredigion Preseli (constituency) 253
Channel Four 88, 99, 140
Channel Islands 241
Chapter Arts Centre (Cardiff) 136
Chilcot Inquiry 51
child poverty 23, 115, 167, 176, 258
China 31
City of London 25, 239
Civil Service 9, 25-31, 34-5, 107, 173, 179, 181, 183-4, 252, 264, 267-70, 272, 275
City Regions 37
'clear red water' 23, 58-61, 166, 249
climate change (also crisis / emergency) 9, 29, 92, 144, 167, 172, 176, 186, 218-19, 245, 248, 257, 260
Clinton, Bill 134
Clowes, Carl 160
Clubb, Gareth 87
Clwyd South (constituency) 149
Clwyd West (constituency) 7
Coal Exchange (Cardiff) 99
Coalisland (N. Ireland) 117
Cole, Stuart 109-10
Coleg Cymraeg Cenedlaethol 254, 265
Commission for Tertiary Education and Research (Medr) 263
Commission on the Constitutional Future of Wales xvii, 10, 225, 235-9, 243, 250-1, 262
Commission on Devolution in Wales 197, 199-200

Commission on the Devolution of Justice Powers to Wales 93, 116, 233
Commission on the UK's Future (Labour Party) 67-8, 233
Committee on Standards in Public Life 193n
Communities First 167
Conservative Party (also Tories / Welsh Conservatives) xviii, 7, 11-13, 16-18, 61, 78, 102, 114, 117, 125-7, 130-1, 140, 146-9, 164-5, 171-2, 180, 201, 206, 217-18, 220, 238, 250, 253, 255
Conservative UK Governments ix, xiii, xx, 3-5, 23, 25, 64-5, 67-8, 116, 141, 172-3, 186, 199, 206, 210, 212, 219, 223, 225, 237-9, 255, 257, 261, 263
consociational democracy 198n
Constitutional Law Association 6
Constitution Unit (University College, London) 188n, 205
Contract Parliamentarianism xi, xiii, 4, 187, 247, 256
  Canada 4, 179, 187
  Denmark 187
  Malaysia 187
  New Zealand 187
  Norway 187
  Sweden 187
Cooke, Phil 18n, 48
Co-operation Agreement vii, ix-xiv, xvi, xvii, xix-xxi, 3-5, 6n, 7, 9-10, 24, 37-8, 40-2, 70-1, 128n, 168, 171, 173-5, 178-80, 182-4, 186-7, 197-9, 203, 207, 212-13, 215-17, 219-25, 228, 230, 235, 244, 248-51, 255, 257-77
  budget arrangements 271
  communication and media arrangements 271-2
  delivery of Agreement 182-5
  implementation unit 179, 267
  Joint Oversight Board 179, 268-9
  legal advice 181-2
  mechanisms for implementation 179, 267-8
  negotiations 172-8
  policy commitments 258-66
  role of Civil Service 269-70
  role of Plaid Cymru Designated Members 257, 259-60, 273-6
  role of Special Advisers 179-80, 256-7, 267-8, 270
  sets precedent in British politics 187
  Swedish precedent 4, 179, 187

Co-Opposition ix, xii, 3, 179-81
Coppieters Foundation 106
Corbyn, Jeremy 56, 77, 98, 101-3, 120, 122, 145, 147, 155, 160
Cork 129
Corporate Joint Committee 262
Council Tax reform 6-7, 9, 24, 176, 186, 220, 248, 259
Covid-19 Inquiry 68, 214-15
Covid-19 pandemic x, xiii, xvi-xvii, xix, 10, 14-15, 23, 42, 55, 68-70, 82n, 171-2, 214-15, 217, 219, 246, 249, 254,
Cox, Alun 94
Crawford, Ewan 146, 151
Crawley, Andrew 35n
Creagh, Mary 111
Crown Estate 225, 238, 255, 260
Crymych 79
culture strategy 253, 264
Curriculum for Wales 253, 264
Customs Union 84, 101-2, 121
Cwmrhydyceirw 227
Cymdeithas Cledwyn 256
Cymru Fydd 133
Cymru Yfory (Tomorrow's Wales) 174, 197n
Cynon Valley 48

Dafis, Cynog vii, 6-7, 17, 18n, 94, 119, 155
Dafis, Llinos 94
Dafydd, Aled ap vii
Dáil Éireann 128
Daily Record 66
Daily Telegraph 7-8
Dance, Charles 111, 114
Dauwen, Günther 104-5, 107
David, Hefin 181
David, Rhys vii
Davidson, George 43
Davidson, Jane 57
Davies, Alun 117, 155, 181, 184
Davies, Andrew 26
Davies, Andrew R.T. 15, 180
Davies, D.J. 43, 52
Davies, David 173-4
Davies, David T.C. 210
Davies, Geraint Talfan vii
Davies, Glyn 117
Davies, John 231n
Davies, Paul 15, 114, 117, 130, 140, 142
Davies, Ron 190-1, 244
Davies, S.O. 52

Index

Day, Geraint vii, 77, 95, 118-19, 122, 125
Delbridge, R. 35n
Democratic Unionist Party (DUP) 111, 117, 120, 122
Designated Members 179-81, 266, 268, 270, 272-7
Development Bank for Wales 214
Development Board for Rural Wales 33
d'Hondt method (see proportional representation)
Dilnot Commission 223
disability rights 265
Disability Task Force 265
Dodds, Nigel 120
Dominion Status 70, 241-3
Drakeford, Mark, ix, x, xii-xiii, xvii, xix-xx, 4, 13-16, 27, 39-42, 55-72, 77, 81, 87, 109, 114, 130-2, 140, 142, 145, 147-8, 152, 155-8, 160, 166-7, 171-5, 178, 180, 187, 203-4, 206-7, 213, 216-17, 221-3, 243, 247-51, 258
   Barnett formula 63-4, 69, 248
   Senedd Reform 206-7
   similarities to Adam Price 39-40
   welcomes potential deal with Plaid 16-7
Dublin 82, 92, 117, 127-30
Dumfries and Galloway 225
DUP (see Democratic Unionist Party)
Dwyfor Meirionnydd (constituency) 172
Dyfed Farmers' Action Group 46

Edinburgh 3, 92, 145, 151, 153, 155, 185
Edwards, Emily vii, 86
Edwards, Jonathan ('Joni Eds') 77-8, 88, 101, 124, 145, 153
EFA (see European Free Alliance)
EFTA (see European Free Trade Association)
Eirug, Aled 58n
Elin, Fflur 86, 152
Elis-Thomas, Dafydd ('Dafydd El') 75, 87, 114, 158, 177, 252
electoral reform 202, 251
Ely (Cardiff) 56-7, 63, 221, 256
English devolution 232-3
English identity 232, 244-6
English jurisdiction 233
Enterprise Ireland 35
Equality Act (2010) 207-11
Equality and Human Rights Commission 210
Eryri (Snowdonia) 139
Essex, Sue 57
European Commission 33, 99, 104, 193

European Free Alliance (EFA) 104-6, 151, 160
European Free Trade Area Association (EFTA) 101
European Parliament xix, 13, 103-6, 121, 140, 151, 165-6, 256
European Parliament election results (Wales, 2019) 165
European Policy Centre (EPC) 99, 106-7
European Research Group (ERG) 120-2
European Union (EU) 13, 15, 20, 28, 48-50, 65, 68, 88, 92-3, 101-6, 108, 111-12, 120-1, 128, 131, 141, 161-2, 165, 232, 239, 252, 257
Evans, Gwynfor 52, 56, 256
Evans, Jill 77, 88, 94, 101, 103-4, 121, 140, 145, 151, 160
Evans, Nerys 216
Ewing, Winnie 161

fair rents xxi, 259
Farage, Nigel 98, 103
farm payments xxi, 261
Faroe Islands 241
Farrell, James 129
federalism 245
   in UK xvi-xvii, 66, 70, 116, 236, 240
Financial Times 16
Fianna Fáil 128
Fine Gael 128
Finland 184
First Minister's Questions (FMQs) 77, 81, 83-4, 89, 109-10, 114-15, 139-40, 145, 151, 155, 180, 182
fiscal gap 24-5
Fleetwood Mac 134
flood review (into 2020-21 incidents) 261
flood management xxi, 58, 249, 260-1
food strategy 250, 261
Ford Motor Company 31, 130
France 184
Free Association 239-43
free childcare xvi, xxi, 9, 38, 186, 219, 247, 258-9
free school meals xvi, xxi, 6-7, 9, 23, 38, 167, 182, 186, 219, 258
Fychan, Heledd 206

Gaelic cultural centre (Derry) 117
Gaelic television (Scotland) xii
Galway 129
Ganz, Marshall 53
Gapes, Mike 144

281

Gatland, Warren 153-4, 162
Gender Recognition Act (2004) 210
General Electric (GE) 31
George, Lloyd 40, 85
German, Michael 17-8
Gething, Vaughan xx, 77, 210, 213-19, 221, 251-2, 256
Glamorgan County Cricket Club 55
Glas Cymru (Welsh Water) 60
Glasgow University 61
Gooberman, Leon 34
Good Friday Agreement 232
Goodhart, David 21-2
Government of Wales Act
   (1998) 198, 238, 247
   (2006) 198
   (2014) 30
   (2017) 200, 206, 242-3
Gramsci, Antonio 19
Grangetown (Cardiff) 82
Greece 105, 160, 239
Green Party (England) 14, 111, 120
Green Party (Scotland) 152, 177
Green Party (Sweden) 179
Green Party (Wales) 165-6, 254
Green voters 13, 22, 147,
Gregynog Hall 115, 138
Griffiths, James (Jim) 43, 52
Griffiths, Leslie 219
Gruffydd, Llyr Huws 80, 88-9, 159
Grŵp Brexit Plaid Cymru (see Brexit, Grŵp (Plaid Cymru))
Guardian, The 57, 100
Guilford, Graeme 28
Gwenllian, Siân vii, 80, 85, 94-5, 122, 132, 153, 159, 174, 211-12
Gwent 133
Gwilym, Eurfyl ap vii, 81, 87, 100
Gwynedd 50, 186, 230

Haf, Gwennol vii
Hague, William 133
Hain, Peter 48
Harris, Carl vii, 83, 90, 93-5, 98, 100, 118, 122, 124, 130, 136-9, 145, 160
health and social care 9, 176, 224
Heath, Edward 124
Heseltine, Michael 111, 114
Highlands and Islands Enterprise 225
Hinds, Michael 17
Holtham, Gerald vii, ix-xi, 28-30, 34, 84-5, 224
Holyhead 129-30

homelessness xxi, 6, 23, 57, 247, 258-9
House of Commons 43, 51, 110-11, 113, 130, 145, 197, 200, 241
House of Lords reform 63-4, 66, 225, 238, 256
housing policy 7, 10, 23, 38, 50, 168, 176, 183, 219, 222-3, 230, 247, 258-9, 265
Howells, John 46
Hughes, Cledwyn 256
Hughes, Peter 214
Hutt, Jane 16, 28, 57, 174, 211, 217

Ibargutxi, Eva Bidania 104
ICM poll (2019, for BBC Wales) 148-9
Insole Court (Cardiff) 100
Institute for Government (London) 67, 206
Institute for International and European Affairs (Dublin) 129
Institute of Public Administration (Dublin) 128
Institute of Welsh Affairs (IWA) 6, 48, 109, 115, 188
International Baccalaureate (IB) 182n
Investment and Development Agency of Ireland 129
Iorwerth, Rhun ap xiii, xx, 75, 80-2, 85, 87, 89, 94, 129-30, 154, 159, 213, 215-16, 219, 251, 256
IRA (Irish Republican Army) 117
Iraq War 23, 51, 144, 166
Ireland, Northern 22, 64, 66, 68, 84, 100-1, 108, 117, 121, 191-2, 232-4, 242
Ireland, Republic of 25, 64, 68, 93, 108, 127-30, 162, 184, 232-3, 241
Irish Free State 241
Irish Northern Aid Committee (NORAID) 117
Isle of Man 241
IWA (see Institute of Welsh Affairs)

James, Julie 80, 110, 219
James, Sioned vii
Jenkins, Nigel 234
Jewell, Delyth 159
Johnson, Boris xix, 14, 55, 65, 112, 173, 249
Jones, Alun Ffred 94, 143
Jones, Carwyn 12-13, 30, 32, 64, 77, 81, 84, 87, 109-10, 114-16, 147, 214, 251
Jones, Elin xiii, 75, 77, 82, 94, 131, 181-2, 200, 207, 208-9

Index

Jones, Gwilym Ceri 107
Jones, Gwyn 30n
Jones, Helen Mary 75, 80, 83, 89, 94, 126, 132, 143, 152, 159
Jones, Hywel Ceri 99-100, 107
Jones, Ieuan Wyn 12, 109
Jones, Ifan Morgan 5
Jones, J. Barry 188n
Jones, Mabli vii, 76, 82, 122, 127, 142
Jones, Richard Wyn 8, 127
Juniper Films 99
justice & policing (powers) 64, 66, 93, 116, 187, 225, 233, 238, 255, 265

Kane, Vincent 133
Kay, John 61n
Kennedy School of Government (Harvard) 53, 128
Kenya 188
King, Richard 44n, 47-8n
Kiribati 187

Labour Party (also Welsh Labour) vii, ix-xiii, xvi-xviii, xix-xxi, 3-5, 7-8, 10-13, 15-19, 23-4, 26n, 29, 32, 37-8, 42, 48-9, 51-3, 55-9, 62-3, 66-7, 69-72, 75, 78, 80, 96, 101-3, 109, 114-15, 117, 120-1, 125-7, 132, 135, 141, 144-5, 146-9, 151-4, 158, 163-8, 171-7, 179-84, 186-7, 190-4, 196-9, 201-4, 212-18, 220-1, 224-5, 227-8, 230, 233-4, 238-9, 242n, 244, 248-56, 272
    attractions of a deal with Plaid 172-3
    disunity under Vaughan Gething 213-5, 217-9, 256
    relations with Plaid Cymru ix, xvi-xvii, 59, 69-71, 212, 228
Lake, Ben 77, 88, 101
Land Authority for Wales 33
Larner, Jac 254
Latvia 105
Law, Peter 16n
Lee, Philip 111
Legal and General 31
Lewis, Gail 133
Lewis, Saunders 244
Lewis, Steffan 76-7, 80, 101, 127-8, 130, 132-5, 138, 140, 158-9
LGBTQ+ Action Plan 266
Liberal Democrats (Lib Dems) xviii, 11-13, 17-18, 22, 57, 96, 111, 114, 120,
145-7, 149, 152, 165, 182, 191, 193, 220, 244, 248, 253
Lightman, Ivor 188n
Lijphart, Arend 198n
Limerick 129
Lindner, Christoph 98
Llamau 57
Llanelli 100
Llanelli (constituency) 124, 149, 217, 253
Llanelli Coastal Park 31
Llantwit Major 182n
Llithfaen 144
Lloyd, Dai 132, 152, 159, 201n
Lloyd George, David 40, 85
Lloyd George, Megan 40
Lloyds Bank 31
Llwynypia (Rhondda) 235n
London ix, xii, 3, 11, 13-14, 23-5, 42-3, 47, 52, 58, 78, 83, 87, 92, 99-100, 103, 111, 113, 120, 140, 160-1, 166-7, 181n, 185, 188n, 193-4, 199, 205-6, 207n, 212, 216n, 220, 239, 247, 252
'Long Revolution' 243-4
looked after children 263
Lucas, Caroline 111, 120

M4 Relief Road 81, 87, 109-10, 115
Macron, Emmanuel 98, 127
Mair, Angharad 144
Major, John 193n
Malachy, Gareth 117
Malaysia 4, 187
Manchester 92
Mandelson, Peter 114
Mansfield College (Oxford) 71n
Marquand, David 61n, 71n, 100
Martin, Ciaran 67
May Day Manifesto (1968) 42
May, Theresa 78, 83, 100, 102, 110-11, 122, 130, 140
McAllister, Laura 180, 195, 200, 235
McCrone, David 145
McDonald, Mary Lou 128
McDonnell, John 101
McEntee, Helen 129-30
McEvatt, Lauren 238
McEvoy, Neil 75, 80, 88, 114, 152-3, 158
McMaster University 48
McMorrin, Anna 144
Mebyon Kernow 133
Medi, Nia vii

media financial support 7, 261-2
Medical school (north Wales) 176
Meirionnydd (constituency) 20, 87, 89, 124, 172
Melding, David 117
Menai Strait 230
mental health policy 265
Menter a Busnes 51, 129
Merthyr (constituency) 201n
Metro (Cardiff and Valleys) 34, 109, 167, 168n, 185, 225, 255, 260
Meurig, Esyllt vii
Michael, Alun 12, 252
Mid and West Wales (Senedd regional constituency) 75, 256
Miles, Jeremy 38, 213-14, 219, 224
Milford Haven 103
Millar, Darren 7
Millennium Stadium (Cardiff) 31
Milne, Seumas 102
Miners' Strike (1984) 39, 43, 45-7, 53, 124
Mitchell, James 145
Mittal Affair 51
Mittal, Lakshmi 51
Monaco 241
Montgomery, General Bernard 'Monty' 105
Montgomeryshire 50, 138n
Montgomeryshire (constituency) 117
Morgan, Eluned xiii, 77, 256
Morgan, Barry 174n
Morgan, Lord Elystan 241-3
Morgan, Julie 57
Morgan, Kevin 32, 48, 184n
Morgan, Prys xx
Morgan, Rhodri ix, xiv, 13, 23, 32-3, 57-60, 69-70, 115, 147, 188, 189n, 192-3, 196, 197n, 252
Morgan, Syd 104, 108
Morris, Steven 100
Mosalski, Ruth 214n
Munday, Max 35n
'muscular unionism' xiii, 11, 64, 67, 173, 249
Mutch, Fergus 146
Mynachlog-ddu 79n

Nant Gwrtheyrn 144, 160n
Narberth 111
Nation Cymru 5, 7n, 26n, 38n, 185n, 210n, 211-12n, 214-16n, 218-19n, 253n

National Assembly (Welsh Assembly) x, xiv, xviii, xxi, 7, 11-12, 17-18, 31-4, 49, 51, 57-9, 75, 83, 87, 96, 109-10, 115-16, 128, 135n, 146-8, 154, 156, 158, 163, 166, 188-9, 190-200, 202, 228, 231, 235, 248, 252
National Care Service 6, 9, 175, 223, 259
National Centre for Learning Welsh 265
National Gallery for Contemporary Art 10, 264
National Infrastructure Commission for Wales 261
National Innovation Strategy 263
National Institute Economic Review 26
National Library xxi, 94
National Museum xxi
Natural Resources Wales 214, 261
National School for Government 128, 262
nature emergency 260 (also see climate change)
Neagle, Lynne 221
Neal, David 214
Neal Soil Suppliers 214
Neath 48, 100
Neath (constituency) 149, 213
Neath Port Talbot Council 50
net zero 186, 257, 260
New Nation 136, 143-4, 152, 154, 160
New Statesman 5, 6n, 147
New York 42, 46n
New Zealand 4, 187, 241-2
Newidiem 51
Newport 109, 133, 167, 168n, 193
Newport West by-election (2019) 150, 152
Nolan Principles (The Seven Principles of Public Life) 30n, 193
Nolan, Lord 193n
Northern Ireland (see Ireland, Northern)
Norway (also Norway-plus) 121, 187
Nova Cambria 86, 122, 136, 143-4, 150, 152, 154, 160

O'Keeffe, Ben vii, 77-8, 88, 94, 102, 108, 123, 135, 140
O'Neill, Michelle 117
O'Sullivan, Marion 128
Obama, Barack 44, 53, 97-8, 139, 145
Objective 1 (European Union funding) 48-9, 252
OECD (see Organisation for Economic Co-operation and Development)
Office for Budget Responsibility 263

Index

One Wales (coalition agreement - 2007-11) xviii, 3, 8, 17-18, 58n, 109, 116, 145, 174, 176, 197-8, 202, 220, 228
Organisation for Economic Co-operation and Development (OECD) 184, 262
Osmond, John ix-xi, xii-xiv, xviii, 18n, 61n, 70n, 79n, 88, 102-5, 107-8, 120, 131-2, 135, 138-9, 143, 145, 151, 153-4, 159, 166, 174, 189, 202, 244-6
Ottawa 145
Owen, David 71n
Owens, Ken, 153

Palestinian Authority 189
Pannick KC, Lord David 181
Paris 42
Parti Québécois 145
Patchett, Keith 188-9
Paterson, Lindsay 145
Peace Academy 176
Pembrokeshire 79n, 117
Penarth 83, 99
People's Vote 77, 101-2, 112, 114, 144, 146, 151-2, 160, 167
Petković, Iva 106
Phillips, Marc 143
Plaid Cymru ix-x, xiii-xiv, xx-xxi, 4, 11-3, 15, 19-20, 22, 25, 30, 35, 37-8, 40n, 52, 54, 71, 79-82, 85-6, 88-9, 106, 121-2, 122-4, 140, 143, 152, 155, 228-9, 216, 224, 231, 239-41, 254
   Dewis 17
   Manifesto (2021) 9n, 16, 50
   relationship with Welsh Labour ix, xiii, xvi-xvii, 69-71, 212, 228, 244
   Robertson Review 90, 118n, 136-9, 142-4
   Senedd election (2021) 171-2, 227
   Shadow Cabinet 79, 82, 85-6, 88-9, 132, 140, 152, 193
Plymouth Brethren 44-5
policing powers (see justice & policing)
Pontcanna (Cardiff) 57
Portugal 25, 188, 239
poverty and inequality 265
Powell, Dewi Waktin 188n,
Powell, Enoch 235n, 247
Powell, Jonathan 253
Price, Adam, vii, ix-x, xiii, xv, xvii-xviii, xx, 4, 8, 11-12, 15, 22, 39-40, 42-55, 76, 78-80, 82, 88, 90-3, 95-113, 115, 117-8, 125-30, 132-40, 142, 144-5, 155-63, 177-8, 218, 249
   approach to policy making 85
   becomes Plaid leader 75
   election strategy (2021) 90-3, 118, 123-7, 149, 163-4
   instinct for compromise 42
   relations with Welsh Labour 19, 51-2
   resignation (May 2023) 216
   similarities to Mark Drakeford 39-40, 114
Price, Adrian 39, 45
Price, Angela 43
Price, Emyr 215n, 256n
Price, Rufus 39, 42-3
Pride 47
Private Finance Initiative (PFI) 23, 166
'progressive universalism' 51, 61-3, 167, 249
property and fair rents 247
proportional representation 33, 71, 174n, 190-1, 196-8, 204
   d'Hondt method 187, 204, 253
   St. Lague method 204
   Single Transferable Vote (STV) x, 33, 192, 194-6, 200, 201-2, 204, 206
Prosiect 2050 (Welsh language usage) 258, 264
Public Accounts Committee 30n
Public Health Wales 156-7
public sector procurement policy 24, 26, 182, 259
public transport 109, 260

qualifications reform 263
quangos (see 'Bonfire of the Quangos')

Race Equality Action Plan 265
'radical federalism' 19
Radical Wales 48, 154-5
rail devolution 225, 238
Rainbow Alliance (2007) 12, 18
Red-Green Alliance 19, 51-2, 52n
Rees, David 4n, 209n
Referendums
   1979 - Welsh Assembly xii
   1997 - National Assembly for Wales 12, 48-9, 57, 190-1, 227, 231, 256
   1997 - Scottish Parliament, 190
   2011 - National Assembly for Wales (legislative powers) 12, 116, 174n

regional partnerships 26n, 28, 35, 124, 184n, 251, 262, 265
renewable energy 7, 26, 82, 167, 260
Renwick, Alan 205
republicanism 71n
Republic of Ireland (see Ireland, Republic of)
reserved powers system 240, 242-3, 247
Rhigos 48
Rhondda 86, 94, 235n
Rhondda (constituency) vii, 75, 123, 172
Rhuthun 100
Richard Commission xiv, 32n, 33, 174n, 189, 192-7, 200, 247
Richard, Lord Ivor 193
Richards, Ceri 103
Richards, Rhuanedd 132, 135n
Roberts, Elin 82-3
Roberts, Liz Saville 77-8, 84, 88-9, 101-3, 117, 120
Robertson, Angus 89, 91, 94, 118, 136-9, 142-4
Robertson, George 190
Robinson, Nick 44n
Roderick, Vaughan 109-10
Rodgers, Bill 71n
Roosevelt, Franklin Delano 76
Rowe-Beddoe, Sir David 30n, 33
Rowlands, David 201
Russell, Mike 152
Runeckles, Jane 173-4

St. Clears, 40
St. Davids Festival of Ideas 82, 86, 111, 145
St. Lague method (see proportional representation)
Salmond, Alex 81
San Marino 241
Sanders, Bernie 98
Sargeant, Carl 110, 135
Save the Children Fund 23
Sayed, Bethan 126, 152, 159
school term (academic year) 221-2, 263
Scotland xii, 35, 40, 64-8, 101, 108, 112, 127, 134, 151, 157, 177, 184, 190-2, 194, 225, 232-4, 238, 242, 245, 247-8, 253
Scottish Borders 225
Scottish Constitutional Convention 192n
Scottish Court of Session Inner House 211
Scottish Enterprise 35, 225
Scottish Government 68, 146

Scottish identity 245-6
Scottish Labour (see Labour Party)
Scottish National Party (SNP) 22, 51, 66n, 88-9, 91, 93-4, 107-8, 111, 118n, 120, 125, 133, 145-6, 151-2, 160, 177
Scottish Parliament 66, 81, 113, 146, 177, 190-1
second (holiday) homes xvi, 7, 172, 175, 186, 219, 222, 247, 259
Secretary of State for Scotland 190
Secretary of State for Wales 30n, 43, 161n, 190, 210, 242, 252
Senedd Cymru 234-5, 240, 244, 246-8, 252, 254, 257
Senedd Cymru (Electoral Candidates Lists) Bill (2024) 207-11
Senedd Cymru (Members and Elections) Act (2024) 205-6
Senedd elections xi, 209-10, 253
  (1999) 11, 51, 57, 58n, 188, 192, 247-8
  (2003) xix 16n, 59, 171
  (2007) ix, xviii, 8, 11, 16-18, 51, 247
  (2011) xix, 171, 220, 247
  (2016) xviii, 12, 16, 85, 128, 134, 158, 166, 174, 256
  (2021) x, xiii, xv, xvi-xvii, xix, 4, 8-9, 14-15, 19, 23-4, 37, 42, 50, 75, 154, 166, 171, 201, 221, 224, 249-50
  (2026) xx, 38, 204, 211, 220, 253-4
  (2030) 211
Senedd reform, x, xiii, xiv, xx, 38, 175, 187, 186-212, 246, 250-1
  closed lists 205-207
  Co-operation Agreement commitment 250
  gender parity 207-2011
  negotiations 203-205
Seren Network 265
Serret, Meritxell 104
Sewel Convention 66, 67n, 241n
Sheen, Michael 114
Shipton, Martin 26n, 40n, 45-6n, 53-4n, 56n, 59n, 63n, 115, 154, 163, 210-11n, 214-16n, 218m, 240n, 242-3n
Sianel Pedwar Cymru (S4C) 46n, 123, 144
Sibelius, Jean 134
Silk Commission 197, 199-202
Silk, Sir Paul 197
Single Transferable Vote (STV) (see proportional representation)

Index

Sinn Féin 78, 117, 128
Singapore 53
Slough 229
Smith, Carmen Ria vii
Smyth, Alyn 108
Snowdonia (see Eryri)
SNP (see Scottish National Party)
social care 6, 9, 23, 38, 172, 175-6, 223-4, 247, 258-9
social care levy 224
Social Democratic Party (SDP) 71n
social housing 10, 183, 222
Socialist Workers Party (SWP) 47
Solva 111
Sony Corporation 31
Soubry, Anna 111, 120
South Glamorgan County Council 57
South of Scotland Enterprise 225
South Pembrokeshire (constituency) 149
South Wales Central (Senedd region) 75, 206, 304
Spain 239
Spatial planning 37
Special Advisers (Spads) x, xv, 3, 5-6, 19, 57, 62, 151, 173-4, 178-80, 267, 269-71
Starmer, Sir Keir 66-7, 101, 213, 216n, 238
Statute of Westminster (1931) 241-2
Stead, Peter 61n
Stirling 108n
Street, Andy 139
Sturgeon, Nicola 55, 81, 146, 151-2
Sullivan, Mike 58n
Sunday Politics (BBC Radio Wales) 109, 150
Sunday Times 55, 173
supply teaching 263
Supreme Court (UK) 209n, 210-11, 249
sustainable farming scheme 261
sustainable public services 263
Swansea xix, 44, 50, 94, 167
Swansea East (constituency) 227
Swansea University 6n, 26, 57-8, 60n
Swansea West (constituency) 81, 110
Sweden 4, 82n, 187
Swinney, John 81

Tertiary Education and Research (Wales) Act (2022) 263
Thatcher, Margaret 40
Thomas, Huw 185
Thomas, Lord (of Cwmgiedd) 93, 233

Thomas, Rhodri Glyn 51
Thomas, Simon 75, 158
Thomson, Harry 6n
three-day week 124
Tonyrefail 86
Tories (see Conservative Party)
tourism levy 260
Transgender people 254
Transport for Wales (TfW) 238, 260
transport policy 24, 26, 34, 50, 79, 109, 238, 260
Trawsfynydd nuclear power station 46, 89
Treasury (UK) 10, 69, 237, 252
tree planting 186, 260-1
Treeware canvassing system 96
Trench, Alan 192-3n
Tripp, David 107
Trump, Donald 98
Trystan, Dafydd 149
Tŷ Gwynfor (Plaid Cymru HQ) vii, 77, 86, 94, 123, 137, 139
Tŷ Hywel (Senedd offices) 78, 83

UK Changing Union Partnership 197n
Unite, the Union 213-214
United Kingdom Independence Party (UKIP) 13, 22, 114, 146-9, 165
United Nations (UN) 193, 232, 240
  Security Council 232
University of Bristol 82
University of Cambridge 105
University of Glamorgan 26
University of Kent 56
University of Leicester 48
Unnos 10, 183, 222-3, 259
Upton, Stevie 31
Urdd Eisteddfod 56

Valentine, Lewis 134
Valles, Marlena 181n
Valleys (southern valleys) 20, 37, 48-50, 167, 176, 178, 184-5, 230, 244, 246, 255, 262
Valleys Development Agency 18, 37, 50, 168, 178, 184, 225, 255
Valleys Regeneration Corporation 18
Vaughan, Elwyn 18n
Vietnam War 42
Vine, Jeremy 110-11
vocational qualifications 263

Wales Act (2014) 30
Wales Act (2017) 200, 206, 242-3

Wales and England relationship 230-5
Wales for Europe 135
Wales Governance Centre 8, 15, 117, 127, 147, 166, 197n, 235, 254, 263
Wales Office 238
Wales on Sunday 50
Walker, Peter 30n
Waters, Lee 217-18, 253, 254
Washington DC 145, 150
Webb, Sir Adrian 26-8
Webb, Harri 134
welfare devolution 225, 265
Wellbeing of Future Generations (Wales) Act (2015) 264
Welsh Affairs Select Committee 65
Welsh Baccalaureate (WelshBac) xiv, 182
Welsh border 55-6, 62, 105, 223, 230, 232-4
Welsh Cabinet 28-30, 56-7, 87, 135, 158, 173, 177, 180, 189, 198, 215n
 Shadow Cabinet (see Plaid Cymru)
Welsh Centre for International Affairs 188n
Welsh citizenship 227, 242-4, 246
Welsh coalfield 231
Welsh Conservatives (see Conservative Party)
Welsh Development Agency (WDA) xiv, xi, 10, 24-5, 30-8, 115, 129, 160, 224, 255
Welsh Development Bank 37
Welsh economic strategies 25-6
Welsh Election Study (July 2024) 254
Welsh Government 6, 11, 26-30, 68, 84, 107, 109, 110n, 140, 158, 163, 167, 171-2, 176, 179, 181, 183-5, 194, 204n, 208, 210, 214-15, 220, 222-5, 228, 234, 246, 254, 257
Welsh Green Deal 176
Welsh history xiii, 7, 10, 45, 133, 186, 229-33
Welsh identity 18, 59, 135, 165, 227, 246
Welsh jurisdiction 116, 187, 233, 238
Welsh language 20, 22-3, 78, 122, 229, 154, 246, 262, 264-5
Welsh Language Commissioner 174, 264
Welsh Language and Education (Wales) Bill (2024) 264
Welsh language place-names 265
Welsh language standards 253, 264
Welsh Language (Wales) Measure (2011) 253, 265

Welsh-medium education 176, 186, 229, 264
Welsh Nation 106, 122
Welsh Office 188n, 252
Welsh SMEs – the 'missing middle' 36
Welsh Treasury (see Treasury, Wales)
Welsh Refugee Council 142
Welsh Water (see Glas Cymru)
Western Mail 4n, 5, 7n, 34n, 45n, 50n, 84, 115, 133, 154, 158, 163, 180n, 184n, 242n
western seaboard (see Arfor)
Whyte, Andrew 216
Wigley, Dafydd 17, 18n, 77-8, 87-8, 101, 120, 124, 140, 145
Wiliam, Math 127, 140
Williams, D.J. 79
Williams, Darren 4n
Williams, David vii
Williams, Gwyn Alf 231
Williams, Hywel 77, 88, 101
Williams, Jane 58n
Williams, Kirsty 114, 177
Williams, Phil 133, 228
Williams, Raymond 105-6, 243-4
Williams, Rowan 235
Williams, Shirley 71n
Williams, Waldo 79n
Wodehouse, P.G. 55
Women's Rights Network Cymru 210
Wood, Leanne xviii, 12, 75-7, 80, 82, 84-5, 89, 94, 114, 123, 126, 128, 148, 152-3, 159
Wrexham 37, 167
Wylfa B power station 80, 88-9, 160n

Y Ddraig Goch 122, 155
Ynni Cymru 9, 167, 260
Ynys Môn 50, 89, 160
Ynys Môn (constituency) 75, 80, 124, 172, 253, 256
YouGov opinion polls (Wales)
 2019 (February) 146-7
 2019 (July) 166
 2024 (June) 254
Ysgol Bryntaf (Cardiff) 256
Ysgol Glantaf (Cardiff) 256
Ystrad Mynach 127

Zuleeg, Fabian 107

Bibliography

Books

Arnade, Chris: *Dignity – Seeking Respect in Back Row America* (Sentinel, 2019).
Barry, Mark: *A Metro for Wales's Capital City Region: Connecting Cardiff, Newport and the Valleys* (Institute of Welsh Affairs, 2011).
Birch, Anthony: *Political Integration and Disintegration in the British Isles* (George Allen and Unwin, 1977).
Davies, John: *A History of Wales* (Penguin, 2007).
Davies, Ron: *Devolution: a process not an event* (Institute of Welsh Affairs, 1999).
Eirug, Aled, and Jane Williams, Jane: *The Impact of Devolution in Wales: Social Democracy with a Welsh Stripe* (University of Wales Press, 2022).
Evans, Rhys: *Gwynfor Evans, Portrait of a Patriot* (Y Lolfa, 2008).
Gooberman, Leon: *From Depression to Devolution: Economy and Government in Wales, 1934-2006* (University of Wales Press, 2017).
Goodhart, David: *The Road to Somewhere: The New Tribes Shaping British Politics* (Penguin Random House, 2017).
Jenkins, Nigel: *Ambush* (Gomer, 1998).
Jones, Carwyn: *The Future of Welsh Labour* (Institute of Welsh Affairs, 2004).
King, Richard: *Brittle with Relics – A History of Wales 1962 to 1997* (Faber, 2022).
Lightman, Ivor et.al.: *Making the Assembly Work* (Institute of Welsh Affairs, 1997).
Lijphart, Arend: *Patterns of Democracy: Government Forms and Performance in Thirty-Six Countries* (Yale University Press, 1999).
Marquand, David: *Britain Since 2018: The Strange Career of British Democracy* (Weidenfield & Nicholson, 2008).
Morgan, Kevin, and Price, Adam: *The Other Wales: The Case for Objective 1 Funding Post 1999* (Institute of Welsh Affairs, 1998).
Morgan, Rhodri: *Rhodri – A Political Life in Wales and Westminster* (University of Wales Press, 2017).
Muller, Wolfgang C., and Strøm, Kaar (Eds.): *Policy, Office, or Votes? How Political Parties in Western Europe Make Hard Decisions* (Cambridge University Press, 1999).

Osmond, John (Ed.): *Welsh Politics Come of Age – Responses to the Richard Commission* (Institute of Welsh Affairs, 2005).
Osmond, John: *Crossing the Rubicon – Coalition Politics Welsh Style* (Institute of Welsh Affairs, 2007).
Osmond, John: *Unpacking the Progressive Consensus* (Institute of Welsh Affairs, 2008).
Osmond, John: *Real Preseli* (Seren, 2019).
Plaid Cymru: *Towards an Independent Wales – Report of the Independence Commission* (Y Lolfa, 2020).
Plaid Cymru: *The Road to Independence: Evidence to the Independent Commission on the Constitutional Future of Wales* (Y Lolfa, 2022).
Price, Adam: *Wales: The First and Final Colony* (Y Lolfa, 2018).
Price, Emyr: *Lord Cledwyn of Penrhos* (Research Centre Wales, Bangor University, 1990).
Richards, Rhuanedd, (Ed.): *Gwladgarwr Gwent/Son of Gwent – Cofio Steffan Lewis* (Y Lolfa, 2019).
Williams, Gwyn A.: *When Was Wales* (Penguin, 1985).
Williams, Phil: *The Psychology of Distance* (Welsh Academic Press & Institute of Welsh Affairs, 2003).
Williams, Raymond: *The Long Revolution* (Penguin, 1971).

Articles, Book Chapters, Lectures, Reports and Speeches

Antoniw, Mick et.al.: *We the People: The Case for Radical Federalism* (Labourlist.org, January 2021).
Bale, Tim, and Bergman, Torbjörn: 'Captive No Longer, but Servants Still? Contract Parliamentarianism and the New Minority Governance in Sweden and New Zealand', *Government and Opposition* (Cambridge University Press, March 2014).
Balsom, Denis: 'The Three Wales Model' in John Osmond (Ed.), *The National Question Again* (Gomer, 1985).
Bradbury, Jonathan, and Davies, Andrew: 'Regional economic development and the case of Wales: theory and practice and problems of strategy and policy', *National Institute Economic Review*, Vol. 261, (Cambridge University Press, 2022).
Crawley, Andrew, Delbridge, Rick, and Munday, Max: 'Selling the region: The problems of a multi-agency approach in promoting regional economies', *Regional Science Policy and Practice*, 12 (3), (Wiley-Blackwell, 2020).
Dewis: *Deffro Mae'n Ddydd* (Awake It Is Day), *Plaid Cymru and the Realities of Coalition Politics in 21st Century Wales* (Dewis, May 2005).

Bibliography

Drakeford, Mark: 'Progressive Universalism', John Osmond (Ed.), *Unpacking the Progressive Consensus* (Institute of Welsh Affairs, 2008).

Will Henson & Harry Thomson: *Our View on the Welsh Government & Plaid Cymru Co-operation Agreement* (Institute of Welsh Affairs, 2021).

Holtham, Gerald: 'Industrial Policy and Infrastructure in Wales', in *Debating Industrial Policy in Wales* (Wales TUC, 2016).

Jones, Elin (Presiding Officer), *The Co-operation Agreement – Senedd Business*, Written Statement, Senedd Record, 15 December 2021.

Martin, Ciaran: 'Can the UK Survive Muscular Unionism' (*Political Insight*, Sage, December 2021.

McAllister, Laura: 'The Best Electoral System', John Osmond (Ed.), *Welsh Politics Come of Age – Responses to the Richard Commission* (Institute of Welsh Affairs, 2005).

Morgan, Kevin, and Upton, Stevie: 'Culling the Quangos' in John Osmond (Ed.), *Welsh Politics Come of Age – Responses to the Richard Commission* (Institute of Welsh Affairs, 2005).

Morgan, Prys: 'The Creation of the National Museum and National Library' in John Osmond (Ed.), *Myths, Memories and Future; The National Library and National Museum in the Story of Wales* (Institute of Welsh Affairs, 2007).

Morgan, Rhodri: 'Clear Red Water', speech to the National Centre for Public Policy, Swansea University (www.sochealth.co.uk, December 2002)

Morgan, Rhodri: 'Welsh Labour's Future', in John Osmond (Ed.), *Politics in 21st Century Wales* (Institute of Welsh Affairs, 2008).

Organisation for Economic Co-operation and Development, *The Future of Regional Development and Public Investment in Wales* (OECD, 2020).

Osmond, John: *Size Matters: Making the National Assembly more effective* (UK Changing Union Partnership, 2014).

Lord Pannick KC and Marlena Valles: *Cooperation Agreement between the Welsh Government and Plaid Cymru: Joint Opinion* (Blackstone Chambers, December 2021).

Price, Adam: *Wales 2030: Seven Steps to Independence* (Self-published, 2018).

Price, Adam: *Wales 2030: A 10-Point Plan for the Welsh Economy* (Self-published, 2018).

Price, Adam: *Arfor: A Region for the Welsh Speaking West* (Self-published, 2013).

Price, Adam: 'Reinventing Radical Wales', in John Osmond (Ed.) *Politics in 21st Century Wales* (Institute of Welsh Affairs, 2008).

Trench, Alan: 'The Assembly's Future as a Legislative Body', John Osmond (Ed.), *Welsh Politics Come of Age – Responses to the Richard Commission* (Institute of Welsh Affairs, 2005).

Party Publications

Labour Party
  Better Governance for Wales - Response to the Richard Commission (2004).
  Moving Wales Forward, Senedd Election Manifesto (2021).
  Report of the Commission on the UK's Future - A New Britain: Renewing our Democracy and Rebuilding our Economy (2022).
  Shaping the Vision: a report on the Powers and Structure of the Welsh Assembly (1995).
Plaid Cymru
  Let Us Face the Future Together, Senedd Election Manifesto (2021).

Government publications

Holtham, Gerald: *Paying for Social Care, An independent report* (Welsh Government, June 2018).

Welsh Government, *Reforming Our Union: Shared governance in the UK* (www.gov.wales, June 2021).

Welsh Government, *Response to the Final Report of the Independent Commission on the Constitutional Future of Wales* (www.gov.wales, March 2024).